PREFACE TO THE VERSION 2003

When I undertook the p   il
guide for the magical Mendo   st
dreams did I expect to sell   y
motivation was to get outside to hike and explore the hidden corners
of my adopted homeland. As I write this sixteen years later, writing
and publishing have become my means of support. I'm deeply grateful
that my passion for hiking has become a large part of my vocation,
and that readers expect me to get out and explore new trails.

The main text of this completely revised, largely rewritten edition
reflects all changes that occurred between 1989 and 1999, adding
more than 50 miles of new trails for your enjoyment. We fully updated
trail descriptions and maps, corrected the errors, expanded the plant
list by 70%, and strived to lead you to more of the magic to be found
just beyond the asphalt ribbon of Highway 1.

Now I'm most thrilled to report that since the May 1999 printing of
this book, over 7500 acres of new public lands have been added on the
Mendocino coast, more than in the previous 15 years. Most exciting of
these is the brand new Big River State Park, 7334 acres that include
that great coastal river, 1500 acres of coastal wetlands, a few immense
trees, and vast amounts of cutover timberlands that are rapidly
reforesting thanks to the lush coastal climate. In the past two months,
I've been fortunate to have the duty of exploring the more than 25
miles of trails in this vast and unpopulated corner of the wild North
Coast. Believe me, it has been a treat. Also new and of note is State
Parks' acquisition of Caspar Headlands, a gorgeous and historic
place to take a walk. These two major changes and all the minor
changes that have occurred since May 1999 are reflected in the
updates on the inside of this book's covers. Please note that further
updates (and more details about Big River State Park) are and will be
available at our website, **boredfeet.com.**

So step inside and find all the information you need to plan a safe
and rewarding trip to explore the wild beauty of California's
marvelous North Coast.

Sweet abalone can be found
upon its rocky shore
While crabs and salmon both abound
And juicy albacore.
Before I tire; ere you go
I would propose a toast:
"We found it clean — let's keep it so"
The Mendocino Coast.

— Conclusion of anonymous poem reprinted
with permission from the Mendocino Beacon.

The
HIKER'S
hip
pocket
GUIDE
to the
Mendocino
Coast

by
Bob Lorentzen

BORED FEET PRESS
MENDOCINO, CALIFORNIA
THIRD EDITION, 1999

© 1986, 1989, 1999, 2003 by Robert S. Lorentzen
Third revised edition, May 1999
3.2003 revised edition, November 2002
Printed in the United States of America on recycled paper.

Illustrations by Joshua Edelman
Symbols by Jann Patterson-Watters and Taylor Cranney
Maps by Bob Lorentzen, Marsha Mello and Liz Petersen.
    Permission to use map on page 99 given by the Mendocino Coast
    Botanical Gardens
Original Design by Judy Detrick
Redesign and composition of third edition by Elizabeth Petersen
Edited by Anne Fox

Published and Distributed by
Bored Feet Press
Post Office Box 1832
Mendocino, CA 95460
(707)964-6629, (888)336-6199
E-mail: boredfeet@mcn.com
Web: www.boredfeet.com

Library of Congress Cataloging-in-Publication Data
(Complete data available from publisher).

Lorentzen, Bob, 1949-
    The hiker's hip pocket guide to the Mendocino coast, third edition

    Bibliography: p.
    Includes index.
    1. Hiking—California—Mendocino County—Guide-books
    2. Mendocino County (Calif.)—Description and travel—Guide-books

ISBN 0-939431-17-3 Softcover

10 9 8 7

ACKNOWLEDGMENTS

I am most grateful to everyone involved in the creation of this book. In particular I wish to thank Joshua Edelman for his sense of humor and his commitment to producing the fine illustrations; Jann Patterson-Watters for her marvelous symbols, enthusiasm and infectious excitement; Judy Detrick for her early encouragement, perseverance and remarkable design talents; Anne Fox for her meticulous and creative editing; Margaret Fox for her acumen in editing and marketing and for believing in this book when it had not yet been created; Carole Raye, Charles Peterson and Carolyn Lorentzen, my mother, for their incisive editing and pithy feedback; Anthony Miksak and Linda Pack of the Gallery Bookshop and Ruth Dobberpuhl for their understanding, patience and book sense; May, China and Leilani Edelman, Jeffrey Garcia, Ray Smith, Marsha Green, David Springer, Maryellen Sheppard and Christopher Kump for testing trails and helping to decide what works; Sue Tavares of the Mendocino Area State Parks, Tom Sutfin of Jackson State Forest, John Jennings of the Sinkyone, Mark Rawitsch of Mendocino County Museum, and everyone at the Kelley House for providing valuable information; Dr. Randy Bancroft for his positive attitude and fine tuning adjustments; Taylor Cranney for her help with the symbols; Karl and Jane Lorentzen, Gina Salamone, Judith Becker and all of the other people, especially readers, who have provided encouragement, enthusiasm and help.

For help with trail changes and new trails in this third edition, I thank Peter Braudrick and Greg Picard of Mendocino State Parks, Bill Wiseheart of Sinkyone Wilderness State Park, Merv Pyorre of Jackson State Forest, Rich Owings of the Mendocino Coast Botanical Gardens, and Lisa Weg of the North Coast Interpretive Association. Special thanks to Marsha Mello and Coastwalk for permission to use several of Marsha's great maps. Thanks to David Springer, Skip Wollenberg and Ted Konigsmark for their geologic expertise, and to Nate Benesi for his botanical knowledge. Many thanks to Liz Petersen for her computer wizardry and perseverance in bringing this book from its antiquated typewritten form into the modern, refined computer version we finally have.

With special thanks to Sam O. Watnick for teaching me to cruise timber and providing a model of hope and determination.

And with apologies and thanks to Edward Abbey for all his passionate and inspiring writings about experiencing, loving and saving the natural world.

CONTENTS

WHAT KIND OF TRAIL ARE YOU LOOKING FOR?

TRAILS FOR BACKPACKING

1. Hidden Valley to Chemise to Whale Gulch
3. Whale Gulch (to Environmental Camps)
5. Bear Harbor (to Environmental Camps)
6. Lost Coast
7. Sally Bell Grove (to Wheeler)
20. North Fork of South Fork Noyo River
22. Mendocino Hiking and Equestrian, Part 1
23. Mendocino Hiking and Equestrian, Part 2
33. Mendocino Hiking and Equestrian, Part 3
38. Fern Canyon (to Environmental Camps)
45. Manchester State Park (to Environmental Camps)

TRAILS WHERE DOGS ARE ALLOWED

1. Hidden Valley to Chemise Mountain (to 6 miles)
2. Chemise Mountain
5. Bear Harbor
8. Usal Waterfall
10. DeHaven Creek to Wages Creek
12. Bruhel Point
13. North to Ten Mile River
14. Laguna Point
17. Glass Beach/Pudding Creek Headlands
20. North Fork of South Fork Noyo River
21. Chamberlain Creek
22. Mendocino Hiking and Equestrian, Part 1
23. Mendocino Hiking and Equestrian, Part 2
28. Blowhole Walk
29. South Headlands Loop
31. Mendocino Headlands West and North
32. Mendocino South Headlands to Big River Beach
33. Mendocino Hiking and Equestrian, Part 3
34. Forest History Trail
35. Montgomery Woods State Reserve
40. Navarro-By-The-Sea—see OTHER SUGGESTION: Navarro Ridge
43. Navarro River Hike
44. Greenwood State Beach
45. Manchester State Park
47. Moat Creek to Bowling Ball Beach
48. Schooner Gulch North to Whiskey Shoals
54. Other Sea Ranch Trails

TRAILS FOR EQUESTRIANS

1. Hidden Valley to Chemise Mountain

2. Chemise Mountain
3. Whale Gulch
5. Bear Harbor
6. Lost Coast (Bear Harbor to Wheeler)
7. Sally Bell Grove
9. Hotel Gulch
13. North to Ten Mile River
16. MacKerricher South Headlands
22. Mendocino Hiking and Equestrian, Part 1
23. Mendocino Hiking and Equestrian, Part 2
33. Mendocino Hiking and Equestrian, Part 3
40. Navarro-By-The-Sea—see OTHER SUGGESTION: Navarro Ridge
43. Navarro River Hike
45. Manchester State Park

TRAILS FOR MOUNTAIN BIKES

1. Hidden Valley to Chemise Mountain
2. Chemise Mountain
7. Sally Bell Grove
9. Hotel Gulch
10. DeHaven Creek to Wages Creek—see OTHER SUGGESTION: Blufftop North to Howard Creek
13. North to Ten Mile River
22. Mendocino Hiking and Equestrian, Part 1
23. Mendocino Hiking and Equestrian, Part 2
27. Waterfall Loop—first 1⅝ miles
33. Mendocino Hiking and Equestrian, Part 3
38. Fern Canyon
39. Upper Fern Canyon to river ford
40. Navarro-By-The-Sea—see OTHER SUGGESTION: Navarro Ridge
43. Navarro River Hike

TRAILS FOR BICYCLES

10. DeHaven to Wages—see OTHER SUGGESTION: Blufftop North to Howard Creek
13. North to Ten Mile River
27. Waterfall Loop—first 1⅝ miles
33. Mendocino Hiking and Equestrian, Part 3
38. Fern Canyon
50. Headlands to Beach Loop

TRAILS FOR HANDICAPPED ACCESS

10. DeHaven to Wages—see OTHER SUGGESTION
14. Laguna Point
15. Lake Cleone
18. Fort Bragg History Walk
19. Mendocino Coast Botanical Gardens
26. Point Cabrillo Preserve
27. Waterfall Loop—first 1⅝ miles

30. Mendocino History Walk
38. Fern Canyon
39. Pygmy Forest (plus dirt trail ½ mile beyond)
41. Gentle Giants Loop
50. Headlands to Beach Loop
   Other trails may be handicapped accessible with assistance or for marginally handicapped.

TRAILS FOR JOGGERS

13. North to Ten Mile River
17. Glass Beach/Pudding Creek Headlands
19. Mendocino Coast Botanical Gardens
23. Mendocino Hiking and Equestrian Trail, Part 2
27. Waterfall Loop
31. West & North Headlands
32. South Headlands to Big River Beach
33. Mendocino Hiking and Equestrian Trail, Part 3
36. Chapman Point
37. Little River Point
38. Fern Canyon
39. Upper Fern Canyon Loop
43. Navarro River Hike
45. Manchester State Park
50. Headlands to Beach Loop
52. Blufftop Trail

CANOE ACCESS

South Fork Eel River: Highway 1 at M.105.00, Highway 101 at many points

Ten Mile River: Highway 1 at M.69.67

Lake Cleone: see Trail #15

Noyo River: Fort Bragg. Access from N. or S. Harbor Drive or logging roads

Big River: N. Big River Road at M.50.35

Albion River: Turn onto Albion River North Side Road at M.43.95

Navarro River: Highway 1 at M.40.15 or various points along Highway 128

Garcia River: Highway 1 at M.18.48 or from Miners Hole Road (M.17.55)

Gualala River: See Trails #50 and 51, or from various side roads

GENERAL
MAP OF THE
MENDOCINO
COAST

INTRODUCTION

THIS BOOK IS FOR RECREATIONAL PURPOSES ONLY

Highway 1 curves and twists for 106 miles along the Mendocino coast, providing access to 131 miles of rugged shoreline. This isolated coast, with its many scattered pocket beaches, is backed by approximately 1000 square miles of forest (and cutover timber land), an intricate labyrinth of ridges, canyons and valleys, through which no less than seven rivers and dozens of creeks flow west into the sea. At its northern end, Highway 1 veers inland and meets its northern terminus at Leggett on Highway 101. But the coast continues north to its most isolated wilderness stretch: Sinkyone Wilderness State Park and King Range Conservation Area—the Lost Coast.

This book tells how to find and walk, hike, jog or ride more than 250 miles of scenic trails through beautiful country. The trails range from easy walks to difficult backpacks, with choices to fit the taste of every nature lover. The trails lead to a variety of habitats: beaches, tidepools, lagoons, dunes, headlands, forests, stream canyons, ridges and mountain tops. You may also hike trails to waterfalls and ghost towns, along old logging railways, through a beautiful cultivated garden, or take a history tour of Mendocino, Fort Bragg or the Point Arena lighthouse. In short, there's something for everyone. So get out of your car and use feet, bicycle, horse or wheelchair to explore the Mendocino coast.

HOW TO USE THIS BOOK

The trails in this book are organized from the north to the south. Highway 1 is the starting point for the directions to all trailheads except Trails #1 through #6. No trail is more than two hours from Mendocino or Fort Bragg.

In the directions to each trail, you'll find a milepost number on Highway 1 listed like this: M.49.88. These numbers refer to white highway mileposts placed frequently (but at irregular intervals) along state highways by CalTrans, the State Department of Transportation. You can quickly determine the

13

location of a trail (and where it is in relation to you) by referring to its milepost number. You don't have to start at the beginning of the book. Simply turn to the trail nearest your location and you'll be on your way. Neighboring trails will be on the adjacent pages.

For each trail in the book you'll find a map (top is always north unless otherwise marked), how to get to the trailhead, the best time to go, appropriate warnings, and a detailed description with some history and/or natural history.

You'll find a group of symbols below the access information for each trail. They tell you at a glance the level of difficulty, type of trail, available facilities, whether there's a fee, and whether dogs are allowed. The list of symbols follows.

After the contents you'll find a table listing the trails most suitable for a particular type of recreation: bicycles, mountain bikes, jogging, equestrians, backpacking and handicap access. It also tells where you can put your canoe in the water along the rivers of the Mendocino coast.

THE DANGERS
TEN COASTAL COMMANDMENTS

When on the trail, *always* keep your senses wide open so that you can best appreciate nature's pleasures as well as her dangers. Don't let nature lull you into complacency. Here are ten rules to keep you out of danger, so that you may safely enjoy the beauty of the coast.

1. DON'T LITTER. Most of these places are unspoiled. Do your part to keep them that way. Show your appreciation for Mother Nature by hiking with a trash bag which you can fill with any trash you find in otherwise pristine places, even matches, cigarette butts and bottle caps.

2. NO TRESPASSING. Property owners have a right to privacy. Stay off private property. There are enough public place without walking through someone's yard.

3. NEVER TURN YOU BACK ON THE OCEAN. Oversized rogue waves can strike the coast at any time. *Watch for them.* They are especially common in winter. They have killed people. More subtle are

THE SYMBOLS

WALK:
Less than 2 miles
Very easy terrain

EASY HIKE:
1 to 10 miles
Easy terrain

MODERATE HIKE:
2 to 10 miles
Rougher terrain

DIFFICULT HIKE:
Strenuous terrain
Backpacking possible

**MOUNTAIN BIKE
TRAIL**

PICNIC SPOT:
May be tables or just
a good blanket spot

BIKE TRAIL

**DOGS ALLOWED
ON LEASH**

CAR CAMPING

**WALK-IN OR
BIKE-IN CAMPING:**
Environmental camps

TIDEPOOL ACCESS

 HANDICAP ACCESS

 RECOMMENDED FOR FAMILIES

 INTERPRETIVE NATURE TRAIL

 TRAIL FOR EQUESTRIANS

 RESTROOMS AVAILABLE

 WATER AVAILABLE

 FEE AREA

 FISHING ACCESS

 NO OIL EXPLORATION OR DRILLING

the changes of the tides: don't let rising tides strand you against steep cliffs or on a submerged tidal island. The ocean is icy and unforgiving, generally unsafe for swimming without a wetsuit.

4. STAY BACK FROM CLIFFS. Coastal soils are often unstable. You wouldn't want to fall 40 feet into the icy sea, would you? Don't get close to the cliff's edge, and never climb on cliffs unless there's a safe trail.

5. WILD THINGS: ANIMAL. All the animal pests of the Mendocino coast are small, unless you get chased by a Roosevelt elk (generally they won't chase you unless you get too close). Watch out for ticks (some carry Lyme disease), wasps, mosquitoes, biting spiders, scorpions and rattlesnakes. Human animals are easily the most dangerous, especially in deer hunting season (from the first week in August until the end of September). Always listen for gunfire, especially outside state parks. *Never* (even in a vehicle) enter an area where logging is in progress. UNDERWATER ANIMALS: When tidepooling or at the beach, always watch for sea urchins and jellyfish. Both have painful stinging spines. Remember, too, that mussels are quarantined each year from May through October; at that time they contain deadly poison.

6. WILD THINGS: PLANT. These mean business

poison oak, *Rhus diversiloba*

too, especially poison oak and stinging nettles, which can get you with the slightest touch. Many other plants are poisonous. It is best to not touch any plants unless you know by positive identification that they are safe; this is most important with mushrooms.

7. POT GARDENS. Don't even think about messing with one, no matter whose side you are on. If you ever stumble onto a pot patch (not likely if you stay on the trails in this book), leave more quietly than you came. Take only memories.

8. TRAFFIC. Coast roads are difficult and sometimes overcrowded. Drive carefully and courteously. Please turn out for faster traffic. You will enjoy the coast more if you do. If you stop, pull safely off the road. A few trails are heavily traveled too. If you share a trail with equestrians, they always have the right of way. Cyclists must yield to hikers and horses and slow to walking speed on blind corners.

9. CRIME. Be sure to lock you car when you park it at the trailhead. Leave valuables out of sight, or better yet, back at your lodging.

10. ALWAYS TAKE RESPONSIBILITY FOR YOURSELF AND YOUR PARTY. This is a trail guide, not a nursery school. The author cannot and will not be responsible for you in the wilds. Information contained in this book is correct to the best of the author's knowledge. Author and publisher assume no liability for damages arising from changes, errors or omissions. **You must take the responsibility for you safety and health while on these trails.** The coast is still a wild place. Safety conditions of trails, beaches and tidepools vary with seasons and tides. Be cautious, heed the above warnings, and always check on local conditions. It is always better to hike with a friend. Know where you can get help in case of emergency.

THE HISTORY

The Mendocino coast was born about 40 million years ago, the result of the collision of two giant pieces of the earth's crust (tectonic plates): as the North American plate moved substantially westward, it collided with and overrode the Pacific plate.

The Coast Ranges were built by the sedimentary material scraped from the Pacific plate in this process. Though the collision became more gentle over the ensuing eons, the plates continue to collide today.

Over the last million years, a series of five to seven marine terraces have been successively uplifted, each one serving its time as the sea coast before being pushed farther above sea level. This process has occurred regularly, creating a complex and fascinating natural history which occurs with such regularity nowhere else in the world. You can see evidence of this process at many places on the Mendocino coast, but the best classroom is the Jughandle Ecological Staircase (Trail #25).

The San Andreas fault now forms the dividing line between the two tectonic plates. The San Andreas runs north into the ocean near Manchester, then continues offshore to Cape Mendocino. The Pacific plate, to the west of the fault, began to move northward about 25 million years ago.

Two distinct plant groups mingle on the Mendocino coast. Plants of a cooler, wetter climate migrated from the north. These include redwood, fir, spruce and tanoak. Representatives of the drier, warmer climate of the south include madrone, manzanita, bay laurel, Bishop pine and ceanothus.

Archeological evidence taken from shell mounds shows that Native Americans lived along the coast for at least 10,000 years before the settlers came. Their culture prospered with California's abundant natural resources until the coming of the settlers.

The first Spanish galleon is believed to have sailed along the Mendocino coast about 1543. The ship's captain named Cape Mendocino (in Humboldt County) in honor of the Viceroy of New Spain, Don Antonio de Mendoza. Though galleons sailed the coast into the 1800s, there was never any record of a landing in what is now Mendocino County.

The Russians also had their time along the coast, establishing Fort Ross (in Sonoma County) in 1812. The Russian fur trappers had been working along the coast even before this time. The name Russian Gulch originated because the local Pomo told of seeing white men there with a large ship. From the Natives' descriptions, the white men were Russian fur trappers; the date was in the late eighteenth century. The Russians abandoned the coast in 1841, having exhausted the fur trade.

With the coming of the California gold rush, beginning in 1848, Americans began to explore the North Coast, seeking timber and other resources to supply California's booming growth. Albion, Greenwood and Mendocino were among the first settlements. By 1900 there were more than three dozen towns on the Mendocino coast, all connected to the timber trade. The tiny mill towns and ports came and went, but by 1940 fifty sawmills were scattered on the coast. A postwar boom increased the number to 129 mills. Then, with improved roads and modernization came the centralizing of the mills. By 1960 only three mills and about a dozen of the towns remained. As you read about and hike the trails, many details of the Coast's history will fall into place.

THE CLIMATE

The climate of the Mendocino coast is cool, but mild enough for year-round hiking if you are prepared for varying conditions. In planning your excursions, keep in mind the following about the seasons along the Mendocino coast:

November to March are the rainy months, time to bring rain coats and waterproof boots. Still, there are often fine sunny days between storms.

April and May are often windy, with occasional rain storms. The wind may be gentle, or fierce and unrelenting. The landscape is at its most lush and beautiful. Bring layered clothing and hats.

June, July and August bring sunny summer days, alternating with thick fog. You may be comfortable in shorts, but bring layered clothing in case the fog comes in. Sometimes you can beat the fog by heading a few miles inland. (This is the most crowded season, especially August.)

September and October are a beautiful time. Fog is less common. Though there may be rainstorms, most of the days are calm and warm. The land is dry, the hills golden, and the sunsets often spectacular.

GET READY, GET SET, HIKE!

You should be chomping at the bit to get out on the trail by now. Here are a few suggestions of what you might need to take on your hike: layered clothing— sweater, sweatshirt, hat, windbreaker or rain coat; insect repellent; sunscreen; sunglasses; and small first aid kit (at least bring moleskin for blisters). Not essential, but highly recommended for all but the shortest walks: water container, extra food, pocket knife, flashlight and extra batteries, matches and fire starter, map, compass (helps if you know how to use it), and of course you would not want to be caught without your *Hiker's hip pocket Guide*!

Additional suggestions: camera; dry socks; binoculars; and field guide to birds, wildflowers and/or trees. If you are backpacking, you should consult an equipment list for that purpose.

When you are out on the trails, remember to slow down, open your senses and enjoy. Most people hike at a rate of 2 to 3 miles per hour. But beach sand or steep terrain may slow all but the most hardy to as little as one mile per hour. Leave ample time to do the hike you plan at a pleasant pace. Hike not to count the miles, but to enjoy and appreciate nature. Happy trails to you!

1

HIDDEN VALLEY
to CHEMISE MOUNTAIN
to WHALE GULCH

LEAST TRAVELED LEG OF THE LOST COAST TRAIL

This old pack trail, now thoroughly reconstructed but still lightly used, connects the northern and southern sections of the Lost Coast. You can start backpacking at the mouth of the Mattole River, walk 25 miles along the beach to Shelter Cove, then hike or hitchhike 3 miles of paved road to Hidden Valley Trailhead. From there a 28-mile hike south will bring you to the Usal Trailhead, 6 miles north of Highway One. That entire route now coexists as part of the California Coastal Trail.

This 7-mile leg from Hidden Valley Trailhead to Whale Gulch (8⅝ miles to Needle Rock Visitor Center) provides a magnificent though rugged experience, passing through diverse habitats: chaparral, pioneer orchard, hardwood forest, old growth fir forest, coastal grassland and, finally, redwood forest, coastal stream canyon and coastal lake. The first 4 miles offer moderately easy walking, then the trail drops 2000 feet in 3 miles, a strenuous trek that offers grand scenery and sweeping coastal views.

Walk past the gate heading southwest on an old road. Young Douglas fir mix with alder, bay laurel, hazel, and thimbleberry. Wild mint grows in the middle of the road. Notice the harsh devastation of a forest fire on the left. This hike winds in and out of the area burned by the Chemise Mountain fire of 1973.

At ⅛ mile the road swings left and crosses a tiny, slow-flowing creek. In spring the purple shades of bush lupine, Douglas iris and ceanothus brighten the path.

You quickly come to a lush green meadow stretching for ½ mile up Hidden Valley, surrounded by chaparral and fire-scarred forest. Poppies and lupine sprinkle the heavenly meadow in spring. Views of the blue Pacific lie to the west and south. In the upper end of the valley, an apple orchard marks

HIDDEN VALLEY
CHEMISE MOUNTAIN
WHALE GULCH:

DISTANCE: 7 miles one way to Whale Gulch, 5 miles round trip to Chemise Mountain.

TIME: Three to four hours.

TERRAIN: Through chaparral to a lush meadow, then climbing through forest to ridge, which you follow to its summit. Then descend the ridge into a deep canyon, following the creek to the coast.

ELEVATION GAIN/LOSS: Round trip to Chemise Mountain: 1040 feet+/1040 feet-. One way to Whale Gulch: 1170 feet+/2880 feet-.

BEST TIME: Spring. Summer and autumn are also good.

WARNINGS: In winter and spring the ford of Whale Gulch Creek may be dangerous or impassable. No water on trail until Whale Gulch. Watch for timber rattlers and poison oak. Nearest year-round facilities at Shelter Cove. Stay on trail and off private property.

HOW TO GET THERE: Leave Highway 101 at Garberville (M.10.8) on the south or Redway (M.14.6) on the north. Take Briceland Road from Redway (2.8 miles north of Garberville on old Highway 101) for 17.5 miles. Go left on Chemise Mountain Road for .25 mile to trailhead on right.

FURTHER INFO: Bureau of Land Management: (707)825-2300 in Arcata; (707)468-4000 in Ukiah.

the site of an old ranch.

At ¼ mile your road forks. You take the left fork; the right fork continues into Hidden Valley. Climb gradually, with views of the valley and the ocean beyond. Before ½ mile you reach the upper end of the apple orchard. Your trail switchbacks to the left and heads north, climbing steeply away from the road. As you climb by several steep, short switchbacks, sweeping views of Hidden Valley reward you.

Climb into unburned forest, dip across a tiny seasonal creek, then ascend by three switchbacks to a rest bench at ⅝ mile. Climb by nine more switchbacks through hardwood forest, then fir forest, rising steeply to a saddle on the ridge at one mile.

Ascend fitfully along the ridgetop past immense fire-scarred firs as the often snow-clad peaks of the Yolla Bollys appear to the east. You dip and rise several times through forest along the ridge to 1½ miles. Then contour and rise through a brush field with sweeping ocean views.

Climb steeply to 1¾ miles, then level at the junction with the trail from Wailaki and Nadelos Campgrounds (see Trail #2). Stay right for Chemise Mountain and Whale Gulch. You climb gradually, heading south to top the ridge.

Before 2½ miles, your climb brings you to the trail's 2560-foot summit, where a brushy side trail on the left climbs 150 feet to the 2598-foot top of Chemise Mountain.

The main trail heads south along the ridge, coming to a less brushy ridgetop knob at 2¾ miles. Your trail descends briefly, then climbs to the brushy top of Chemise Flat at 2⅞ miles. Then you descend gently on a rocky, well-cleared path until 3⅛ miles. Your trail descends steeply, then moderately, along the west side of the ridge before it climbs to a top at 3¼ miles where bay laurel grows. Descend again with more views south.

You may hear the distant roar of surf as you climb to another top at 3¾ miles. Then a shady portion of trail descends along the ridge before climbing briefly to the summit called Manzanita at 4 miles, with a grand view south over the convoluted terrain of Sinkyone Wilderness. A USGS bench marker beside the trail indicates an elevation of 2120 feet. This is a good place to turn back if you're day hiking. From here the trail descends steeply almost to sea level in less than 3 miles.

What the heck, you say? Let's go! You can reach the beach in an hour or two. Your trail descends southeast. By 4¼ miles you enter cool, mature Douglas fir forest. You leave the ridge to descend steeply by switchbacks into a gully, then contour to return to the ridge at 4⅜ miles.

The trail descends steeply along the ridge, then levels briefly at a grassy clearing, a sign of what lies ahead. You wind left and descend through mixed forest before climbing to another knob on the ridge at 4¾ miles. Your trail levels along the shady ridgetop, then descends gradually beyond 5 miles before leveling again. Wild rose, Douglas iris, sugar stick and huckleberry grow beneath the dense forest canopy.

Before 5½ miles you make a brief steep descent, then climb along the crest of the razor ridge with grasslands to the west. This quickly brings you into a grassy clearing with excellent views south into the Sinkyone Wilderness. Descend, then climb through the grasslands, then descend steeply through the forest for ⅛ mile. At 5⅞ miles you again descend through grasslands sprinkled with poppy, yarrow, redwood sorrel, tall brodiaea, buttercup, purple bush lupine, paintbrush and sticky monkeyflower. You soon meet a road from the left that the trail follows, climbing to a flat top on the ridge at 6 miles. An unfinished hip-roofed building sits beside the trail. From here you should stay on top of the ridge or on its west face; private property lies to the east.

Enjoy the easy descent through the grasslands. The trail will soon turn steep. At 6¼ miles you return to

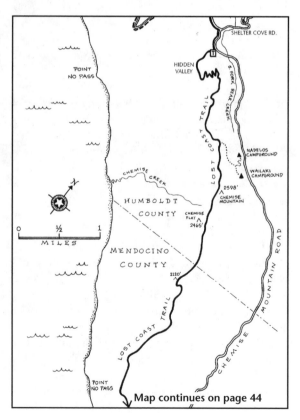

Map continues on page 44

forest as you descend steeply along the narrow ridge. As you pass the bench marker called Red Hill (elevation 1418 feet), you can see a private house below on the left. Stay on the trail along the razor ridge to avoid the private property.

Beyond the house, the trail steepens. Watch for poison oak from here to the bottom. At 6⅜ miles the trail veers left and follows the east side of the ridge through hardwood forest. Return briefly to the ridge. Then, at 6½ miles, the trail descends east by switchbacks. Slink pod and hazel grow on the forest floor. The broad, cleared path descends steeply, zig-zagging toward Whale Gulch Creek.

At 6¾ miles your path drops to a shady, slippery ford of the creek. As long as the water is not too deep, rock-hop across the creek, a pleasant spot for a break.

From there you follow a well-beaten trail climbing by switchbacks, then winding south through small gullies. Ascend to a summit and an overlook of Whale Gulch Creek where it empties into the Pacific Ocean.

Descend toward two small lakes, 7 miles from the Hidden Valley Trailhead. The lakes are a favorite haunt of the immense Roosevelt elk that live in Sinkyone Wilderness State Park; stay clear of these seemingly docile, but potentially dangerous wild animals. The trail soon climbs southeast, coming to Jones Beach Environmental Camp at 7⅝ miles. Three campsites cluster around a eucalyptus grove beside a small creek. It's one mile farther south along the bluffs to Needle Rock Visitor Center, where you must register if you wish to camp. If you plan to continue on the Lost Coast Trail to Usal, you must walk the dirt road south for 2¾ miles to its end at Orchard Creek. From there it is 16¾ miles to Usal (see Trail #6).

2.

CHEMISE MOUNTAIN from NADELOS or WAILAKI

GREAT VIEWS OF THE COAST

This well-engineered trail climbs up the wooded side of an otherwise brushy mountain to link with the California Coastal Trail for commanding views up and down the coast and over the surrounding countryside. Chemise Mountain marks the southern end of the King Range Conservation Area. For more trails in the King Range Conservation Area, see The Hiker's hip pocket Guide to the Humboldt Coast.

Your trail starts at pleasantly wooded Wailaki Campground, crossing a small bridge over Bear Creek. Just 150 feet beyond the bridge you pass the short King Range Nature Trail on the right, meandering near the creek. Beyond the junction Chemise Trail starts climbing, crossing two tiny tributaries that may be flowing in spring. Woodwardia ferns grow on the north-facing slope beneath a mature fir forest. Salal and huckleberry grow on the drier south-facing slope.

Continue the steady climb for ¼ mile to the junction with the trail from Nadelos Campground. Just beyond the junction, you will find a trail register. Sign in, please.

Your trail steepens to ½ mile. Then the ridgetop looms ahead. You switchback to the left and meet the Hidden Valley Trail, branching to the right (see Trail #1). Take the left fork.

CHEMISE MOUNTAIN:

DISTANCE: 2¾ miles round trip to Chemise Mountain, 3¼ miles round trip to knob.

TIME: Two hours.

TERRAIN: Steep mountain near the coast, covered with alternating brush and forest.

ELEVATION GAIN/LOSS: 750 feet+/750 feet-.

BEST TIME: Spring. Autumn and summer are good, too.

WARNINGS: No water along trail. Timber rattlers live in this area. Nearest year round facilities at Whitethorn, Redway.

HOW TO GET THERE: Leave Highway 101 at Garberville on the south or at Redway on the north. Take Briceland Road from Redway (2.8 miles north of Garberville on Redwood Drive) for 17.5 miles. Go left on Chemise Mountain Road 1.75 miles to Wailaki Campground. Trail leaves from south end of campground. (If you are riding horses it is better to leave from Nadelos Camp, .5 mile north.)

FURTHER INFO: Bureau of Land Management (707)468-4000.

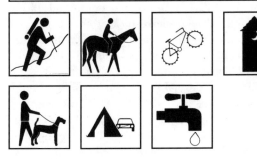

Your climb becomes gradual as you head south just below the ridgetop. The mixed conifer forest changes to predominantly hardwoods. About one mile from the trailhead, your trail levels. The snow-covered Yolla Bolly Mountains appear through the trees to the east. At 1⅛ mile you top the ridge, but tall brush conceals the views. At 1¼ miles the brush parts for a view of Shelter Cove to the northwest.

Just 1⅜ miles from the trailhead, the trail reaches its summit. From there a sometimes overgrown, unmarked side trail on your left winds to the very top of Chemise Mountain in about 150 feet. The side trip is worthwhile, as the brush parts sufficiently at the 2598-foot summit to divulge fine views in all directions. Except for a few houses visible from the

summit, the land is largely uninhabited. To the south, at least 13 coastal ridges can be spotted on a clear day. Immediately to the south, Chemise Mountain drops off into the deep canyon of Whale Gulch, the Sinkyone Wilderness and precipitous Anderson Cliffs just beyond. Beyond are Cape Vizcaino, Kibesillah Hill, Ten Mile River mouth and dunes, the Georgia-Pacific smokestack in Fort Bragg and Sherwood Ridge. Greenwood Ridge forms the southern horizon. To your east, all of the Yolla Bollys rise to their 7000-foot summits.

Returning to the main trail, you can follow it south along the ridge. In less than ¼ mile, it comes to a knob, one of several around Chemise Flat. Though not as high in elevation, this peak is more open on top, providing better views directly south into the Sinkyone. The improved trail continues south along the ridge (see Trail #1), a portion of the 58-mile route traversing the entire Lost Coast, from the Mattole River on the north to Usal Creek on the south. Return on the same trail you ascended.

SINKYONE WILDERNESS STATE PARK

INCLUDES THE NEXT SEVEN TRAILS

Located in the extreme northwestern corner of Mendocino County, the Sinkyone (sing-key-own) preserves a sample of the rugged wilderness that once existed all along the Mendocino coast. Though the Sinkyone was settled in the 1860s, and was logged and ranched for much of the next century, it now stands as a largely pristine wilderness. The State Park was established in 1976.

The Sinkyone contains numerous interwoven environments within its 7567 acres: black sand beaches, tidepools, coastal cliffs, lush coastal streams, grassy headlands, old homestead and town sites, untouched virgin forests, logged-over areas, and high ridges. All of these can be reached on one or more of the following trails.

Sinkyone Wilderness State Park is unlike any other park in the state system. It can be reached only by isolated, unpaved mountain roads that are often impassable in winter. Usal is the only campground where you can park next to your campsite; you must hike at least 200 feet to reach all other camps. There is no entrance station and the visitor center occupies a rustic old ranch house with no electricity or telephone, although a faucet with filtered water stands by the path to the building. The nearest gas station and store are far from the park boundary. Though rangers do patrol the park regularly, do not expect to find one at a moment's notice, or even see one every day.

If this scenario does not appeal to you, you would do best not to visit the Sinkyone. While you can visit the park as a long day trip, you will enjoy it far more if you can stay overnight, or even better, a week.

The Sinkyone was named for the tribe that originally inhabited this rugged country. They were the southernmost of the Athabascan language tribes on the coast. Though known for their backwoods skills, the Sinkyone tribe was small and loosely organized. They were quickly overrun by the white settlers.

On the brighter side, a group of four-legged

31

SINKYONE WILDERNESS STATE PARK:

GENERAL DIRECTIONS: Exit Highway 101 at Garberville (M.10.8) on the south or Redway (M.14.6) on the north. Take Briceland Road from Redway (2.8 miles north of Garberville on Redwood Drive). In 12 miles turn left and go through Whitethorn. In 4.5 more miles, you come to the junction known as Four Corners. Go straight to reach the visitor center, 3.6 miles down a steep and narrow winding dirt road (never advisable for RV's or trailers, may be impassable in rainy months to most vehicles).

You may also reach the Sinkyone during the dry season (generally May–September) via the Usal Road. It leaves Highway 1 at M.90.88. The first 6 miles to Usal are not bad, but the next 19 miles to Four Corners make a long, wild ride. Usal Road provides access to the Sally Bell Grove Trail (Trail #7), and eventually reaches Four Corners, but the road gets rougher at its north end.

FURTHER INFO: Sinkyone Wilderness State Park (707)986-7711, 247-3318.

ENVIRONMENTAL CAMPS: The park has 6 walk-in camps with a total of 17 campsites in the Needle Rock-Bear Harbor area.

FEES: Day use parking: $3/vehicle (May–Sept.), $2/vehicle (Oct.–April). Primitive camping: $7–11/night. Needle Rock Barn Camp (out of the weather!): $12–16/night. $3/person/night in Lost Coast Trail camps.

Sinkyone natives live in the park. At last count 75 Roosevelt elk lived within park boundaries. These large animals stand five feet at the shoulder. The males grow up to 1200 pounds, with antlers up to six feet, which they shed in fall. Elk originally inhabited all of Mendocino County, but were hunted nearly to extinction.

If you meet elk on the trail, give them plenty of room, especially in rut season in September. The half-ton bulls may resent sharing their territory; they can run as fast as 35 miles per hour.

If you'd like to get a copy of the park map to plan your visit, send a check payable to R.G.I.A., 1600 U.S. Hwy 101, Garberville, CA 95542.

3.

WHALE GULCH
COASTAL STREAM AND LAKE HABITAT

*This often overlooked corner of this lightly visited
state park offers grand scenery, especially when the
weather's clear: lush canyons, coastal lakes, hidden waterfalls, and a chance to see the park's resident herd of Roosevelt elk. While it offers a pleasant
and easy day hike, you also have the option of camping at Jones Beach Camp or one of the closer walk-
in camps.*

Your trail leaves from the east side of the barn (north
of the visitor center). It winds past the Needle Rock
Environmental Camp, then heads out to the edge of
the bluff above eroding Needle Rock, following the
California Coastal Trail north.

At ¼ mile you cross a small creek and come to
Streamside Environmental Camp. Your trail
promptly returns to the edge of the eroding bluff,
then traverses coastal prairie.

At ½ mile you cross a bridge over another creek,
then meet the base of the Low Gap Trail. Continue
north across more prairie where you might encounter elk. At ¾ mile you meet the deep canyon of Low
Gap Creek on your left. You soon cross it on another
bridge, then traverse another expanse of prairie.

At one mile you approach a grove of large eucalyptus and meet the old upper trail. Nestled in the
trees is the first of the Jones Beach campsites. In
100 feet a restroom and the trail to the second campsite are on the left. You then cross a small creek.
Long ago an old car was used as fill at this creek
crossing. You can see it in the creek bed on the left,
with a tree growing through it. Another camp is just
beyond, under beautiful trees with calla lilies
growing nearby.

The trail forks shortly, the left fork heading down
to Jones Beach. Take the right fork to Whale Gulch.
At 1⅛ miles you can look down a deep gully to the
beach. Then your trail draws closer to the deep canyon. Perhaps this canyon was once a tidal estuary
before geological forces uplifted this old marine

33

WHALE GULCH:

DISTANCE: 4 miles round trip.

TIME: Two hours.

TERRAIN: Deep, verdant coastal stream canyon running parallel to the coast, including two coastal lakes at an elevation of 100 feet.

ELEVATION GAIN/LOSS: To Jones Beach Camp: 80 feet+/180 feet-. To Whale Gulch: 120 feet+/200 feet. To Chemise Mountain: 2870 feet+/500 feet-.

BEST TIME: Spring. Summer is OK. Rather dry by autumn.

WARNINGS: Stinging nettles and poison oak abound. Isolated country with no services.

HOW TO GET THERE: Follow general directions to Sinkyone State Park and park near visitor center.

ENVIRONMENTAL CAMPS: This trail leads to Needle Rock, Streamside and Jones Beach Environmental Camps, respectively 200 feet, ¼ mile and one mile from the trailhead.

FURTHER INFO: Sinkyone Wilderness State Park (707)986-7711.

FEES: Day use parking: $3/vehicle (May–Sept.), $2/vehicle (Oct.–April).

terrace to its present level.

At 1¼ miles your trail crosses a small stream. Just to your left, the creek plunges into the deep verdant canyon. As you top a short hill, you may glimpse the ocean over the razor ridge to the west. Sounds of creek and waterfall mingle with the crashing of the surf.

Now your trail descends gradually into the canyon. The next section can be very marshy, especially in spring. You cross and recross the main creek at 1⅜ miles. After you cross the creek again, you come to the first of two lakes. Water irises and cattails grow in the shallows. If the stream was in fact a tidal estuary in eons past, then these lakes were salt-water tidal lagoons.

The trail continues to the right of the lake. You climb to higher and drier ground at 1⅝ miles, where the trail forks between the two lakes. Go right, climbing above the second lake. At 1¾ miles the ocean comes into view to the northwest. In another 300 feet, you are overlooking deep, rugged Whale Gulch. Driftwood logs are jammed into the small lagoon at the mouth of Whale Gulch Creek. To the right is the creek's steep canyon and a small waterfall.

The trail turns north up the gulch, then descends to a ford in a pleasant spot on Whale Gulch Creek at 2 miles. The trail to Chemise Mountain climbs steeply from the other side of the creek. See the end of Trail #1 for a complete description. Retrace your steps back along the canyon and across the prairie to your car.

OTHER SUGGESTION: The LOW GAP TRAIL, 1½ miles long, crosses the park road ½ mile north of the visitor center. It follows the original Needle Rock wagon road, climbing 900 feet to Usal Road.

4.

NEEDLE ROCK to FLAT ROCK CREEK

LONG DARK-SAND BEACH

This wild, hidden beach offers a pleasant and remote place to saunter along the Pacific shore. This description descends a steep path to the beach from the visitor center, while the easiest path is the Jones Beach Trail a mile north. It makes a moderately steep, short descent to the north end of the beach. Either way it's well worth a visit. You might find whale bones and see whales, pelicans and loons here, and you'll often see the tracks of deer, elk, raccoon and even bear in the fine sand.

While a vague trail starts directly across the road from the visitor center, take the better path 150 feet north. Go west over gently sloping grassy headlands. In 200 feet it passes to the right of a giant fallen, bleached eucalyptus snag and follows the canyon's edge. Just 350 feet from the road you come to a long, steep winding stairway that takes you to the beach

just east of Double Rock. The path is very steep and rough, not for those afraid of heights. It reaches the beach around ⅛ mile. Needle Rock is visible not far to the north. (You may also walk north along the beach past Needle Rock to Jones Beach, one mile north, where a better and maintained stairway leads up to the Whale Gulch Trail, see end of report.)

The described walk heads southeast along the dark-sand beach beside high, eroded cliffs. Pass the first seasonal creek before ¼ mile. Beyond here the cliffs are cut by several steep gulches which may have waterfalls in spring. The deepest gulches, around one mile, generally have year-round streams.

Around ⅜ mile you round one point composed of tiny aggregates atop bedrock, then another. The beach broadens and curves south toward the rocky point, the destination for this hike. After the beach narrows around ⅝ mile, it soon broadens for its final sweep south to the flat-rock point. Around ¾ mile you pass the mouth of a year-round creek as it tumbles down its steep twisting canyon. You soon pass another small creek, then clumps of paintbrush along the base of the cliff.

Around one mile many small streams tumble down steep, eroded gorges to the dark-sand beach. Near its south end, the beach becomes very broad, then narrows at one last canyon. Continue to the flat rocky point with its several small tidepools. The tidepools, mostly scoured of life by the powerful surf, are best left to oystercatchers and gulls—hazardous due to the big wave potential here.

To the southeast is Secret Beach, accessible only

NEEDLE ROCK to FLAT ROCK CREEK:

DISTANCE: 1¼ miles one way, 2½ miles round trip, or up to 4⅝ miles round trip via Jones Beach Trail (add up to ½ mile if you visit Secret Beach).

TIME: Two or three hours.

TERRAIN: Grassy headlands, steep stairway to a long broad, dark-sand beach.

ELEVATION GAIN/LOSS: 180 feet+/180 feet-.

BEST TIME: Medium to low tide.

WARNINGS: Trail may be closed periodically, in which case you should use the Jones Beach Trail (see Trail #3). Never turn your back on the ocean; rogue waves can strike any time, especially in winter. Moderate to low tide only, especially in winter.

HOW TO GET THERE: Follow general directions to Sinkyone Park Visitor Center. Trail leads west from there.

FURTHER INFO: Sinkyone Wilderness State Park (707)986-7711.

FEES: Day use parking: $3/vehicle (May–Sept.), $2/vehicle (Oct.–April).

at a low tide of less than +2.0 feet. It extends another ¼ mile, but don't get caught there by the rising tide.

Just 300 feet before the point, where the beach narrows and comes to a creek, a rough emergency-exit trail leads up the canyon and across the bluffs on a vague path to reach the main road just north of the rough crossing at Flat Rock Creek. It is much easier, however, to walk back the way you came.

If you want to walk north on the beach from the steep path from the visitor center, it's slightly more than ⅛ mile to Needle Rock's twin wave tunnels beneath its guano-bleached razor edge. Continue north past more small creeks. The third stream before ⅝ mile, Low Gap Creek, the largest that drops to this entire beach, has a pretty cascade about 200 feet from its rocky mouth. Continue north past a 25-foot rock spire on the beach around ¾ mile to the broadest canyon yet. This is Jones Beach Gulch where the trail climbs east to Jones Beach Camp on the Whale Gulch Trail (Trail #3) at just beyond one mile.

From Jones Beach Trail you can also continue north-northwest along this wild beach at tides lower than +3.0 feet in summer. You might make it all the way to the mouth of Whale Gulch if the tide is right.

5.

BEAR HARBOR
FROM ROAD'S END TO AN OLD HOMESTEAD

The name Bear Harbor fittingly describes the wild and remote nature of this spectacularly rugged place. It's a place of legend—you might have heard some adventurer mention it without giving any hint how to get there. Still, as the word harbor implies, this isolated corner of the world once bustled with commerce. Captain John A. Morgan died while trying to establish a shipping point here in 1868. Morgan Rock is named for him. Dr. William McCornack of Mendocino finally built a loading chute here in 1892, selling it the following year to a group that became the Bear Harbor Lumber Company. The company laid nine miles of railroad track over the ridge and down Indian Creek in 1898, but in 1899 a tidal wave struck, demolishing their wharf and loading chute and drowning a man.

After the disaster they sold out to Sam Anderson's Southern Humboldt Lumber Company which spent a half million dollars extending the railway down Indian Creek to meet the planned Northwestern Pacific route through the South Fork Eel River Canyon. At the start of April 1906 the Southern Humboldt Company had finished their railway and nearly completed the new sawmill that would process their logs. Then the big earthquake hit, throwing the grand plan into chaos. The new NWP line was relocated east, bypassing the South Fork canyon. When a heavy beam struck Anderson in the head and killed him, the mill never opened and the rails and rolling stock of the Bear Harbor and Eel River Railroad rusted in the woods.

BEAR HARBOR:

DISTANCE: ¾ mile to 3¾ miles round trip to Bear Harbor, depending on road conditions. You can add ¾ mile round trip along the beach unless it's high tide.

TIME: One half hour to two hours.

TERRAIN: Verdant coastal stream canyon leading to a secluded beach.

BEST TIME: Spring is best. Summer, autumn OK.

WARNINGS: Watch for stinging nettles and poison oak along the trail. Isolated country with no services. If not camping, leave ample time before dark to walk back to your car.

HOW TO GET THERE: Follow general directions to Sinkyone State Park. One mile beyond the visitor center a sign says NO VEHICLES ADVISED BEYOND THIS POINT. The main problem lies .5 mile beyond the sign in a deep gully at the Flat Rock Creek crossing. Generally a four-wheel-drive or any high-clearance vehicle can easily cross the gully, except perhaps at high water. Some passenger cars have even gone beyond. If you have doubts, consult with the ranger. Do not take chances: no tow truck is around to pull you out. Walk or drive to where the road is blocked by a fence near Orchard Creek. Bear Harbor is ⅜ mile beyond.

FURTHER INFO: Sinkyone Wilderness State Park (707)986-7711.

ENVIRONMENTAL CAMPS: Orchard Creek Camp is 200 feet upstream (to the northeast) at the end of the road, by a pioneer apple orchard. Railroad Creek Camp is ⅛ mile down the trail from the end of the road, in a eucalyptus grove planted by pioneers. Bear Harbor Camp sits around an old homestead site, just a stone's throw from the beach of Bear Harbor.

FEES: Day use parking: $3/vehicle (May–Sept.), $2/vehicle (Oct.–April).

The trail to Bear Harbor crosses Orchard Creek on a small wooden footbridge, following the route of the California Coastal Trail. The nearly level trail follows the creek through lush riparian vegetation. Before ⅛ mile you enter a grove of tall eucalyptus trees, quickly coming upon the path to Railroad Creek Camp on the left. Just beyond the low brushy ridge on your right lies a narrow beach.

Railroad Creek acquired its name in the early days of logging. The railroad ran up this creek to the area where many big redwoods were felled. The bucked-up logs were loaded onto the short line railroad and hauled to Bear Harbor to be loaded onto the lumber schooners that called there. As you cross a footbridge across Railroad Creek, your trail follows the old railroad bed for most of the next ¼ mile to Bear Harbor. Just before you reach the campground at the site of Bear Harbor Ranch, the railroad bed veers to the right across the creek and starts to climb the overgrown ridge to the location of the loading chute at the tip of the point. Iron rails can still be seen protruding from the cliff there.

At ⅜ mile the trail forks. The Lost Coast Trail (and California Coastal Trail, Trail #6) forks left up a canyon past one last camp and a holly bush. Our described trail takes the right fork across a bridge and past the old Bear Harbor Ranch house site (on your left) before coming to the dark sand cove of Bear Harbor. Scattered near the junction of the two creeks are many domesticated plants from the old ranch garden now gone wild: calla lilies, narcissus, yellow water iris, blue creeping myrtle, Port Orford cedar and an old holly bush. The creek has been diverted around the old home site by a stone wall. Notice how the old ranch house was sited to give it maximum protection from the strong winds blowing here most of the time.

From Bear Harbor beach you look south along a jagged, cliffy shoreline torn by immense landslides. It feels like the end of the world. The jagged Anderson Cliffs on the southern horizon soar a thousand feet skyward beyond the mouth of Jackass Creek. Along the tideline of the beach can be found bits of brick and pottery from the old ranch. Watercress and brooklime grow nearly to tideline at the creek's sloping mouth. Seabirds nest in the cliffs above and in the sea stacks offshore. The large sea stack directly offshore is Cluster Cone Rock, the tallest of four spires off the point.

Unless it's high tide, you can walk about ⅜ mile south along the dark-sand beach. As you walk along the beach, keep an ear cocked for the sound of landslides from the precipitous slopes above you. You can see evidence of several slides, most prominently the one inhibiting passage to the jagged point at the south end of the beach, consisting of rocks up to the size of houses. Beyond the point there's no way other than swimming to reach the next sandy beach.

As you return along the beach, keep an eye on the rocky promontory where the loading chute once was. Hawks and ravens frequent this perch, perusing the area for food or intruders. You can walk west across the driftwood at the mouth of the creek and out to the point. At low tide it's an easy scramble over the rocks to the otherwise inaccessible beach west of the ridge. Just be very careful that the rising tide does not trap you on the wrong side of the point. To the northwest lies Morgan Rock, bleached white with guano. Notice its flat top; another loading pier, known as Bear Landing, once reached out to it.

It's a short, easy walk back to your car if you were able to drive to the end of the road. Consider extending your walk by following the Lost Coast Trail south (no dogs, please) It's about 3¾ miles round trip to the virgin forest at Duffy's Gulch. It takes most of a day to walk the 8¼ miles round trip to Wheeler where the trail next drops to sea level. Leave extra time, however, if you had to park 1½ miles farther up the road.

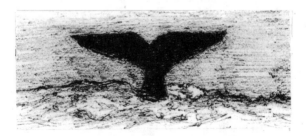

6.

SINKYONE'S LOST COAST

The Lost Coast Trail traverses the most spectacular portion of the Mendocino coast, rugged untamed country. Thomas Merton, famed religious writer and world traveler, considered the Sinkyone one of the most beautiful places in the world. Upon visiting in 1967, he said of the virgin forests here, "Who can bear to see such trees and be away from them."

This trail was completed in 1987. These 17 miles are the most rugged portion of the entire 1200-mile California Coastal Trail. The Lost Coast Trail passes remnants of century-old homesteads and logging camps, even a ghost town abandoned in 1960. The trail is shown on USGS topo maps revised in 1994. Wilderness Press publishes Trails of the Lost Coast, *a map with 250-foot contour lines that shows both Sinkyone State Park and King Range National Conservation Area. On the ground, the trail is well marked. Map and compass are recommended, as is hiking with a friend. You must register to camp along the trail. The cost is $3 per person per night.*

From the road-end trailhead, the trail crosses Orchard Creek on a small footbridge. The nearly level path parallels the creek through lush, riparian vegetation. At ⅛ mile a spur forks left to Railroad Creek Environmental Camp. At ⅜ mile you come to the site of Bear Harbor Ranch, where Bear Harbor Environmental Camp lies near the beach (see Trail #5).

The Lost Coast Trail heads east along a creek, passing one last campsite. Grasslands give way to lush forest as you begin to climb. Around ¾ mile you cross the creek at a verdant, easy ford where five finger fern, pig-a-back plants and salmonberry thrive. Then your trail switchbacks to the right and climbs steadily out of the canyon. Before 1¼ miles your trail joins the first of many old logging roads it follows. It ascends to grand views of the rugged coast.

At 1½ miles the trail switches away from one logging road and promptly joins another. Redwood,

SINKYONE'S LOST COAST:

DISTANCE: 16¾ miles one way.

TIME: Two to three days.

TERRAIN: Rugged coastal canyons and ridges of mixed forest and grassland.

ELEVATION GAIN/LOSS: Orchard Creek to Wheeler: 1440 feet+/1440 feet-. For entire trail: 5300 feet+/5300 feet-.

BEST TIME: Spring. Summer and autumn are next best.

WARNINGS: Isolated country far from towns and traveled roads. Hike with a companion. Requires map and compass and the ability to use them. Timber rattlesnakes, scorpions, ticks, poison oak and stinging nettles all occur along the trail. Watch out and keep away from them. Beyond Wheeler (at 4½ miles), this route is one of the most arduous in this book. You must have a permit to hike overnight on this trail. When you get your permit, inquire about trail conditions. Camping allowed only in designated areas.

HOW TO GET THERE: Follow general directions to Sinkyone State Park, then proceed to Bear Harbor. (If you cannot drive beyond Flat Rock Creek, add 1½ miles to total distance.) The trail is marked LOST COAST TRAIL at the fork near Bear Harbor Environmental Camp.

FEES: Day use parking: $3/vehicle (May–Sept.), $2/vehicle (Oct.–April). Permit required for overnights: $3/person/night.

FURTHER INFO: Sinkyone Wilderness State Park (707)986-7711.

huckleberry, wild rose, iris, and slink pod grow along the trail. You top a ridge, then descend into Duffy's Gulch. The trail leaves the logging road and joins a portion of the original Humboldt Trail, built in 1862 when the coast to the south was opened to homesteading. A Pomo Indian was the last person known to traverse the old trail. He rode a horse from Usal to Shelter Cove in 1922.

As you descend east into Duffy's Gulch, you spot virgin redwoods. As you descend more steeply, the

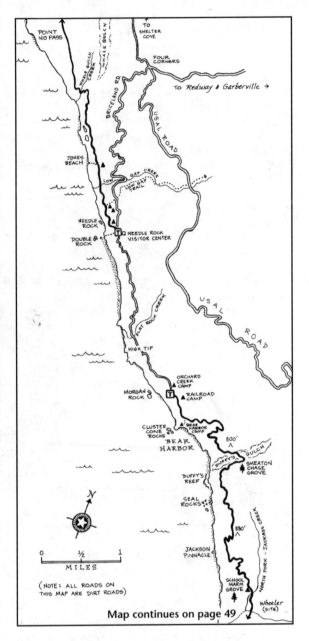

Map continues on page 49

gurgling of the stream can be heard over the roaring of the surf. The trail switchbacks down to the creek crossing, passing ancient redwoods ten feet in diameter, grand fir, Douglas fir and bay laurel. Look up to your left at a towering rock overhang; a large fir tree grows atop the rock. Over the creek crossing grows a giant big leaf maple with a crown 80 feet across.

44

Take a minute to quench your thirst, fill your canteen, and marvel at the virgin beauty of this place. Along the creek grow five-finger, woodwardia, leather, sword and lady ferns. Pacific waterleaf (with odd green flowers), redwood sorrel, pig-a-back plant, huckleberry, Douglas iris and an occasional calypso orchid thrive in this moist habitat, as does poison oak, which you should watch for. You have come 2¼ miles from Orchard Creek.

Leave the forest for steep coastal grasslands around 2¾ miles. Your trail traverses grassy bluffs through a series of small gullies and rises. Paintbrush, buttercup, blue-eyed grass, lupine, dandelion and golden poppy add color as the roar of surf rises from below. Expansive views of the Sinkyone lie to the north.

You soon plunge into the first of several dark forests along the ridge. After more grasslands, you enter another fir forest as you wrap around a sinkhole or slough pocket, a natural drainage with no above ground outlet. The sinkhole formed as coastal uplifting occurred to the west of the drainage, causing it to find an underground outlet. As your trail follows the western edge of the sinkhole, notice the dense vegetation in its protected microclimate. Pass a gnarled, wind-topped redwood, then come to more grasslands.

You come to a nice stand of redwoods at 3¼ miles. Your trail switchbacks left and climbs to a ridge. Ascend steeply along the narrow ridge to its top, passing trillium, iris, redwood sorrel, one-leaved wild onion, slink pod, miners lettuce, toyon and columbine. You parallel an old fence before descending steeply east, then south. Climb steeply again to another top, then descend more switchbacks before climbing to a third top at 3¾ miles. From here you can look east into the heavily wooded canyons of Jackass Creek, site of the logging ghost town of Wheeler.

Descend gradually along the east side of the ridge through mixed conifer forest. Then you switch sharply right and descend bluffs of low brush and grass with foxglove, ceanothus, tall brodiaea, blue-eyed grass, sticky monkeyflower, beach strawberry and poison oak.

Parallel the edge of a forest around 3⅞ miles. You soon approach a gnarled old redwood grove, the trees windswept and stunted, but surviving. Behind their dense vegetation lies another slough pocket. Two narrow paths into the depression are guarded by poison oak and easily missed. If you find your way, however, you enter a small virgin redwood grove, a refuge where the silence of the trees overcomes the roar of surf and wind outside.

At 4⅛ miles your trail turns northeast, leaving the coast and the ridge you have been following. As you come to a clearing, you can see the old Wheeler road in a flat grassy opening 600 feet below; you will be there soon. The trail drops rapidly now by a series of long switchbacks.

Pass two large redwoods surrounded by smaller redwoods, then descend into a fern-filled gulch. You soon come to big trees at the bottom of the canyon. Known as Schoolmarm Grove, it was named for the Wheeler schoolhouse once located nearby. In another 100 feet you come to a campsite beneath two large redwoods in a clearing beside the North Fork of Jackass Creek. A second campsite lies 200 feet downstream, near the creek crossing. A spring box lies in the gulch west of the outhouse.

If you need to hike out the same day, be sure to leave three hours of daylight to get back to your car or camp.

Wheeler was established in 1950, one of the last company logging towns and probably the newest ghost town in the west. The town lasted ten years, abandoned as improved roads allowed the logs to be hauled to larger mills. Wheeler housed 32 families who harvested the timber, worked in the sawmill, and hauled the cut lumber to Willits by truck. The modern town had electricity, telephones and a water system.

The trail into "town" fords the creek, then heads south on the old road, passing crumbling foundations, rusting logging relics and side streets. Domesticated plants grow wild here: foxglove, spearmint, red hot poker and alyssum. About ¼ mile from the creek crossing, you reach the heart of town. The sawmill was located here at the confluence of the two forks of the creek.

The trail fords the creek and heads south, paralleling the beach at 4⅞ miles. A large grassy flat and a lagoon lie between the trail and the beach. High

cliffs guard the dark-sand beach at both ends. Harbor seals and seabirds frequent the strand.

The trail turns southeast and climbs a grassy gulch where the bosses lived. At 5⅛ miles you come to a wildflower garden at the top of the cleared portion of the gulch. The trail ascends steeply through dense brush, then into tall forest. From 6¾ miles you climb by several switchbacks to top a ridge at 800 feet elevation.

Descend along the border between forest and grasslands. At 7¼ miles a vernal pool lies west of the trail. Continue your descent into a hanging valley of grasslands sprinkled with wildflowers. At 7½ miles you approach the creek at an elevation of 450 feet. Be careful as you cross it because stinging nettles cover deep holes in the creek; one false step and they will sting you.

Then your trail climbs east, following the south fork of the creek. At 7⅝ miles you switchback to the right and climb a ridge at the top of Anderson Cliff by a dozen switchbacks. Several of the westernmost switchbacks have side trails that lead to the top of Anderson Cliff for magnificent views.

The long climb ends as you gain a grassy ridge at 8⅜ miles (1100 feet elevation). An old jeep road on your left climbs to meet the Wheeler Road. After a brief level stretch, your trail descends gradually east, then steeply south toward Little Jackass Creek. At 8⅞ miles you veer left and descend by several switchbacks through grasslands with great views. You might hear a herd of sea lions barking on the beach below. Wildflowers brighten the way: foxglove, paintbrush, yarrow, monkeyflower, poppy and brodiaea.

Come to the floor of the canyon at 9¼ miles, near an old corral, all that remains of a pre-1900 logging camp. An outhouse at the junction serves two adjacent campsites. The magnificent beach lies about ⅛ mile west, bordered by sea caves and the towering Anderson Cliff. A herd of sea lions sometimes lives on the south end of the beach. Please stay at least 200 feet from the wild animals.

The main trail heads up the canyon, crossing the creek at 9⅜ miles. In another 500 feet, you come to the upper camp with two more sites and an outhouse near the creek beneath large redwoods and maples.

The trail south starts climbing immediately, crossing the creek and ascending along it before switchbacking to the right. Ascend steadily by six switchbacks into the upper canyon, a checkerboard of clearcuts and virgin stands. At 10¼ miles the trail meets an old road. You follow it east, then south above Northport Gulch. The road stays generally level, crossing a small creek at 10½ miles, then passing whole hillsides of sticky monkeyflowers.

Beyond 10⅞ miles you reach a broad landing where the road turns northeast. Your trail leaves the road here, descending south, with views down to the mouth of Northport Gulch. Switchback left, then descend steeply by eight switchbacks into Anderson Gulch. At 11¾ miles you reach the camp, with a view down to the mouth of Anderson Gulch.

Descend two more switchbacks to a ford of the creek. Climb steeply to precipitous, grassy headlands, where you contour above the shore. Make a short descent into fern-filled Dark Gulch, where towering Big White Rock and a pyramid-shaped blowhole rock lie offshore. The trail follows Dark Gulch upstream, crossing the creek at 12⅞ miles.

Now you make one last long ascent, climbing 900

feet in 1¼ miles to just below the 1320-foot summit of Timber Point. Your trail meanders south through the forest, crosses a seasonal creek, then descends to grasslands at 15¼ miles. The unusual red and green brodiaea called Chinese firecracker grows beside the trail in spring.

You follow the ridge southeast, with great views of the coast to the south and the wooded canyons of Hotel Gulch and Usal Creek to the east. The last ⅞ mile you descend east by 20 switchbacks to meet Usal Road, 16¾ miles from the northern trailhead.

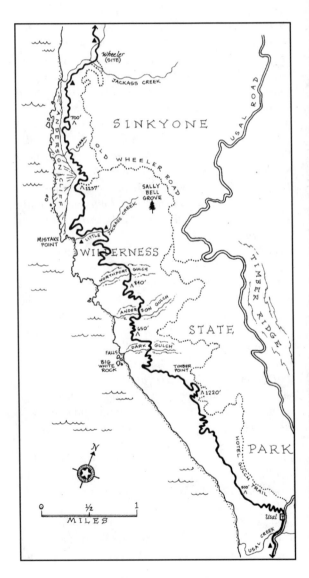

7.

SALLY BELL GROVE

OLD WHEELER ROAD

In autumn of 1983, word spread around the north coast that Georgia-Pacific was logging the last of the big virgin trees around Usal. About 200 action-oriented environmentalists decided to try to stop the logging of the biggest trees along the Wheeler Road. They went out to the Lost Coast by cover of darkness and prepared for civil disobedience. When the loggers arrived at dawn to cut the trees, they found people sitting, lying, standing between them and the virgin redwoods, blocking their bulldozers, and preventing work from beginning. The confrontation vented much anger between the opposing sides. When sheriff's deputies arrested one of the protestors, she said her name was Sally Bell. In fact, Sally Bell was one of the last full-blooded members of the Sinkyone tribe. She had died about 80 years before. The eco-defenders wanted to show their support for the Native American practice of living in harmony with the land, the antithesis of the clearcutting that was going on. The name Sally Bell caught on, and from then on the press referred to the ongoing confrontation as occurring at the Sally Bell Grove.

After continuing showdowns between the loggers and the lovers of the forest, a court injunction delayed logging at the site. The grove was finally saved when the Trust for Public Land purchased the grove and the surrounding lands. The last of the once-extensive virgin forests of the Sinkyone was saved. While there are bigger groves and bigger trees elsewhere, the victory for the environment instilled a special spirit in this place, and gave momentum to the efforts to save the last of the virgin redwoods.

The old Wheeler Road leaves the Usal Road at M.10.5. An orange gate stands 100 feet from the Usal Road, blocking the Wheeler Road to motor vehicle traffic. Behind the gate the road bends right and heads west, descending through cutover timber lands where Douglas fir and redwood are regenerating the forest. You pass hardwood and brush species along

SALLY BELL GROVE:

DISTANCE: 2⅛ miles round trip to grove, 8¼ miles round trip to Wheeler.

TIME: One hour to grove, four hours to Wheeler, round trip.

TERRAIN: Well graded old logging road through cutover forest to small virgin grove. Steep descent on road to reach Wheeler.

ELEVATION GAIN/LOSS: Round trip to grove: 240 feet+/240 feet-. Round trip to Wheeler: 1960 feet+/ 1960 feet-.

BEST TIME: Spring for wildflowers.

WARNINGS: You must obtain a permit before going to Wheeler to camp. Isolated country far from services; hike with a friend. No water along trail. Road to trailhead may be impassable in rainy season. Due to steep curves, it is never passable to RV's or trailers. Bikes not allowed on last 2 miles of Wheeler Road.

HOW TO GET THERE: Turn west off Highway 1 at M.90.88 onto unpaved, unmarked Usal Road. The road climbs to 1000 feet, then descends by abrupt, steep switchbacks to Usal Campground, then climbs steeply again to M.10.5, where you will see an orange gate on a spur road on your left, the Wheeler Road. (While you can also reach the trailhead from Four Corners, 15 miles north, that portion of the road is even rougher.)

FURTHER INFO: Sinkyone Wilderness State Park (707) 986-7711. See map, page 49.

the way: tanoak, madrone, chinquapin, ceanothus and manzanita. The deep canyon of Anderson Gulch lies on your left. At ⅜ mile your descent steepens.

Beyond ⅜ mile the road levels and meets a junction with the Hotel Gulch horse and bike trail (marked as Road 4500 on a chunk of rusting saw blade). You continue on the Wheeler Road, turning north and climbing. Rhododendron and wax myrtle mix with the other hardwood species. Douglas iris cluster at the edge of your path.

Beyond ¾ mile your road descends west, winds, then climbs. At ⅞ mile you pass a small redwood grove. Your route soon climbs northeast, lined with pampas grass. You level again at one mile and head due west. Passing huckleberry bushes, you climb slightly for 300 feet and come to virgin redwoods on the left of the road.

This is the upper end of the Sally Bell Grove, a small but special grove named for Sally Bell, the last member of the Sinkyone tribe that once called these wild lands home. A path heads west into the grove. The grove has several fire-scarred redwood giants up to eleven feet in diameter and 200 feet in height, as well as several large Douglas firs. While this area was disrupted by heavy logging equipment before it became part of Sinkyone Wilderness State Park, it has recently been restored to its original form. It still harbors scattered pockets of huckleberry, redwood sorrel, evergreen violets and salal. The grove extends downhill into the headwaters of Little Jackass Creek.

Take a few minutes to enjoy the stately quiet of the grove. Imagine what this wilderness was like before the loggers took the big trees from most of the land. Even this small virgin stand would be gone without the bold action of a few committed conservationists.

From here you have a short and easy return to your starting point. Or you may continue along the road to the site of the ghost town of Wheeler on the coast.

If you choose to continue, the road heads west. Soon an opening on your left looks out to the ocean. You can hear the surf pounding far below. At 1¼ miles you approach more virgin redwoods and Douglas firs on the right of the road.

Near 1⅜ miles you come to a grand view down into Little Jackass Canyon, with the Pacific beyond. Wood rose grows at your feet. Your route descends west, passing woodwardia ferns, then sticky monkeyflower and bush lupine. Soon another grand view south opens up, this one of the rugged coast south to Fort Bragg and beyond.

At 1½ miles your road bends and descends steeply. Just before 1¾ miles, a view opens up to the north. You have an end-on vista of the Sinkyone and Lost Coast, including High Tip, Chemise Mountain, Shelter Cove, Shubrick Peak and Punta Gorda. At 2 miles from the Usal Road, you come to a level wide spot in the road. From here a rough trail climbs steeply, then descends to meet the trail to Little Jackass Creek in ⅜ mile. The main road bends right, and comes to a sturdy locked gate. Bicycles are not allowed beyond the gate. Wheeler Road descends 1200 feet in elevation to Wheeler, meeting the Lost Coast Trail at 4⅛ miles. Keep in mind that you must have a permit to camp along the Lost Coast Trail, while camping is not allowed along the Wheeler Road.

If you do continue to Wheeler, save some time, energy and drinking water for the steep climb back out to the Usal Road.

8.

USAL WATERFALL
SOUTH END OF THE SINKYONE

Usal Beach and the adjacent steep bluffs were the southern end of the Sinkyone tribe's territory. The Sinkyone name for the place was Djokniki. The name Usal (Youshal on early maps) is believed to have originated in the Pomo word for southeast.

After 1867 Usal saw a number of white travelers since it was on the Humboldt Trail, which led along the coast from Fort Bragg to Eureka. But not until

USAL WATERFALL:

DISTANCE: 4½ miles round trip.

TIME: Two to three hours.

TERRAIN: Rocky beach at the foot of steep cliffs.

BEST TIME: Spring. By summer the falls are just a trickle. Extreme low tide is best, though passable at moderate low tide.

WARNINGS: Requires a tide of +2.0 feet or lower. Always watch the ocean for oversize rogue waves. Wear sturdy boots to walk the rocky beach. Isolated country; nearest services: south at Westport and east at Leggett. Water faucets now in campground. Road may be impassable in rainy season. Due to steep curves, it is never passable to RV's or trailers. Use of off-road vehicles prohibited.

HOW TO GET THERE: Turn west off Highway 1 at M.90.88 (road on left when going north) onto unpaved, unmarked Usal Road. The road quickly climbs to 1000 feet, providing spectacular coastal views. It then descends by abrupt, steep switchbacks to Usal Campground near the mouth of Usal Creek. Cross a narrow wooden bridge over the creek, then turn left at M.6.00 onto the rough, short road to the beach.

FURTHER INFO: Sinkyone Wilderness State Park. (707)986-7711. See map, page 49.

FEES: Day use parking: $3/vehicle (May–Sept.), $2/vehicle (Oct.–April). Car camping: $7–11/night.

1889 did the first whites settle at Usal, where they installed a lumber mill and loading wharf for the Usal Redwood Company. Usal had some of the largest trees in Mendocino County. The large mill was in operation by 1892, along with a 1600-foot-long wharf (!) and 3 miles of railroad up the creek.

In 1894 Robert Dollar bought the whole operation. Apparently Dollar was able to purchase it because he owned the steamship Newsboy and was able to land where other ships refused to call, Usal being the most dangerous of all the doghole ports. The mill shut down in 1900, largely because the huge trees were inferior to (though probably older than) those used for lumber elsewhere on the coast, yield-

*ing only half the lumber that their size indicated. In
1902 the idle mill and most of the town burned down.*

*Robert Dollar went on to build his fortune with
the Dollar Steamship Line, later President Lines.
Usal became one of the first of many logging ghost
towns along the Mendocino coast. Logging resumed
after World War II, and informal use by hunters,
fishermen and off-road vehicles became common.*

*The state acquired the land in 1987, banning hunt-
ing and off-road vehicles, removing garbage, and
providing rangers and volunteers to enforce the new
rules. This wild land became subject to state park
regulations: dogs must be leashed, fires are permitted only in the fire rings provided, camping is $7-11
per night ($3 more for each additional vehicle and
$1 per dog). All refuse must be packed out.*

*The beach hike to the waterfall at Dark Gulch
Creek is one of the most strenuous moderate hikes
in this book. I recommend sturdy boots because of
the uneven rock hopping beyond the first mile. It's
this rock dance that makes the otherwise level trek
so strenuous.*

Have you checked your tide table? Make sure you
are interpreting current tide information correctly,
as the cliffs behind this narrow beach are unforgiving. It is best to start this hike two hours or more
before low tide. You can only reach the waterfall at
a tide of +2.0 feet or less.

This beach hike starts where the beach road ends,
just north of the mouth of Usal Creek. You walk
northwest along the dark-sand and gravel beach, at
the base of 400-foot cliffs. Large rocks lie scattered
along the beach, mostly at the base of the slide-torn
cliffs.

Within a mile large boulders lie along the beach.
The cliffs on your right become even higher as you
walk toward the waterfall, which can be seen falling
to the beach near the point. At 1¼ miles, 1320-foot-
high Timber Point lies hidden above you at the top
of the cliffs, less than a half mile away. This is more
than a 100% slope (a 45° angle). Also near this point,
two small seasonal streams cascade down to the
beach. They are not dependable as a water source,
drying up by summer.

Continue northwest on the narrowing beach. It
becomes more rocky than sandy for the rest of the

hike. In fact, the walking over uneven rocks makes the rest of the hike rough-going. A few sea stacks lie offshore. Several rock outcrops along this stretch bar passage at a tide of +2.0 feet or more. Beyond 2 miles, you pass 100-foot-tall Big White Rock offshore. Beyond the pinnacle, the waterfall, when flowing, pulls at your attention. When it is in full force, billows of spray fly in all directions. As you walk around one more rocky outcrop, the falls are not far ahead.

At 2¼ miles you come to the falls. Here the beach ends, with the waterfall tumbling out of Dark Gulch onto rocks just short of the point. A pyramid-shaped, 50-foot-tall seastack rises offshore. When the waves and tide are right, a blowhole shoots spray high in the air.

It takes a minus tide of -1.5 feet to be able to walk around the point. Even then, be sure you do not get trapped on the wrong side of the point by the rising tide. You cannot climb the crumbly cliffs above the beach.

As you walk back along the beach, you have spectacular views south along the coast to the jagged point of Cape Vizcaino and the rest of the Mendocino coast beyond.

OTHER SUGGESTION: LOST COAST TRAIL, SOUTH END, leaves the Usal Road at M.6.14, climbing quickly to spectacular views of the beach and Usal Creek in the first mile. It is 5 steep miles to Anderson Gulch, 7½ miles to Little Jackass Creek.

HOTEL GULCH HORSE & BIKE TRAIL (Trail #9) follows an old logging road from the northwest corner of Usal Campground north for 6 miles to join the Wheeler Road.

9.

HOTEL GULCH
BIKE & EQUESTRIAN TRAIL WORKS FOR HIKERS TOO

Usal in Sinkyone Wilderness State Park sits in one of the most beautiful and remote corners of the Mendocino coast, a land of breathtaking vistas and towering ridges and cliffs. If hiking the Lost Coast Trail from its south end seems too steep for your taste (1330 feet+/160 feet- in 2½ miles), try this moderate hike on an old road. While this old road climbs as high, it's gradient overall is more gradual, especially beyond Timber Ridge.

The Hotel Gulch Trail follows the eastern park boundary, climbing over Timber Ridge, then dipping through the upper reaches of Dark Gulch and Anderson Gulch before ending at the Wheeler Road. From there you can return or extend the loop as described below.

Your hike starts at the junction of Usal Road and Hotel Gulch Trail at the north end of Usal Campground. Hotel Gulch Trail, an old logging road, heads west on a gentle incline through forest. Pass a silver gate at ⅛ mile and climb gradually to ½ mile where you cross a tributary of Hotel Gulch Creek. Ascend moderately on good track to 1½ miles. At big bends left and right, look south for the first views along the coast.

Continue climbing moderately beyond 1½ miles with intermittent steep hills. Beyond 1¾ mile the ascent eases at a big bend right where you overlook the nearby Lost Coast Trail and the rugged shoreline beyond. The double track continues its moderate ascent over Timber Ridge, with some gradual inclines providing relief. After another coastal view at 2⅛ miles, ascend moderately by switchbacks to top Timber Ridge at 2⅝ miles.

At the 1320-foot summit, vistas suddenly expand to include the heavily logged but spectacular watersheds of Dark Gulch and Anderson Gulch to the northwest. As you start to descend, a big bend to the right at 2¾ miles offers views west down steep Dark Gulch to its mouth, where Big White Rock

HOTEL GULCH

DISTANCE: 11½ miles round trip, or 5¼ miles round trip to Timber Ridge. Add one mile round trip to Sally Bell Grove.

TIME: All day.

TERRAIN: Steady ascent through cut-over areas to a high ridge, then down and up through two watersheds.

ELEVATION GAIN/LOSS: 2200 feet+/2200 feet-. Add 40 feet+/40 feet- to grove.

BEST TIME: Spring and autumn.

WARNINGS: Watch for and yield to equestrians. Watch for cyclists.

HOW TO GET THERE: Follow directions in Trail #8 across bridge over Usal Creek. Continue straight to the second intersection after the bridge and park.

FURTHER INFO: Sinkyone Wilderness State Park (707) 986-7711, 247-3318.

FEES: Day use: $3/vehicle (May–Sept.), $2/vehicle (Oct.-April). Camping at Usal: $7–11/night.

towers offshore. Hotel Gulch Trail descends moderately to 3¼ miles then crosses Dark Gulch.

Above the creek crossing, Dark Gulch Creek tumbles over a 12-foot-tall rock shelf draped with five-finger ferns, a lovely weeping wall. Your double track descends gradually for about a mile. Pause at 4 miles for another great view down Dark Gulch. Look south to Timber Ridge, where several large trees 200 to 300 feet tall pierce the skyline. Imagine this entire watershed filled with an immense forest of redwoods and firs, many with bases twenty feet or more in diameter. Such a forest was here until 1980, and may grow back in another 500 years.

Hotel Gulch Trail bends to the right and crosses to the north side of a ridge, entering the Anderson Gulch watershed. The descent continues until 4¾ miles, where you cross the first of several forks of

Anderson Gulch Creek. Ascend moderately through an area where recent restoration and repair of logging damage makes for rough tread. After crossing the creek's main fork at 4⅞ miles, climb steeply, with occasional relief, to 5¼ miles. Tread improves as the incline turns moderate to the end of Hotel Gulch Trail at the old Wheeler Road at 5¾ miles, where you have several choices.

You can return from here for an 11½-mile round trip. Or you can go left at the end of Hotel Gulch Trail to descend the Wheeler Road ½ mile to Sally Bell Grove, a remnant stand of virgin redwoods with a commanding view down Little Jackass Creek to the shore when it's clear. You can continue down Wheeler Road beyond the grove. This stretch offers more coastal views north and south. At one mile a locked gate marks the end of bicycle access, but hikers can continue to Wheeler on the coast to link with the Lost Coast Trail. If you continue to Wheeler, however, you'll probably want to have overnight gear unless you're a marathon hiker.

10.

DeHAVEN CREEK to WAGES CREEK

SANDY WALK ALONG ROCKY SHORE OF
WESTPORT-UNION LANDING STATE BEACH

Officially only 60 acres, tiny Westport-Union Landing State Beach sprawls along 4 miles of spectacularly rugged coast. When the tide is high you can only reach isolated pocket beaches here—they're pleasant, but don't amount to a hike. But when the tide is +2.0 feet or lower, you can hike along 2½ miles of tidepool-rich rocky and sandy shore, an easy and invigorating walk following the route of the California Coastal Trail through a natural marine wonderland.

Both the Westport and the Union Landing of the park's name refer to historic towns, one at each end of the state-held shoreline. Westport to the south boomed during the last two decades of the nineteenth century, with 60 or more ships loading at the town's

DeHAVEN CREEK to WAGES CREEK:

DISTANCE: 1½ to 2¾ miles round trip.
TIME: One or two hours.
TERRAIN: Sandy beach.
BEST TIME: Low tide.
WARNINGS: Impassable at tide of +2.0 feet or more.
   Always watch the ocean for killer waves. Private
   property at south end. Stay on sand.
HOW TO GET THERE: Turn west off Highway 1 at
   M.79.3, north of Westport. Parking lot is 150 feet
   north of entrance.
FURTHER INFO: Mendocino State Parks (707)
   937-5804.

*two wharves each year. One account claims Westport
had 14 saloons in its heyday. Though fires consumed
much of Westport in the first half of the twentieth century, the sleepy town managed to survive.*

*Fate dealt more harshly with Union Landing. The
sawmill town on the bluffs south of Juan Creek
hummed with activity from 1899 until 1924, but no
trace of it has been visible for many years.*

The trail starts 100 feet south of the parking lot. A
sign indicates no motor vehicles beyond the
trailhead. The trail drops quickly to a rocky beach.
You soon come to a ford of DeHaven Creek. It's an
easy ford in summer, but in winter you'll probably
get wet feet.

Just over ⅛ mile from the trailhead, you come to a
rocky point. Here you must gauge if the tide is low
enough to continue. If the tide is rising and the water is coming over the tidal rocks onto the beach,
don't go.

The beach widens just around this point. Rocky
tidepools are on your right, blanketed with seaweed
and very slippery. At ¼ mile you round a second
rocky point. The view opens up to the south; you
can see Wages Creek Beach ½ mile ahead, the buildings of Westport visible beyond.

The beach widens again near ⅜ mile. The rocky
tidepools on the right give way to scattered small

rocks. The cliffs to your left are lower here.

A little beyond ½ mile, the cliffs end. You come to a very wide beach at the broad canyon of Wages Creek. A private campground is up in the canyon—please KEEP OUT unless you're camping there! At ¾ mile you come to Wages Creek, running along the cliff at the south end of the beach. Here you must decide whether to return for a 1½-mile round trip or continue, if the tide is still low enough.

If you decide to continue, it's easiest to ford the creek about 100 feet upstream from its mouth. Return to the mouth of the creek and follow the beach south along the base of the cliff, coming to a narrow passage or, if the tide is too high, an impassable spot. If you can get by, you soon reach a sea stack on your right at the edge of the beach. You can walk into its wave tunnel at low tide to examine the tidal creatures. Gooseneck and volcano-shape barnacles, limpets and a few mussels grow on the east side. The seaward side has more mussels and some anemones.

Beyond the sea stack, the narrow sand strip broadens to another beach. This ends ¼ mile beyond at yet another rocky point. Just 200 feet before the south end of the beach, a trail climbs 87 steps to reach the bluffs, a convenient escape route if the tide is rising. To continue south, you must scramble over rocks for 150 feet. (Again, make sure the tide is low enough!) Then another long beach extends for ⅛ mile to more rocks. You're now 1⅜ miles from your car. If you walk out on the rocks beyond the

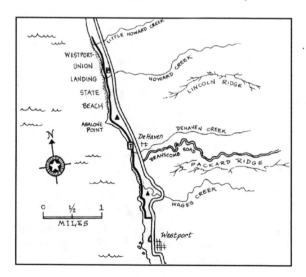

point, you can see yet another small beach, above which are the houses of Westport. If you continue over slippery, seaweed-covered tidal rocks, you'll probably get your feet wet. Many varieties of seaweed cover the rocks.

As you return, you may want to walk along the top of the beach at the base of the cliff, observing the tangled mass of soft chaparral thriving there. The plants include:

horsetail fern	poison hemlock
angelica	coast buckwheat
lupine	bracken fern
wild mustard	sea rocket
ice plant	seep-spring monkeyflower
hen and chicks	northern dune tansy
golden poppy	purple seaside daisy
paintbrush	creeping myrtle
thistle	coastal manroot
plantain	beach morning glory
blackberry	salal
cow parsnip	yellow sand verbena

OTHER SUGGESTIONS: The paved road along the BLUFFTOP NORTH TO HOWARD CREEK provides a good place to explore on bicycles, on foot or in a wheelchair. Watch for vehicle traffic on the 1¼-mile ride. At low tide you can also walk the

ROCKY BEACH NORTH TO ABALONE POINT and
beyond to Howard Creek Beach.

PETE'S BEACH TRAIL provides access to the ¼-
mile long beach south of Wages Creek no matter
what the tide. It leaves Highway 1 at M.77.78 and
descends 87 steps to the south end of the beach.

11.

ANGELO PRESERVE

OLD GROWTH SANCTUARY PROTECTS
BIOLOGICAL DIVERSITY

*The Angelo Preserve, until recently called the North-
ern California Coast Range Preserve, straddles the
South Fork Eel River near its headwaters, protect-
ing one of California's larger remaining virgin forests. The Kato people, the southernmost
Athabascan-speaking tribe in California, roamed
these hills for centuries, inhabiting the meadows and
harvesting abundant food found in diverse habitats:
pure and mixed forest, grassland, chaparral and
riparian. The Kato inhabited a triangular area
roughly defined by the contemporary towns of
Branscomb, Laytonville and Cummings. They were
relatives of the Sinkyone and Wailaki people to the
north. The Kato creation story views:*

> our earth as a vast horned animal that wal-
> lowed southward through the primeval waters
> with Nagaicho (the great traveler) standing on
> its head, until the beast came to rest lying down
> in its present position.

*Most of the Kato had already been forced onto
reservations when the first white settlers reached
the Branscomb Valley in 1885. Over the next twenty
years, eight families homesteaded land now in the
Preserve. Like the Kato, they lived in the meadows
and relied on the land's natural resources for sur-
vival.*

*The settlers' lives were never easy, but twentieth
century economics added additional pressures.
When the depression hit in 1929, many settlers had*

ANGELO PRESERVE:

DISTANCE: 7¼ miles round trip or 7¾ semi-loop.

TIME: Half day to full day.

TERRAIN: Follows dirt road up and down through virgin forest and meadows along canyon of wild river, descends to homestead beside meadow, climbs to brushy ridge, descends and returns.

ELEVATION GAIN/LOSS: 400 feet+/560 feet- to White House, 900 feet+/960 feet- with upper loop.

BEST TIME: Spring or summer.

WARNINGS: Watch for poison oak. Don not disturb any plants, animals or historical artifacts. Watch for rattlesnakes, ticks and scorpions. No mountain bikes, pets, radios, smoking or camping allowed.

HOW TO GET THERE: FROM HIGHWAY 1: Turn east north of Westport at M.79.1 onto steep, winding, recently paved Branscomb Road. Go 12.9 miles, then turn left on Wilderness Lodge Road and go 3.5 more miles to headquarters. Register, pick up a map and perhaps make a donation. Then drive 500 feet to parking. FROM HIGHWAY 101: Turn west in Laytonville onto Branscomb Road (M.70.). Go 13 miles to Wilderness Lodge Road, which forks right just beyond Eel River bridge. Go 3.5 miles to Preserve.

FURTHER INFO: Angelo Preserve (707)984-6653.

already moved on. Heath and Marjorie Angelo bought the boarded-up Elder homestead in 1931, later acquiring adjacent lands. The Angelos loved the area's wilderness nature and acted to preserve it. In 1959 they sold to the tiny Nature Conservancy, the organization's first venture in the western states. The Bureau of Land Management added adjoining virgin forests, completing today's 7520-acre sanctuary.

This richly layered biome, catching 85 inches of rain in an average year, supports a vast botanical diversity: 450 species of vascular plants, 93 mosses and 78 lichens. More than 60 mammal species reside or visit. Flying squirrels, ringtails, ermines and endangered spotted owls inhabit the forests. Pristine riparian corridors bring steelhead and salmon runs which in turn sustain river otter, mink, bear and mountain lion. Chaparral on south slopes shelters brush rabbits, wood rats, chipmunks and bobcats. Today the Angelo Preserve is managed by the University of California Natural Reserve System. Please watch for and do not disturb ongoing research projects, efforts to better understand, protect and preserve this pristine complex of interweaving habitats.

California hazel and vanilla grass grow beside the parking lot 500 feet beyond headquarters. Follow a footpath that drops north to the dirt road beside interpretive panels, then walk northeast past the gate on narrow Wilderness Lodge Road paralleling the South Fork Eel River below on the left. Climb gradually through mixed forest to ¼ mile. Perennials in the lush understory include creeping snowberry, wood rose, wood strawberry, evergreen huckleberry, rattlesnake plantain, saxifrage, honeysuckle and poison oak, all common along this hike. In spring look for flowers of evergreen violet, milkmaids, inside-out flower, redwood sorrel, trillium, starflower, wood anemone, fat Solomon's seal, Indian warrior and vanilla leaf.

Pass sedum and leather fern on a rocky cutbank, then descend east to wind along the river where large virgin redwoods and Douglas firs mix with tanoaks, madrones, big leaf maples and bay laurels in mature forest.

Cross a bridge over Skunk Creek, lined with woodwardia and sword ferns, at ⅝ mile. Soon a beautiful grove of redwoods stands between road and river. As you continue down canyon, you might spot tiger lilies in May. Sinuously shaped madrones stretch for sunlight.

Pass the Conger Trail on the right at one mile. (It climbs 1500 feet in 5½ miles to the Conger homestead.) Your road crosses a bridge over beautiful Elder Creek, then bends right, leaving the river to follow the creek upstream. Walker Meadow Trail soon forks left to cross the river, rejoining the road near Wilderness Lodge (summer bridges at crossings, fords required rest of year).

As you continue on the road above Elder Creek, look for red larkspur on the left and serviceberry, miner's lettuce and soap plant on the right. Pass the old Angelo place at 1¼ miles. Homesteaded by the Elder family in 1892, it now serves as the caretaker's residence. Two outhouses stand on the left beside the pleasant clearing and orchard.

Your road starts climbing, offering fine views of Elder Creek's pristine canyon. You soon pass a hydrologic bench mark station used to monitor the creek for flow and quality. Ascend along the lovely canyon passing ocean spray beneath mixed forest.

Climb through oak woodlands around 1⅝ miles After a rolling glade on the right, your route climbs north to meet the Black Oak Mountain Trail on the right at a saddle. (It forks right to ascend the 3708-foot peak on the Preserve's eastern boundary.)

Follow the road as it descends northeast, leaving Elder Creek watershed and returning to mature conifer forest. Look for slink pod, hazel, giant trillium and Oregon grape on a long steady descent, soon overlooking the Eel in its canyon far below. Pass a large redwood at 2⅛ miles and return to the river-

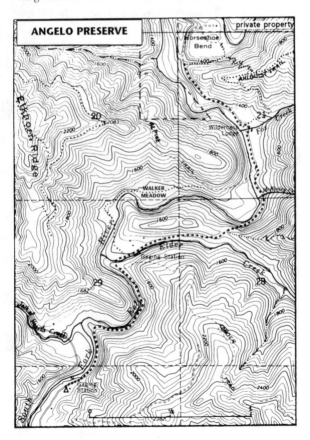

side, lined with red alders. Your trail contours north, then climbs above a grassy flat beside the river at 2¼ miles. You meet the north end of the Walker Meadow Trail on your left in 250 feet.

Your road threads between the river and big South Meadow. The Preserve's broad, flat clearings like this are former river terraces, shaped before the river cut its deeper canyon. The Kato people enlarged and managed these clearings by burning them, encouraging food plants like the white oaks, canyon live oaks and manzanitas growing here. Baby blue eyes, poppies, irises, lupines, buttercups and popcorn flowers color the lush green clearing in spring. The road soon bends right, wrapping around the meadow's north end.

Cross a bridge over Fox Creek at 2⅝ miles and meet a junction. The Ahlquist Trail forks right past old farm equipment rusting beneath fruit trees. The loop at the end of the described hike returns by that trail. Follow the main road as it bends left past Wilderness Lodge, now used by researchers and educational groups. The original Wilderness Lodge, which burned in 1937, was a resort for city dwellers during the first quarter of the twentieth century.

The road heads northwest along the edge of the meadow past shooting star, woodland star and yarrow. A spur forks left at 2¾ miles, descending to a big emerald pool on the river. Your road climbs gradually above the winding Eel, becoming a narrow, less-traveled track lined with yerba de selva as it returns to the forest. The ascent steepens as the terrain gets rocky. Bare slopes around 3⅛ miles sprout exquisite, petite rose-purple blooms of Kellogg's monkeyflower.

At 3¼ miles a hand-painted trail sign points right. (The road leaves the Preserve in ¼ mile, encountering private property.) From the junction you look west to Elkhorn Ridge and the rugged northwest corner of the Preserve. Take the narrow trail on the right, signed WHITEHOUSE, TEN-MILE CREEK, WILDERNESS LODGE LOOP, heading east through mature forest. Watch for poison oak, Pacific dogwood and calypso orchids as you traverse the steep slope. Descend to a fork at 3½ miles. Turn left, descending through a berry patch and apple orchard into a very large meadow and quickly come to the White House.

The stately, two-story Lovejoy homestead sits on

the edge of the big meadow at Horseshoe Bend. Built in 1895, the White House still has many of its furnishings including paintings and mirrors on the walls, old wood-burning stoves and the hand pump at the kitchen sink. It looks as if the family might have left last month for a trip to visit relatives. The home's isolation amidst such splendid natural beauty speaks eloquently of the adventure and hardships faced by the settlers who came here to carve a living from the wilderness.

You're welcome to look around, contemplating what it might have been like to live in such a place. Remains of a blacksmith shop (where two-eyed violets now grow), barn, outhouse and other outbuildings surround the abode, along with old roses, daffodils, narcissus and foxgloves. Please disturb nothing and stay off adjacent private property to the north. In keeping with the Preserve spirit, take only memories or photographs, leave only footprints.

If you want the easiest hike, return on the same trail for a 7¼-mile round trip. Our described hike continues on Wilderness Lodge Loop, which adds 500 feet elevation gain/loss and ½ mile to the total distance.

Return to the junction south of the house. Bear left, climbing steeply southeast through the forest. A old cross-cut saw blade leans incongruously against a six-foot diameter Douglas fir giant. Before 3¾ miles you switchback to the right as your steep climb eases slightly. Ten more switchbacks bring you to the top of the slope and a junction on the brushy ridgetop at 4 miles. Ahlquist Trail goes left, climbing east along the ridge before descending to Ten-Mile Creek.

Turn right and descend west on the ridge through chaparral of manzanita, canyon live oak, chamise, coyote brush, coffeeberry and various kinds of ceanothus. The trail veers left around 4¼ miles, coming to a rest bench with a fine view of the wilderness. Sit and enjoy the view unless the sun is too hot on this south-facing slope. On your left Black Oak Mountain towers southeast. The ridge south of it forms the Preserve's southern boundary. South Meadow and Wilderness Lodge lie below in the river canyon. You can hear the river but cannot see it from here. Elkhorn Ridge is due west.

Your trail descends east, then bends right. The trail levels in shady hardwood forest at 4⅜ miles. Resume your descent through forest of madrone, live oak and bay laurel. Your descent steepens as conifers mix with the hardwoods. The path levels briefly, high above the rushing waters of Fox Creek. The trail winds right then left, descending steeply to the meadow and your junction opposite Wilderness Lodge.

From here it's about 2¾ miles back along the road to your starting point. If you want to explore more of this rugged country, consider returning on the Walker Meadow Trail if you can ford the river. It adds 1⅛ miles to the return trip.

OTHER SUGGESTIONS: CONGER TRAIL (5½ miles one way), WALKER MEADOW TRAIL (May to October only, 2⅞ miles one way), BLACK OAK MOUNTAIN TRAIL (2¾ miles one way) and AHLQUIST TRAIL are mentioned in text where they leave main trail.

12

BRUHEL POINT

MARVELOUS HEADLANDS AND TIDEPOOLS

The territory of the Coast Yuki tribe extended along the coast from Rockport to Ten Mile River. Here at Bruhel Point, Mussel Rock, or Lilim as the Coast Yuki called it, provided a popular and important seafood-gathering place for the Yuki and most of their neighbors—the Kato and Huchnom to the east, the northern Pomo to the south, and the Sinkyone and Wailaki to the north.

The tribes would come to Lilim to pry mussels, limpets and abalone from the rocks, net surf fish and spear salmon in nearby streams. (Most small streams on the coast had salmon and steelhead runs before logging and the resulting erosion filled them with slash and silt.) When the white settlers arrived, they learned of the sea's bountiful harvest here. Mussel Rock continues to be a popular harvesting place today.

In the last half of the nineteenth century, two lumber towns were built just south—Kibesillah (Kibasilla) and Newport. Kibesillah, a mile south, prospered until 1885, when its mill moved to Fort Bragg, followed by the town's population. Newport, the shipping port for Kibesillah, also blew away in the dust of the move to Fort Bragg.

The Humboldt Trail from Fort Bragg to Eureka went along the bluffs at Bruhel Point. At several places along this walk, especially the north end, you can see the old, two-rutted wagon track. In one spot the track leads off the edge of the eroded bluff, a victim of the wearing action of the waves. Today this hike follows the route of the California Coastal Trail along these bluffs.

Your trail heads west down 19 steps and across the sloping grassy headland. In 200 feet your return trail branches right. Continue west, passing the westernmost cypress and coming to the bluff's edge at ⅛ mile, where narrow-leaved mule ears bloom in spring.

Many points and coves punctuate the coast here.

BRUHEL POINT:

DISTANCE: ¼ mile to 2¼ miles round trip, plus 1¼ miles round trip south of access trail.

TIME: One or two hours.

TERRAIN: Sloping grassy headlands leading to several small coves and extensive rocky tidepool area (at low tide).

BEST TIME: Low tide. Wildflowers best in spring.

WARNINGS: These tidal areas are very exposed to strong surf. Never turn your back on the ocean. Watch for killer waves. You need a California fishing license to harvest mussels, fish or shellfish. Tidal rocks are very slippery, so wear shoes with good traction, and watch your step. Mussel gathering is prohibited during quarantine season, usually May-October.

HOW TO GET THERE: Turn west off Highway 1 into the vista point at M.74.09, south of Westport, near a stand of cypress trees.

FURTHER INFO: CalTrans (707)445-6444.

There are a couple to your south (you can go ⅝ mile south to a deep cove, see end of report), but most of them extend their rocky fingers into the surf to the north. If you look north from here to the east side of the highway, you will see round, grassy Kibesillah Hill (650 foot elevation).

The described trail winds north along the blufftop from the top of the cove before you. At low tide you can head down to the beach and onto the tidal shelves here for a look at an incredible variety of intertidal marine life. From the bluffs west, you are on your own. USE CAUTION. Even if you're not tidepooling, it may be worth your while to walk 150 feet west to the tip of the point for a grand overview of the tidal rocks.

Walk northwest on the meandering trail along the edge of the bluff. You pass a big wild strawberry patch and asters in late summer. Before ¼ mile, come to a point littered with bits of shells, an Indian shell midden. It overlooks the large tidal zone to the north. To the north and east, a narrow sandy cove extends far inland. Your trail turns east, winding along the lip of the cove. The next cove overlook is surrounded by coastal scrub—Douglas iris, salal, angelica, gum plant, Mendocino paintbrush, bracken fern and more huddle together against the sea breeze. Follow the trail southeast to the head of the cove.

At the head of the cove, turn north along the bluff edge above its eastern shore. The path winds through a tangle of coastal scrub. At ⅜ mile you pass coast silktassel and California rose on your left and a blackberry thicket on your right and head northwest along the bluff's edge over open coastal prairie. Iris, narrow-leaved mule ears, poppies and other wildflowers line the trail in spring.

Near the mouth of the cove, another access path leads down to a broad tidal shelf. Bisecting this shelf is a deep submarine channel through which the waves surge, creating a blowhole effect. The blufftop trail turns north. At ½ mile, where the upper path

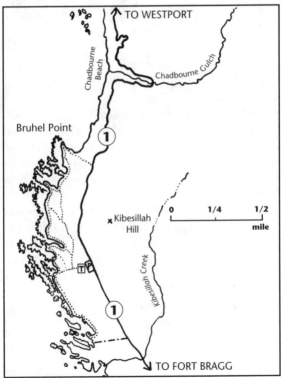

enters from the east, another spur descends to the tidal shelf.

Continue north along the bluff, heading for the point visible ahead. You reach the point beyond ⅝ mile, where two more trails descend to tidepools.

Your bluff trail now climbs briefly. In 150 feet you come to another point, where a trail leads down to a sandy beach. Directly offshore is a favorite haunt of harbor seals. (Please do not disturb!) The blufftop trail continues, climbing east and quickly returning to bluff's edge. You top a rise and veer left, staying near bluff's edge.

Descend to a point with yet another path to the tide zone before ¾ mile. When it's clear, you have a grand vista of the Lost Coast to the north and northwest, from Cape Vizcaino to Punta Gorda. If you want to continue, veer left on the fork that ascends southeast away from the shore. In 300 feet, the trail forks. The right fork ascends east to the highway north of the trailhead. Take the left fork climbing northeast following the bluff edge.

Around ⅞ mile the path turns northwest and descends to bluff's edge. The trail north to the tip of Bruhel Point becomes rough and hard to follow. To go on, take the left track west on a steep and slippery descent for 100 feet. Then take the steep trail on the right that descends to the tiny beach. Cross the beach and scramble up to the rock shelf on its

73

far side. You will soon find rough steps that climb back up to the headland.

Walking becomes easy again as you head north across the bluff. But watch out for poison oak. At 1⅛ miles from the trailhead, you reach the tip of Bruhel Point. The wave-swept beach of Chadbourne Gulch lies to the north, while to the south lies the convoluted shore of this tidepool wonderland.

Return by the same route. If you want the shortest trip back to your car, take the trail before the blackberry thicket that forks left and veers southeast toward the pines. It leads to the parking area in about ¼ mile.

If you haven't had your fill of this great place, descend west to the edge of bluff once again and take the trail south along the edge of the blufftop. It passes more spurs to the tide zone. Beyond ⅛ mile the track heads straight across the blufftop. From ¼ mile, deep water lurks and surges around the offshore rocks. A vertiginous spur on the right before ⅜ mile drops to an outstanding deep-water fishing spot. Continue south to the tip of a point overlooking a deep emerald cove to your south.

To leave the point and continue south above the shore, backtrack briefly until you find an obvious path. Follow it east 200 feet, then take the right fork and head south through a broken down fence around ½ mile. Continue south, climbing along the bluff edge. At the top of the hill you look back northwest at a deep cove and the point you were just on. Go west on a path that descends to end on a grassy north slope at ⅝ mile. From here you have a grand panorama of the convoluted shore and surging ocean with the Lost Coast beyond. Retrace your steps to the parking lot.

Tidal animals commonly seen in the area:

mussel	limpet
barnacle	gooseneck barnacle
purple shore crab	hermit crab
abalone	sea star
sea anemone	spiny sea urchin
turban snail	chiton
giant chiton	Pacific octopus

OTHER SUGGESTION: Just north of Bruhel Point at M.75.42 is a mile-long, narrow, dark-sand beach at CHADBOURNE GULCH. The beach is virtually inaccessible at high tide, but is a fine walk at medium to low tide. It is a popular place for surf fishing and bird watching.

MacKERRICHER STATE PARK

INCLUDES THE NEXT FOUR TRAILS

Just north of Fort Bragg lies MacKerricher State Park, 2299 acres of beach, bluff, headland, sand dune, forest and wetland. The park, west of Highway 1, stretches from Ten Mile River on the north (10 miles from Noyo River), to Pudding Creek Beach on the south, within the Fort Bragg city limits. MacKerricher offers the Mendocino coast's largest campground as well as abundant hiking opportunities.

Coast Yuki and Pomo Indians inhabited the area for thousands of years. They lived abundantly upon the rich variety of sea creatures and native plants to be gathered here. Their lands became part of the Mendocino Indian Reservation, founded 1856.

After the reservation closed in 1867, Duncan MacKerricher settled here in 1868. He rode to Eureka on the then-new Humboldt Trail to file land claims at the State Land Office, paying $1.25 per acre. The MacKerricher family worked the land until 1949, when they gift-deeded it to the State Park System.

The main entrance to MacKerricher State Park is three miles north of Fort Bragg, at M.64.87 on Highway 1. Most of the trail descriptions start from there. This is also where you should go if you need information or plan to camp. Several other points provide access to the old Haul Road, and from there to other trails in the park. All access points are west of the highway, listed here (in order) from north to south:

M.69.67 South end of Ten Mile River bridge. North access to Trail #13.

M.65.2 Ward Avenue. Drive west for .5 mile to parking area where Ward makes sharp left. Alter-

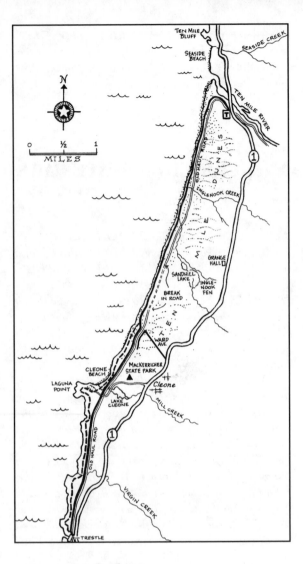

nate access to Trail #13.

　　*M.65.06 Mill Creek Drive. Drive west for .5 mile
into the park.*

　　M.64.87 Main park entrance.

　　*M.63.7 Virgin Creek trail leads west from high-
way to meet the Haul Road.*

　　*M.62.7 Old Haul Road entrance; park in lot near
silver gate. Access to Trail #16.*

　　M.62.3 Pudding Creek Beach.

13

NORTH to TEN MILE RIVER

ALONG THE OLD HAUL ROAD

In 1916 the Union Lumber Company of Fort Bragg laid tracks north near the shore from their sawmill all the way to Ten Mile River (and upriver to vast forests of redwoods). The tracks ran where the old haul road runs through MacKerricher Park today. The last train made the run to Ten Mile and back on June 18, 1949, after which the tracks were covered by a paved truck road. When storm surf in the winter of 1982 destroyed part of the road, the timber company stopped using it and it quickly became a favorite spot for park visitors. The State Park System finally purchased the haul road in the 1990s. Much more of the haul road was eroded over the winter of 1997-98, especially north of Ward Avenue. This hike follows the route of the California Coastal Trail.

From the upper tier of the Laguna Point parking lot, walk east to a break in the fence and follow a dirt path southeast past picnic tables to the elevated haul road in 300 feet. Turn left and follow the haul road north. The elevated road crosses the creek that drains Lake Cleone, passing above 1500-foot-long Cleone Beach on your left and Lake Cleone on the right. Before ¼ mile a side trail forks left to Cleone Beach, then another forks right, leading to Lake Cleone at its parking lot. Continue along a section of the haul road reduced to a narrow dirt track by several winters of storm surf.

Continue north past a midden on your right as the road resumes, passing low-growing shore pines. At ⅜ mile a horse trail leads east to Pinewood Campground. Soon Cleone Beach ends as a bluff-edge spur forks left, then another trail forks east. A horse trail leads west to the beach before ½ mile. As you follow the haul road north, use caution at a washed-out creek crossing at ¾ mile. Yellow and pink sand verbena, poppies and lupine grow on vegetated dunes beside the road. At 1⅛ miles you pass the Ward Avenue access point. Wild mustard, reeds and

grasses grow beside the road.

At 1¼ miles an interpretive panel discusses the sensitive, ever-changing dune environment. Here you're in fact surrounded by dunes cloaked in dense vegetation. In another 250 feet you reach the section of road washed out by the voracious winter surf of 1998. A side trail on the right leads into the dunes—no bikes or horses please due to sensitive and endangered plant and bird habitat. Sand Hill Lake and Inglenook Fen lie hidden in the dunes to the east. (A fen is a wooded marsh where the soils are composed primarily of decaying vegetative matter.) This is the southernmost fen remaining on the Pacific Coast, a prime bird habitat.

Descend the steep gravel path straight ahead that drops to the beach and follow the tideline north. Where you reach the beach, a few rocks stand in the tide zone, but from here north it's one continuous beach stretching to Ten Mile River. Notice that the last few rocks you pass have flat west-facing sides that are aligned nearly due north. These rocks are

NORTH to TEN MILE RIVER:

DISTANCE: 5⅛ miles one way, 10¼ miles round trip.
TIME: Up to five hours.
TERRAIN: Paved old logging road and sandy beach.
BEST TIME: Anytime.
WARNINGS: Watch for killer waves on beach. Blowing sand can make this walk miserable in strong winds.
HOW TO GET THERE: SOUTH END: Park at MacKerricher Laguna Point lot. NORTH END: On Highway 1 (M.69.67) south end of bridge.
FEES: Car and walk-in camping: $16/night.
FURTHER INFO: Mendocino State Parks (707) 937-5804.

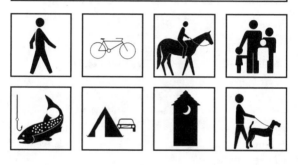

the surface expression of a newly recognized fault uncovered by the winter storms of 1998. The fault formed when part of the earth's crust underlying the Ten Mile dunes sank and tilted to the north. The several sandy layers visible in the sea cliff reveal the slope of this block. The layers descend gently in the direction of Ten Mile River until they disappear into the beach about 275 feet north of the last trail descending from the haul road. At the point where the sandy layers disappear a canyon jammed with driftwood logs has been cut through the dunes. Several organic-rich soil layers are exposed in the sea cliff here. These layers are remnants of marshes and woodlands drowned when faulting dropped them below sea level. Radio carbon dating indicates the organic layers are between 4000 and 20,000 years old. Local geologist David Springer has been studying the fault.

Continue north along the tideline. Roughly 1¼ miles of the haul road have been obliterated. (California State Parks is considering plans to build a boardwalk or other path through the dunes to bridge the gap.) At 2½ miles you can return to the road where the rails of the old railroad protrude from beneath the road surface. If you prefer you can continue north along the beach. Sand verbena, ice plant and beach morning glory thrive in the sandy, salty environment.

After the pavement resumes, look northeast to the big forested canyons of Ten Mile River, 4234-foot Cahto Peak visible beyond. The site of an Indian camp lies east of the road. The coastal tribes cooked and shelled their harvest of shellfish here, leaving the large piles of shells. A creek lies to the east, where the Indians found drinking water. What's odd is that no tidal rocks support shellfish within a mile of this spot today. Springer believes the tidal rocks that were once nearby have been buried by shifting along the fault.

At 2⅝ miles the haul road passes an old farm gate on the right. The State Park System has gradually been acquiring ranch lands surrounding the park. The area behind the gate is still private property; please stay out. At 2¾ miles the road crosses a creek that runs into a small lagoon on the left. Invasive European beach grass grows on low-lying areas of the mostly bare dunes.

Continuing north, at 3¼ miles the haul road passes another farm gate, then crosses another small creek with a lagoon. Rushes, willows, lupine, beach sweet pea and Himalaya blackberries grow along the road. The dunes to the right are heavily covered with vegetation.

Around 3⅝ miles, at a slight bend in the road, the dunes reach their broadest point, extending east for about a mile to a height of 130 feet. They're backed by groves of tall blue gum eucalyptus, the ridges beyond covered with conifer forests. Even though you can see a few houses and ranch buildings at the edge of the dunes, there's a true wilderness feeling here. To the north by northwest lie the sparsely settled grasslands around Kibesillah Hill and Bruhel Point. Farther up the coast, on a clear day, you can see the rugged shoreline of the Sinkyone Wilderness and the Lost Coast stretching to the rounded point of Punta Gorda.

Continue north with the beach now immediately west of the road. Beyond 4½ miles the road begins a big bend to the right. Tall grass growing on the dunes to the west of the road hides the ocean beyond. At 4⅝ miles, as the road continues its big bend, a trail heads north to the mouth of Ten Mile River, beyond the rolling grassy dunes.

If you continue on the road, it now heads east, paralleling the river. At 4⅞ miles it crosses the state park boundary. In another ⅛ mile, a path on the right climbs the dunes to the parking area at M.69.67 on Highway 1. The paved trail continues east under the highway bridge, a favorite nesting place for mud swallows. The road ends in another ⅛ mile, where a new logging road blocks the old railroad bed. The marshlands along the river and the dense thicket of willows, cypress and vines along the road near the bridge provide another fine bird habitat, a treat for those willing to sit quietly and watch and wait.

If you turn around and head back to the central part of MacKerricher State Park, you will be looking west along Ten Mile River to the sea stacks and sea tunnels at Seaside Beach. As you return through the dunes, keep an eye out for birds and other small animals. Think about the time over 140 years ago when this area (and virtually all the coast) was a wilderness inhabited only by Native Americans and wild animals.

OTHER SUGGESTIONS: You can also walk the HAUL ROAD SOUTH: In 2 miles it passes the silver gate where another parking area lies beside the highway. About ⅛ mile beyond, the Haul Road crosses the original railroad trestle over Pudding Creek, closed until it can be refurbished.

DUNE WANDERING: The extensive dunes to the east of this route are a great place to wander and discover. Creeks, shell middens, Sand Hill Lake and the Inglenook Fen lie nestled in this small wilderness. Please try not to walk on the plants!

SEASIDE BEACH lies just north of the mouth of Ten Mile River. When the river is low, you can ford it at the mouth and continue north for ½ mile on Seaside Beach, or you may reach the beach from Highway 1 at M.70.64.

14

LAGUNA POINT

SEALS, WHALES, TIDEPOOLS AND SHOREBIRDS

This short, level walk is very popular for its easy access to the grassy point, tidepools and seal and whale watching. It's prime habitat for both grassland birds and shorebirds. A wharf and loading chute at the point operated from 1883 until 1918, supplying ships with lumber, tanbark and other goods. A gravity powered railway brought lumber from two nearby mills. The name Laguna came from the original name of the town we now call Cleone.

The trail follows a raised boardwalk from the northwest corner of the parking lot adjacent to Cleone Beach. Follow the boardwalk through the split rail fence and west above grassy headlands scattered with short, windblown cypress trees. Stay to the right at the first fork in 200 feet. You quickly reach an overlook of the rocky tidal zone where an interpretive panel discusses continental drift and the San Andreas fault offshore. Continue west on the boardwalk through a thicket of cypress.

You pass another viewing platform, then pass through another split rail fence where a side trail on the right leads immediately to a small rocky beach and tidepools. Another viewing platform has panels showing that this was the take off point for the wharf and loading chute supplied by the gravity railroad. The boardwalk continues southwest to a fourth platform with a fine panel about the local Coast Yuki and Pomo people harvesting seafood here.

Continue along the boardwalk as it heads west toward the tip of the point. Beyond ¼ mile you come to a broad platform with a bench, the "Laguna Point Seal Watching Station." Harbor seals lounge on the rocks to the west or play and fish in the surf nearby. They live here year round. The open water beyond the rocks is prime whale-spotting territory when the gray whales are migrating, from December through April or May. To the right of the point are tidepools where you can see tidal creatures even at a moderately high tide. (Use caution on the slippery rocks.)

DISTANCE: ⅝-mile or ¾-mile loop or 4¼ miles round trip.

TIME: One half hour to two hours.

TERRAIN: Boardwalk across flat headland leading to rocky point, rocky tidepools, and bluff trail south.

BEST TIME: Anytime.

WARNINGS: Watch for rogue waves at the point, especially in winter. Never turn your back on the ocean.

HOW TO GET THERE: Turn left off Highway 1 into MacKerricher State Park main entrance at M.64.87 on or onto Mill Creek Drive at M.65.06. Go past Lake Cleone (Trail #15) and under the old Haul Road to the paved parking lot facing Cleone Beach.

FURTHER INFO: Mendocino State Parks (707) 937-5804.

You can return directly from here to the parking lot, taking the right fork for a ⅝ mile loop, or continue south following the bluff's edge along the shore, passing above offshore sea stacks and tidepools, prime shore bird habitat. If you are lucky (or patient), you may see a brown pelican or a black oystercatcher. Beyond ⅜ mile your trail turns east with the edge of the bluff. At ½ mile a side trail leads to another small but protected gravelly beach. Nearby a trail on your left heads northeast to return to the parking lot at ¾ mile.

If you want to continue south along the bluff, at ¾ mile the trail rounds the bluff above a pretty blond pocket beach and joins the pleasant horse trail south. The horse trail draws beside the paved Haul Road at ⅞ mile. It joins the Haul Road at 1⅛ miles to pass above Virgin Creek Beach, then follows the shore south to Pudding Creek near Fort Bragg.

15.

LAKE CLEONE
HAVEN FOR TROUT AND BIRDS

Lake Cleone originally formed as a tidal lagoon of Mill Creek, long ago when the level of the Pacific Ocean was higher than it is now. As the level of the sea receded, the lagoon was flushed by winter storms and eventually became less saline. The fresh-water lake we see today was created when Duncan MacKerricher closed off the ocean entrance, using the lake for water for his ranch. MacKerricher chose the name Cleone for the town just east. Cleone is a Greek word meaning gracious and beautiful. The fine bird habitat around the lake is a permanent home to quail, gulls, hawks, blackbirds and jays. In fall and winter, many migratory fowl stop here: more than 90 species have been identified.

Your trail follows a boardwalk east from the east end of the parking lot. The walkway follows the shore of the lake through a forest of willows, alders, tanoaks and pines. The understory has a tangle of native blackberry, California rose, wax myrtle, twinberry, coffeeberry, thimbleberry, honeysuckle, hedge nettle and ferns. Before ¼ mile the boardwalk ends as it crosses a service road, then resumes.

At ¼ mile a wide spot in the boardwalk overlooks a marsh east of the lake where cattails, sedges and

LAKE CLEONE:

DISTANCE: 1¼-mile loop.

TIME: One half hour to one hour.

TERRAIN: Gentle shoreline of 15-acre lake, partially forested, partially marshy. Great bird habitat.

BEST TIME: Anytime, although non-boardwalk portion of hike may be muddy after rains.

WARNINGS: Be quiet, or you may be the target of a bird watcher's wrath.

HOW TO GET THERE: Follow directions in Trail #14 but stop at Lake Cleone, just before beach parking area.

FURTHER INFO: Mendocino State Parks (707) 937-5804.

tall grasses provide prime bird habitat. Be quiet here; there are birds all around you, hidden in the tall foliage. You may be rewarded with the sounds and perhaps sightings of resident or migratory birds.

Before ⅜ mile your wooden trail turns south into a swamp where skunk cabbage and pig-a-back plant grow. The boardwalk ends at the end of the swamp before ½ mile. Wheelchair riders will need to turn back here.

The trail continues as a dirt path, climbing to higher and drier ground where you should watch for poison oak. You continue circling the marsh with views of cattails and yellow pond lilies. Climb to a view of marsh, lake and ocean before ⅝ mile. Follow the shore of the lake west through a forest of mature Bishop pines. Cross a rustic bridge dwarfed by the huge skunk cabbages beside it. Just before ⅞ mile, you cross a series of floating bridges, then head northwest. Soon your path hugs the shore of the lake. After passing a magnificent display of purple aster blooms, you meet the paved road. Turn right and follow the path north to return to the parking area.

16.

MacKERRICHER SOUTH HEADLANDS

FLOWERED BLUFFTOPS ABOVE SHELTERED BEACHES

Everybody comes here to visit the old Haul Road, a scenic and level path that runs north from here into the heart of the park. But I most like to explore the spectacular bluffs and pocket beaches west of the Haul Road as this hike does. If you're on a bike, pushing a stroller, or riding a wheelchair, you'll want to stay on the pavement to the east. The California Coastal Trail follows either the headland or the road route.

From the silver gate, cross the Haul Road and head west on the unmarked dirt path toward the bluff's edge. It traverses a grassy headland tangled with iris, gum plant, purple seaside daisy and native blackberry.

In 400 feet the path reaches the bluff edge and forks. If you want to descend to a lovely beach of fine sand that stretches north ⅜ mile, continue straight. Our described hike forks right to follow the winding bluff-edge path north. You pass abundant sea thrift, poppy, lupine, angelica and ice plant. Only as you get beyond the intrusive motel row to the east do you begin to see coast buckwheat, brilliant Mendocino paintbrush and beach silverweed.

At ¼ mile you can take the bluff edge path as it dips across a seasonal creek, though in winter and spring you may want to detour east slightly to cross the stream on the pavement. (If you do, return to the blufftop path in 100 feet.) The bluff edge path soon veers inland around a sandy cove to join the horse trail, but where the equestrian path returns to the pavement, you angle northwest across open grassy headlands sprinkled with salal and woolly sunflower. At ⅜ mile you pass a river of dried concrete that angles down to the beach at its north end. Continue north across level headlands more or less following the bluff edge. A left fork rounds a point while the right fork maintains a northward path.

At ½ mile you dip down to an easy creek ford,

MacKERRICHER SOUTH HEADLANDS:

DISTANCE: 4 miles round trip or 4¼-mile loop.
TIME: One half hour to two hours.
TERRAIN: Grassy headlands and pocket beaches.
BEST TIME: Spring and summer for wildflowers. Low tide for beach walking.
WARNINGS: Never turn your back on the ocean. Watch for poison oak in coastal scrub.
HOW TO GET THERE: Turn west off Highway 1 just north of Fort Bragg at M.62.7 into gravel parking lot beside silver gate.
FURTHER INFO: Mendocino State Parks (707) 937-5804.

passing above the first of several tiny but pristine pocket beaches. After the climb back to the level blufftop, continue along the bluff edge path as it traverses another point, then winds east around another cove at ⅝ mile. Heading east you might notice grassy Bald Hill inland from the coastal terrace. Bald Hill marked the eastern boundary of the Mendocino Indian Reservation of the 1850s.

North of the cove you pass short loop trails that explore small grassy promontories. Look northwest for a sandstone arch in an offshore rock. Harbor seals haul out nearby. Follow the blufftop north and east, crossing the head of a small sandy cove around ¾ mile. Head east across a small gully and up to the top of a sandy hill for the best vista. Or in summer when Virgin Creek is fordable, drop north down the gully and comb the beach for up to one mile.

From the hilltop you can survey the entire beach backed by rocky Laguna Point, with round Kibesillah Hill and the Lost Coast tracing the distant shoreline. To the east Virgin Creek winds toward Bald Hill. To the south Fort Bragg hides behind industrial clutter. Many bits of shell lay scattered at your feet around this vantage point.

When I continue north from here, I like to head east to the Haul Road at one mile, follow it across Virgin Creek and up the hill to return to the grassy headlands via the horse path that forks left from the Haul Road at 1⅛ miles. After 200 feet you can leave the horse trail and follow a bluff edge path. In summer it passes the purple and white blooms of the unusual parasitic plant California orobanche or broomrape. At 1½ miles it passes a side trail to a pristine pocket beach of fine blond sand. At the next junction, where the horse trail forks right, you veer left and follow the bluff edge track. If you continue to Laguna Point at 2 miles, you can loop back via the boardwalk and the Haul Road to return to the trailhead.

OTHER SUGGESTION: Stay on the paved HAUL ROAD and follow it up to 3½ miles to where it's washed out (up to 7 miles round trip).

17.

GLASS BEACH
PUDDING CREEK HEADLANDS
DOWN AT THE OLD DUMP

The beach at the west end of Elm Street served as a dump both for the city of Fort Bragg and the Union Lumber Company well into the 1960s. Many other small coastal towns had similar dumps based on the assumption that the salt water and tides would purify and carry away all the rubble. The absurdity of this idea today shows how far we've come in the last 30 years. Still, over time the ocean has not only scoured the old refuse site, it has ground the rubble into wondrous bits of glass, pottery and miscellany, a beachcomber's paradise. While Glass Beach is fascinating, consider expanding your visit with a walk along the spectacularly convoluted bluffs and their adjacent wildflower-rich headlands, where several rare and endangered wildflowers mingle with wooly sunflower, coastal wild onion and acres of goldfields. The rare plants include abundant Mendocino paintbrush, Menzie's wallflower, Phacelia insularis and the early yellow blooms of blennosperma. The headlands route follows the California Coastal Trail.

Behind a yellow gate, follow the paved road heading

88

GLASS BEACH
PUDDING CREEK HEADLANDS:

DISTANCE: ½ mile round trip plus optional 1⅛-mile headlands loop.

TIME: One hour.

TERRAIN: Gently rolling headlands leading to convoluted bluffs surrounding old dump sites.

BEST TIME: Medium to low tide for the beach. Spring for wildflowers, but worth a visit any time you're in town.

WARNINGS: Parts of this beach are particularly exposed to large surf. Use extreme caution when the waves are big. Never turn your back on the ocean. Do be aware that this is an old dump site. For example, do not let young children put objects in their mouths.

HOW TO GET THERE: In Fort Bragg the northernmost street west of Highway 1 is Elm Street at M.62.0. Go west 2 blocks to parking area at Old Haul Road.

FURTHER INFO: Mendocino Coast Chamber of Commerce 961-6300, 800-726-2780.

west from the parking area. Wildflowers and berry vines thrive on the ¼ mile path to the beach. On your left the new Pacific Marine Farms, an aquaculture enterprise growing salmon, shrimp and abalone, is being built.

Where the path forks, take either trail. Both descend to coves littered with sparkling bits of glass and pottery worn smooth by tidal action, a mosaic artist's dream come true. For beachcombers this is great territory.

If you want to walk rather than hit the beach, take the right fork which descends gently beside a seasonal creek jammed with willows. At a second fork, go right again to a third fork where you can go left to the north end of Glass Beach. Our described trail turns right and descends to a bushy cypress tree. Veer to the right up a short hill and dip through a second gully at ¼ mile where driftwood logs lie on your left and willows grow on the right.

Climb out of the gully to meet a fork. Two paths

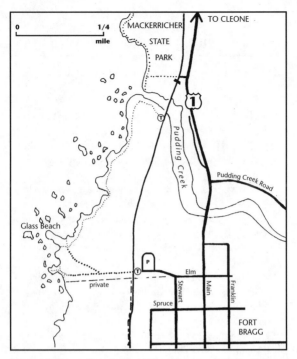

lead north across the headlands, one winding along the bluff's edge, the other taking a straighter path across lush grasslands carpeted with flowers. Turn left on the path along the bluff edge above the beach. (You'll return via the right fork.) Following the faint bluff-edge path, you quickly encounter botanical diversity, with patches of beach strawberry, iris, purple seaside daisy, poppy, wooly sunflower and non-native ice plant. After rounding a small point, continue along the meandering bluff-edge path. Much of the tread before ½ mile is on beach sand eroded from the uplifted bluff.

Around ½ mile you reach a high point above the breakers. From here you can stay to the left on a sandstone path or follow the dirt path on the headlands just above. Continue past abundant sea thrift and coast buckwheat. Pass a narrow promontory, then round rocky coves above a pocket beach. Around ⅝ mile a steep path descends to the strand, but continue along the bluff-edge track. You're soon forced onto the dirt headland trail. Follow it 200 feet, then return to the bluff edge.

Around ¾ mile lupine, beach knotweed, blennosperma and silvery beach sagewort join the tangle of plants. In 250 feet you come to the Pudding Creek Headlands. The mouth of Pudding Creek lies 40 feet below. Beyond the broad beach there stand the headlands of MacKerricher State Park, the Lost Coast beyond.

The bluff trail turns due east, heading for the Pudding Creek Trestle (future CCT) and the north parking area. But turn right in just 100 feet, taking the broad path south across the heart of the headlands. Beyond ⅞ mile you're once again above the pocket beach. Continue south on the upper track.

At one mile you come to Glass Beach Heights. No, I'm not referring to the new subdivision marring the view southeast. The high mounds left of your trail are vegetated dunes where an abundance of coastal scrub species thrive. Continue along the center path past two spurs on the left leading toward the development. After passing more dune hills around 1⅛ miles, it descends southwest to the cypress at 1¼ miles. Retrace your steps to the trailhead, or go take a break on Glass Beach.

18.

FORT BRAGG HISTORY WALK

AN OUTDOOR TOUR

In l856 the United States government established the Mendocino Indian Reservation, the fourth reservation in the nation. It extended along the coast from the Noyo River north to about a mile north of Ten Mile River and inland to the first ridge, about 25,000 acres in all. The government tried to relocate all the Native Americans from Marin County north to the Oregon line onto this reservation, though many were overlooked.

In 1857 Lieutenant Horatio G. Gibson was sent to establish a military outpost for the growing reservation. When he arrived at Mendocino in June, there was still no road or trail north to the Noyo River, so Gibson booked passage on a schooner to Noyo. The new outpost was officially begun on June 11, l857. It was located where downtown Fort Bragg is today. The site was then a beautiful glade, sloping gently west and totally surrounded by dense forest.

Lt. Gibson named the post for his West Point classmate and compatriot in the Mexican war, General Braxton Bragg, later a general in the Confederate Army.

The post was abandoned in 1864 when the Native American population was being moved inland to Round Valley, near Covelo, where a reservation still exists today. In 1885 lumbermen established the new town of Fort Bragg at the site of the old fort.

The tour below was developed by the Mendocino County Museum, the Georgia-Pacific Corporation and Will Kelsey, whom the author thanks for allowing it to be reprinted here. The tour guides you through downtown Fort Bragg, featuring many of its oldest buildings.

1. RAILROAD DEPOT (built 1924) is the home of the California Western Railroad (Skunk Train). The town's railroad was established in 1885 to serve the Union Lumber Company. By 1904 the rail line provided a link to Alpine, 18 miles east of town, where travelers could transfer to stagecoaches and proceed to Sherwood and the main line Northwestern Pacific Railroad. In 1911, C.W.R.R. connected

directly to the Northwestern Pacific Railroad at Willits.

You may catch the train here or walk around the railroad yard to view the Skunk (a diesel-powered trolley), the other rolling stock and the big steam locomotive.

Walk south, then east to the nearby Guest House on the hill. You pass a picnic area and climb to a view of the Pacific.

2. GUEST HOUSE MUSEUM (built 1892), constructed for T.L. Johnson, brother of Union Lumber Company founder C.R. Johnson. In 1912 it became a company guest house, used in this capacity until 1969. This was also the site of the 1857 military post hospital. C.R. Johnson lived in that building from 1885 until 1902. The Guest House now houses a museum run by the city of Fort Bragg, open Wednesday through Sunday, 10 to 2 (Saturday only, November to March). Admission $2 ($1 with any local receipt), kids under 13 free.

Walk east to Main Street (Highway 1) and go right to:

3. 319 N. MAIN (built 1904, now law offices) This is the only brick building that survived the 1906 earthquake. Emerging from the side walls are truss rods, installed as reinforcements after the quake.

Walk south to:

4. 303 N. MAIN (built 1912, now the Company Store mall) was originally the company store of the Union Lumber Co. A building was constructed here in 1886 and, after surviving the 1906 quake, was replaced by the present structure for $30,000 in 1912.

Cross to the east side of Main and walk north:

5. MAIN STREET (ca. 1890–1950) reflects a blend of commercial architectural styles typical of American towns during the first half of the twentieth century. You'll pass the Chamber of Commerce and several shops and cafes. Historically this block housed a saloon and general store as well as restaurants and shops.

Still walking north, across the street is:

6. 363 MAIN (built 1912, Ten Mile Judicial District Courthouse until the library fire of 1987) was originally constructed as the Fort Bragg Commercial Bank. The building was later taken over by the Bank of Italy, later renamed the Bank of America, which occupied the site until 1960. In September

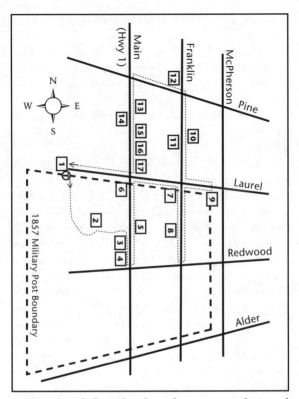

1987, a fire, believed to have been arson, damaged this building and destroyed the adjacent old library.

Go east on Laurel Street (the Rodeo Drive of Fort Bragg) for one block, to the southeast corner:

7. 363 N. FRANKLIN (built ca. 1890, now Cheshire Bookshop) was protected from the flames of the 1906 fire by the south-facing brick fire wall. The fire wall was here because the building was a bakery at the time. Only slightly damaged by the tremors, the wall now hides behind the building's south facade.

Walk south on Franklin to:

8. 335 N. FRANKLIN (built 1906) was the White House Hotel starting in 1888. It burned down in the fire of 1906 along with virtually every building in a two-block area. The hotel was quickly rebuilt. Later remodeled into nondescript ugliness, it was restored in 1980.

Walk back north to the corner of Franklin and Laurel. One block east is:

9. 248 E. LAUREL (built 1909, now the Footlighters Little Theatre) was originally opened May 9, 1909 as the Sequoia Theatre, Fort Bragg's

first conventional movie house. It has been used as a theatre since its construction. Old fashioned melodramas are now performed there every summer.

You are at the eastern edge of the old military post. In the 1890s there was a Chinese neighborhood one block south.

Walk back to Franklin and go north past City Hall ½ block to:

10. OLD FORT BUILDING (built 1857) was relocated from its original location near the southwest corner of the post. Believed to have been the quartermaster's storehouse and fort commissary, this is the last known surviving structure of the Fort Bragg military outpost. It houses a small museum. Notice especially the 1863 photographs, the scale model and painting of the fort, and the 1857 map of the coast, commissioned by the superintendent of Indian Affairs.

Across the street is:

11. 435 N. FRANKLIN (built ca. 1910) was constructed as a community hall by electric plant superintendent William Bennett, a local legend. Bennett was a lonely bachelor who created an entire "family" for himself carved from redwood, a wife and five daughters.

There were dances, I remember Mr. Bennett had his dolls...and he had them all dressed up. He had a skating rink there and certain nights of the month...he would have a dance with all of these wooden dolls (and the whole town). I'm telling you he was a character.

—from *Mendocino County Remembered: An Oral History*

Walk north to Pine Street. On the northwest corner is:

12. FIRST BAPTIST CHURCH (built 1912), constructed for $15,000, survives as one of the finest examples of California Mission Style architecture in Mendocino County. In 1912 an 1890 New England Style church (not unlike the Presbyterian Church in Mendocino) was moved to the rear of the lot, remodeled, and now remains as the north portion of the present structure. Look for the 1890 church in the central stained glass window of the main floor's south wall.

Walk west to Main, then go south.

13. THE PARSONAGE (now the North Coast Brewing Company) is all that remains of the old Presbyterian Church. The church, where the parking lot is today, burned in a spectacular dawn fire in

1980. If you're thirsty, stop in for one of their great brews on tap.

Across the street is:

14. 435 N. MAIN (built ca. 1889, now Clark's Musical Instruments) was originally the home of the Fort Bragg Advocate-News, founded in 1889. The newspaper's large rotary press moved several inches during the 1906 quake, but the building was only slightly damaged.

Back on the east side of the street:

15. 428 N. MAIN (built 1908, I.O.O.F./Masonic Hall) was constructed after the earthquake destroyed the large brick building that previously occupied the site.

16. 418 N. MAIN (built 1896, now The Restaurant), one of Fort Bragg's first hospitals, was pelted by bricks during the 1906 temblor when the south wall of the I.O.O.F. Hall collapsed. The building housed the hospital, Dr. Lendrum's office and H.R. Baum's pharmacy.

17. 400 N. MAIN (ca. 1890s, now Fiddles and Cameras). Extensively altered over the years, this building once housed Weller Hall, site of the founding of the Presbyterian (1885) and Baptist (1887) congregations. At the turn of the century, the building housed Shafsky Bros. Workingmen's Cash Store. On Admission Day 1899, an acrobat balanced his way across Main Street on a tightrope stretched between Shafsky's and the livery stable across the street to the west.

This concludes the History Walk. The railroad depot is directly to your west. For information about buildings not included in the walk, stop at the Guest House Museum across the street.

OTHER SUGGESTION: Ride the Skunk train from Fort Bragg through the redwoods along the Noyo River. Trains leave daily both mornings and afternoons, except in December when schedule varies. Reservations advised.

19.

MENDOCINO COAST
BOTANICAL GARDENS

CORNUCOPIA OF PLANTS

These 47 acres harbor the coast's premier garden spot. A spectacular mix of exotic and native plants grows here and the collection gets better all the time. Several thousand varieties of plants thrive in the mild Mediterranean coastal environment of the Botanical Gardens.

This described hike follows the paved South Trail, ideal for wheelchairs and baby strollers, to the spectacular ocean bluffs. It returns by the North Trail, which may not be appropriate for wheeled transport. Many other dirt paths wander all over the 47 acres, so don't feel compelled to limit yourself to the paved trails described here. A quick walk on this loop takes less than an hour. Better yet, plan to spend the day here with a picnic lunch. Many sheltered lawns and meadows provide space to spread your blanket and revel in the horticultural and natural beauty. In numerous choice corners you'll find picnic tables and benches as well. Signs at the bases of many plants denote common and scientific names of plants to help you identify them.

The gardens' entrance is to the left of the Gardens Grill. Beside the ticket window is the delightful and compact Gardens Store. Your purchases from the store and from the nursery you walk through beyond the entrance directly benefit the nonprofit Botanical Gardens.

Take the gravel trail that leaves the nursery, winding north past many ornamental shrubs beside the deck of the Gardens Grill. In 250 feet it meets the paved path. Turn left and descend the pavement past cypresses and a dawn redwood, a rare deciduous species from China that was thought to be extinct until 1944. Continue past the perennial garden until the pavement forks.

Turn left and follow the South Trail past grevilleas, a favorite of hummingbirds, and the cactus, Mediterranean and heather gardens. Beyond the cacti at

97

MENDOCINO COAST
BOTANICAL GARDENS:

DISTANCE: 1¼-mile loop or more.
TIME: One hour or all day.
TERRAIN: Mostly level through coastal meadows, forest and headlands.
BEST TIME: Spring and summer, but something is blooming all the time.
WARNINGS: Please stay off adjacent private property.
HOW TO GET THERE: On the west side of Highway 1 at M.59.08 just south of Fort Bragg.
FURTHER INFO: Mendocino Coast Botanical Gardens (707) 964-4352.

FEES:		
General	$6.00	
Children	3.00	(age 13 to 17)
6-12	1.00	
Under 6	free	
Senior	5.00	(Age 60 or over)
Residents	3.75	(Westport to Elk)
AAA members	1.00 discount	
Gardens	$20/year individual	
Membership	$25/year family	

A membership supports the work at the Botanical Gardens and entitles you to bring guests at half price.

⅛ mile, you encounter the first rhododendrons, which represent a large part of this Botanical Garden's collection. The grounds are scattered with large native Bishop pine, tanoak, wax myrtle and redwood trees. You'll find many exotic cultivated trees in smaller numbers.

Descend west along the Garden's south boundary briefly. In 250 feet the bog, or freshwater marsh, on your right supports dense cattails. Continue along a broad promenade lined with an amazing array of rhododendrons, with species that bloom from March through June. Where your South Trail meets the

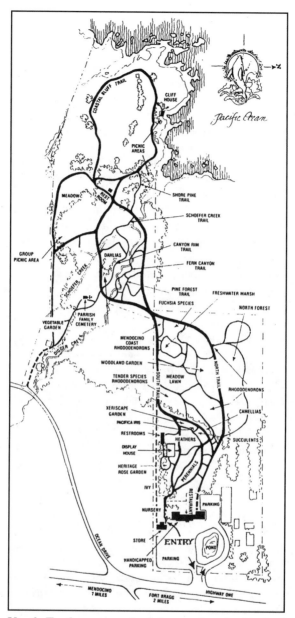

Pacific Ocean

North Trail, veer to the left, passing the big leaf rhododendrons growing beneath stately tanoaks. These huge rhodos, native to the Himalaya, have been here since 1988, but first bloomed in 1997.

At ¼ mile your trail dips across tiny Digger Creek. Just before the bridge, the narrow Pine Forest Trail and Fern Canyon Trail fork right, offering an intimate look at the creek. Continue along the South Trail, ignoring forks left and right. (Still, the Can-

yon Rim Trail on the right is one of my favorites.)
Soon the Dahlia Garden on your right may be worth
a look.

Before ⅜ mile you cross tiny Schoeffer Creek,
named for the founder of these Botanical Gardens,
then more side trails through the dense vegetation.
From here west, nearly all the plants you'll see are
native to this coastal habitat. Soon you can see the
shoreline to the north. Notice that the trees do not
grow as tall here near the ocean. The farther west
you go, the more they are sculpted into irregular
shapes by the strong winds common here.

You quickly come to another important junction.
A paved trail that enters from the left has two outhouses, one wheelchair accessible. On the right is
the end of the paved North Trail, by which this described hike returns. Don't turn back yet, however.
Continue west on the Coastal Bluff Trail to the Botanical Gardens' wild side. You pass through a
forest of Bishop pine, shore pine, Monterey cypress
and the scrubbier, indigenous Mendocino cypress.
Pass the Shore Pine Trail on your right at ½ mile.
You immediately come to the bluffs above the mouth
of Digger Creek. A rocky shore sprawls north to Fort
Bragg, the Lost Coast stretching seaward beyond.
The plume of Georgia Pacific's smokestack billows
from behind Todd's Point.

Your trail continues west along the shore to a rocky
point. In 300 feet the pavement ends. A broad fork
on the right descends steps to the Cliff House, which
has sheltered picnic tables and benches with an ocean
view. Another path leads northwest to the top of the
rocky point above the grassy coastal bluffs. The
headlands sparkle with wildflowers most of the year.
Convoluted sea cliffs stretch north and south. The
described loop angles left on the broad main path,
swinging southwest to a grassy point on the rim of
the bluff. At the westernmost point at ⅝ mile,
several side trails explore the shore.

Continue along the broad path as it swings southeast and east through coastal grasslands with several rest benches. Beyond ¾ mile you pass through
a corridor lined with shore pines and come to the
Wildflower Meadow. The trail splits here. The fork
on the right eventually returns to the entrance too.
Our described loop takes the left fork, returning to
the two-privy junction at ⅞ mile.

I recommend returning on the North Trail straight ahead unless you're using a wheeled vehicle. (Wheels go right, returning by the South Trail.) The North Trail descends across Digger Creek just upstream from its mouth, then climbs past the Fern Canyon Trail beneath mature Bishop pine forest.

By one mile you return to the cultivated gardens. Veer left at the junction with the South Trail and continue along the North Trail past the Woodland Garden and its wondrous collection of fuchsias. Once again you encounter many different rhododendrons.

Soon the new North Forest Garden borders your path on the left. This once heavily wooded area was opened to cultivation recently when many of its big trees toppled in winter storms.

At 1⅛ miles three young redwoods shelter native wild ginger and fringed corn lily. Continue east, quickly meeting the east end of the South Trail. Retrace your steps, more or less, to the nursery and store at 1¼ miles. Remember that all your purchases here benefit Mendocino Coast Botanical Gardens.

JACKSON STATE FOREST

Jackson State Forest was established in 1947 when the State purchased most of the land of the Caspar Lumber Company. This 50,000 acre forest stretches from Fort Bragg to Mendocino and inland for up to 18 miles. This extensive tract of land is used for timber harvesting and forestry studies. It is also open to public recreational use.

A network of dirt logging roads crisscrosses the State Forest. Many older roads, closed to vehicle traffic, are suitable for hiking, riding or mountain biking. Numerous primitive campsites lie in the north and east portions.

This book includes five trails in Jackson State Forest: #20—North Fork of South Fork Noyo River's Trestle Trail, #21—Chamberlain Creek Waterfall and #22, Part 2 of the Mendocino Hiking and Equestrian Trail, which follow directly. The two other trails appear later in the book since they are in the south° part of JSF: #33—Part 3 of the Mendocino Hiking and Equestrian Trail, and #34—Forest History Trail.

Contact the State Forest headquarters for more information, to get their topographic map, or for the location of other places you may hike.

20.

NORTH FORK of SOUTH FORK NOYO RIVER'S TRESTLE TRAIL

SECLUDED REDWOOD CANYON

The Trestle Trail and the dirt road leading to it follow the route of the Caspar Railroad, used by the Caspar Lumber Company when it cut the virgin forest here in the first half of the twentieth century. The access road descends to Camp One, then traces a spur line up the canyon of the North Fork of South Fork Noyo River, where you can see remnants of the railway's trestles along this hike. The lumber railway originated in the early 1870s in Caspar, first running on wooden "rails" because of a steel shortage following the Civil War. Horses and oxen pulled the trains until 1875, when the Caspar Railroad brought the first steam locomotive to the coast.

Over the years the railroad extended its line north and east, seeking new forests to cut. All the activity was south of the Noyo River until a 1000-foot tunnel was dug in 1903, running from Bunker Gulch on upper Hare Creek into the South Fork of the Noyo watershed. The tunnel passed beneath Highway 20 near your turnoff.

Camp One, now the site of the egg-collecting station, was the biggest and longest-lasting camp in the woods for the Caspar Lumber Company. The

NORTH FORK OF SOUTH FORK NOYO RIVER'S TRESTLE TRAIL:

DISTANCE: 13½ miles round trip to waterfall, 14½ miles round trip to end of trail. 19½-mile loop with Roads 1070 and 330 and Bob Woods Trail.

TIME: Full day round trip to waterfall, two or more days for loop.

TERRAIN: Along a steep, wooded stream canyon to its headwaters. Then you may climb through a logged area to a ridge road before descending to your starting point.

ELEVATION GAIN/LOSS: Add 120 feet+/120 feet- for Road 360/361 from gate. From Trestle Trailhead: 1000 feet+/1000 feet- to waterfall; 1240 feet+/1240 feet- to end of trail. Loop: 2600 feet+/2600 feet-.

BEST TIME: Late spring and all summer, also pretty in autumn.

WARNINGS: Prime habitat for poison oak. Use extreme caution when driving back roads to trailhead. Narrow and winding road doubles as Mendocino Hiking and Equestrian Trail (see Trails #22 and #23). May be impassable in rainy season. Avoid in deer-hunting season, August-September. Watch and listen for gunfire.

HOW TO GET THERE: Turn east off Highway 1 onto Highway 20 at M.59.8, just south of Fort Bragg. Go 5.9 miles to Road 350 on left, leading downhill by some redwoods. In .3 mile, take the right fork. You pass several spur roads on the left, but stay on main road. In 3 miles from the highway, you come to the Noyo Egg Collecting Station. Just past the station at 3.2 miles, you come to a big intersection. Take Road 360 heading north to a gate at 3.7 miles. If gate is locked, this is your trailhead. Turn around and park, not blocking gate.

If gate is open, continue on this road past a junction at 4.4 miles where it turns into Road 361 (Road 360 makes a sharp left). Road 361 continues (may be big mud holes in spring) past several campgrounds until road's end at 7 miles, where you park.

FURTHER INFO: Jackson State Forest (707) 964-5674.

small town there provided bunkhouses for single men, bungalows for families, a store, a cookhouse, an ice plant, a school, an engine house and switching yard for the cluster of engines used in the woods. The town was occupied until the railroad was abandoned in 1945.

Other more temporary logging camps, many of which are now campsites, dotted the way along Road 360/361 leading north, reaching Camp 8, near the start of the Trestle Trail, by 1915. Over the next nine years, the company built and logged its way up the canyon where the trail is today until the area was logged out. Though the rails were removed and laid elsewhere, the wooden crossties and trestles were left to rot in the woods.

The Trestle Trail provides access to a very pretty canyon with a waterfall and logging relics. As of press time you need to walk or bike 3⅛ miles to reach the start of the Trestle Trail since Road 361 is no longer open to vehicle traffic. A bike offers considerable advantage since the road closure requires 6¼ additional miles just to get to the Trestle Trail. The Trestle Trail connects with a little-traveled road system on its east end, allowing the avid day hiker or backpacker an opportunity to make a beautiful 19-mile loop through great scenery. Several walk-in camps along Road 361 offer the opportunity of camping near the start of the Trestle Trail.

Please note that the rustic trestles are disintegrating rapidly after 65 years, with much damage and decay occurring in the past 12 years. Schedule a visit here sooner rather than later to see the trestles.

Park at the locked gate and walk or bike the road 3⅛ miles on a gentle ascent to its end. By 2⅝ miles you pass the Bob Woods Trail and Camp 8, the last walk-in camp before the Trestle Trailhead. Continue along the narrowing track to its end at 3⅛ miles. There the river forms a small pool with a roughhewn trestle on its far bank. It's a pleasant spot beside the stream and may be enough to satisfy your curiosity.

If it's not, take the footpath on the left heading northeast. Mileage counts from zero again here. The trail follows the stream past young redwoods, then climbs to join an old road bed. Just beyond ⅛ mile, you pass through a stile and cross a small footbridge over a small side stream. The trail switchbacks twice

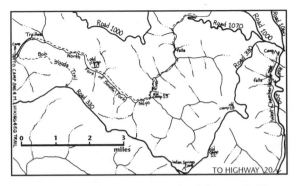

to climb above the steep cutbank of the creek. From
¼ mile the trail contours across steep canyon walls.
Notice that the hillside environment on your left is
much drier than the streamside. Redwoods still
thrive on the drier south-facing slopes of this deep
canyon as do Douglas iris, California hazel,
ceanothus, redwood sorrel and starflower.

Beyond ⅜ mile you descend steeply to the creek.
You soon near the old logging trestle you will follow
for the next 3 miles. Notice that it's not made of fancy
cut lumber, but of roughly cut logs, probably from
the first trees cut here, then quickly slapped into
place. At ½ mile you are alongside the trestle, where
ferns, berry bushes, hazel, poison oak and even a
young fir sapling grow out of its rotting wood. Old
rusted spikes are exposed, with a few of the crossties
still in place.

About ⅝ mile the trail passes along a steep
cutbank. The forest here consists almost entirely of
bay laurel growing where redwoods used to be. You
will soon reenter deep redwood forest. As you cross
a small bridge, the old trestle is still on your right.
You pass redwood sorrel, evergreen violet, trail
plant, coltsfoot, red larkspur and columbine in the
understory, big leaf maple, tan oak and California
nutmeg in the forest.

Beyond ¾ mile grow healthy young redwoods up-
wards of 3 feet in diameter. You cross several more
roughhewn redwood bridges. The trestle (across the
creek) widens into a broad platform that may have
been a landing for the old logging operations. Large
trees, only 60 to 70 years old, grow through the platform.

Your trail soon climbs steeply to a grassy clearing
beyond ⅞ mile. You soon switchback to the right and
drop back down to the bottom of the canyon. Be-

105

yond one mile you're walking atop the old railroad bed where some of the original crossties remain in place. Wood rose, berries, rhododendrons and poison oak grow at trailside. Cross a small bridge over a tributary, then again follow the rail bed. Two old apple trees grow above the creek on your right beyond 1¼ miles, marking the site of an old homestead.

At 1⅜ miles the trail veers left as the trestle shoots diagonally across the canyon. Contour above the creek, then climb a steep short hill, coming to the top of a large slide. Watch your step! It's a steep drop on your right. Just beyond in a small gully grow scouring rush, wild strawberries and sword, five-finger and woodwardia ferns. The trail continues to climb high above the creek.

From the summit around 1⅝ miles you can see the canyon's steep and wooded north face. Descend toward the sound of the creek, then to the old rail bed. The environment here is cool and lush with healthy redwoods. At 1⅞ miles you climb more steps, then follow the lay of the land into a shady northeast slope.

At 2 miles the trail drops by 20 steep steps to a bridge across the creek. Head east briefly on the old track bed, then make a steep, short climb before quickly returning to streamside, where you continue northeast. You are back on the rail way by 2⅛ miles.

At 2¼ miles, where a trestle spans the canyon, you recross the North Fork of South Fork on a large old beam. Rejoin the old trail to head generally north upstream from a big bend in the river.

Your trail rejoins the rail bed at 2⅜ miles and comes to a few rusting relics. Have you ever tried to lift a railroad wheel? Continue through some healthy second-growth forest. Soon after 2½ miles, you cross the stream on old trestle pieces lush with ferns. Then you head northeast along the rail bed.

You cross another bridge over the fork at 2⅝ miles. Climb steep steps heading north to where the trail crosses an old cable from the 1920s logging operations. It is tied to the big stump just above the trail.

Descend back to the floodplain of the river and cross a dry side gulch. You soon ford the main stream and continue northeast up the canyon. Beyond 2⅞ miles you ford the stream again. You come to a broad portion of the canyon.

At 3 miles you cross a bridge where five-finger and sword ferns grow. Continue northeast on the right

side of the canyon, climbing briefly, then returning to the level canyon floor. At 3⅛ miles you cross a bridge over an eastern fork of the North Fork of South Fork.

Continue up the canyon, crossing a bridge over the main stream again at 3¼ miles. An elevated landfill between you and the stream was the rail bed here. Now it is much eroded, with trees growing on it. Cross another bridge at 3⅜ miles, then soon another, with a roughhewn trestle on your right.

As you climb steeply at 3½ miles, you see the last remnant of the trestle below you. While old stumps up canyon indicate that the line went farther, no trace of it remains.

You come to a view of a pretty, 15-foot waterfall where the canyon steepens. The trail crosses two bridges over side streams. Then, at 3⅝ miles a side trail forks right to a rest bench overlooking the falls. This is a good turnaround point if you do not plan to hike the long loop. The trail ahead soon enters a recently logged area.

The main trail continues north, then northeast up the canyon. Climb above the canyon floor at 3¾ miles, then return to it at 3⅞ miles. As you come to a ford of the stream, recent logging activity mars the beauty of the canyon. The trail continues, climbing more steeply up the canyon. After another ford, you come to a logging landing and the last ford of the North Fork of South Fork Noyo River, 4⅛ miles from the Trestle Trailhead.

If you want to continue on the long loop, keep in mind that you still have 9⅛ miles and a lot of climbing to go just to return to Camp 8 (plus another 3⅛ miles to the parking area on Road 360). You're game? Go west on Road 1070, before it switchbacks and heads generally east to meet Road 1000 at 5⅞ miles.

Then go immediately right on Road 330, climbing for the next mile.

Beyond 7¼ miles Road 330 becomes mostly level. You follow an old ridge line of the Caspar Railroad, with more trestles and logging camps along the route. At 8⅞ miles you come to Indian Springs Camp, the only place on the route beyond Camp 8 where backpackers can spend the night.

At 11⅝ miles Road 330 meets the Bob Woods Trail, which descends north, then west through attractive forest and meadows for 1⅛ miles, to return to the North Fork of South Fork at Camp 8. It is 3⅛ miles west along Road 361 to your starting point.

21.

CHAMBERLAIN CREEK

WATERFALL WALK

For me, this virgin grove will always be known as the Glenn Watters Memorial Grove. In most any weather, Glenn would go out to this special place in his Birkenstocks. It was Glenn who first told me about this fine place. This grove is one of the few places in Jackson State Forest where a significant virgin stand of redwoods survives. It was overlooked during successive timber harvests because of the steep and deep canyon in which it lies.

A wooden railing and steps lead downhill from the parking area. Continue descending steeply (watch your step), then turn right into cool, young-growth forest. In 300 feet you drop by two switchbacks into a moist environment where rhododendrons, redwood sorrel and sword ferns thrive. After one more switchback near a big rock, descend into virgin redwood forest near the creek.

Follow the trail beneath two large fallen redwood logs and the waterfall is suddenly before you. At the base of the 50-plus-foot falls grow five-finger and other ferns. Also growing in this moist pocket are trilliums, false Solomon's seal, and fragrant vanilla leaf (three large wedge-shaped leaflets).

The virgin redwoods extend west into a side canyon. You may cross the creek on a large fallen log,

CHAMBERLAIN CREEK WATERFALL:

DISTANCE: ¼ mile to 2 miles round trip.

TIME: A half hour to one hour.

TERRAIN: Short steep walk into creek canyon with virgin redwoods, then climbing up creek to a campsite near headwaters.

ELEVATION GAIN/LOSS: 85 feet+/85 feet- to falls; 445 feet+/445 feet- to upper camp and back.

BEST TIME: Late winter or spring, when waterfall is in full glory (after a big rainstorm is best); a pretty spot anytime.

WARNINGS: The trail is quite steep but mercifully short. This trail can be slippery, especially when wet, but even when dry.

HOW TO GET THERE: From Highway 1 south of Fort Bragg, turn east onto Highway 20 at M.59.8. Go east to M.17.4, where, just past the Chamberlain Creek bridge, you turn left onto Road 200. In 1.2 miles, the road splits. Take a sharp left, following Road 200 as it climbs gradually then more steeply, until you are 4.7 miles from Highway 20. There the road widens with parking for four cars on the left shoulder. A wooden railing leads downhill.

FURTHER INFO: Jackson State Forest (707) 964-5674.

or you may ford the creek near the base of the falls if the water is not too high. In 200 feet you come to a picnic spot (no camping or fires, please). From there a newly worked path climbs north up the side of the canyon. It follows the canyon of Chamberlain Creek for ⅞ mile to a campsite near the headwaters. From there you may return on the same pleasant path, or walk the road back down to your car.

OTHER SUGGESTION: At M.17.3 on Highway 20, just west of the Chamberlain Creek bridge, turn right and park by the steam donkey engine just south of the highway. The CHAMBERLAIN CREEK DEMONSTRATION FOREST TRAIL leaves from there. It consists of a short loop with an easy climb or a longer, steeper loop. The interpretive

22.

MENDOCINO HIKING & EQUESTRIAN TRAIL

PART ONE: SHERWOOD ROAD

This hike along remote Sherwood Road, even more than the other two sections of the Mendocino Hiking and Equestrian Trail (also known as the Little Lake-Sherwood Trail), is not so much for the casual walker as it is a place to strike out on a long all-day or overnight hike. The route of the old Sherwood stagecoach Road follows high ridges through rugged, wild country. The hike has its charms, but it doesn't reveal them easily since the traveler must endure steep ascents, clearcuts, trash and other scars on the landscape in order to discover the long vistas and hidden charms along the route.

For the quickest rewards, consider starting your hike from the east end where it's a relatively short hike to reach the area near the summit of Sherwood Peak or the year-round spring a mile beyond. Whether you start from Fort Bragg or Willits, you're not likely to see many people out here. You might consider using this long dirt road as a mountain-bike route in spring or autumn. Summer can be very hot here and in winter many trees may be down across the route.

Head east through forest on unpaved Sherwood Road, which quickly narrows and starts looking like the old stagecoach road it is. Contour or ascend gradually for ⅝ mile. As late as April or May large mud holes may lurk around the first bend, recurring intermittently all along the route. Then the road bends sharply left and climbs, gaining 400 feet in the next mile, with good views east and south.

An unmarked spur road branches to the left, the

110

MENDOCINO HIKING & EQUESTRIAN TRAIL
Part One:

DISTANCE: 24½ miles one way. (From Company Ranch Road, Sherwood Road junction to eastern trailhead, near Sherwood Indian Rancheria). Part of 42-mile Mendocino Hiking & Equestrian Trail.

TIME: Two to three days.

TERRAIN: Old dirt stagecoach road up and down along rambling ridges through severely logged area.

ELEVATION GAIN/LOSS: 3780 feet+/1320 feet- (to Willits another 900 feet-).

BEST TIME: Late spring, autumn next best.

WARNINGS: Road passes through rugged, sometimes confusing terrain with a maze of logging roads; carry map and compass. Active logging may make the route even more confusing; best to inquire before going. May be impassable in rainy season. Open to motor vehicles, although not heavily traveled. Watch and listen for motor traffic. The road passes over private timber lands. Do not trespass. No water available except at Coon Camp and near Sherwood Peak. Watch and listen for hunters and "recreational shooters." Avoid in deer hunting season, August to September.

HOW TO GET THERE, WEST END: Turn east off Highway 1 at Oak Street (M.61.3), near the center of Fort Bragg. Go 5.3 miles to end of pavement at unmarked intersection of Sherwood Road and Company Ranch Road. (At Fort Bragg city limit, Oak becomes Sherwood Road. The mileage markers count from there.) Park off road. Though you can drive farther, road quickly becomes steep, narrow and rough beyond this point.

HOW TO GET THERE, EAST END: Turn west off Highway 101 at north end of Willits (M.47.2) onto Sherwood Road. Go 12.4 miles to end of pavement and an intersection where Sherwood Road turns left. Park near intersection.

FURTHER INFO: Mendocino County Road Department (707)964-2596.

ENVIRONMENTAL CAMPS: Coon Camp is located at M.11.8. Wanhalla Camp is at M.27.50.

first of many. Be careful along this entire route not to mistake these spurs for the main ridge route. Notice that spurs are generally rougher and often lead downhill, while the main route generally does not change suddenly.

At ¾ mile Sherwood Road becomes very steep. You soon encounter more deep mud holes (or their dried up remains). By 1⅛ miles, after another steep climb, you gain a ridgetop clearcut. From the clearing, look north to see the watersheds of Pudding Creek (foreground) and Ten Mile River.

At a fork around 1¼ miles, stay to the right. Another very steep climb brings you to a level top around 1½ miles, where a clearcut on your left allows a look west down canyons to the coast around Fort Bragg. Ascend to the first summit before 1⅝ miles.

At a fork just beyond, Sherwood Road descends on the right, dropping with views east past iris and Oregon grape to 1¾ miles. Climb steeply again on an often muddy section of road. When the road is muddy, a narrower track to your left may be better. At 2⅜ miles you come to a top around M.6.5. The brief level stretch is soon followed by a downhill stretch marked by a steep and rutted sharp right turn, wrapping around a large redwood.

Adjacent to the redwood is a large stump with a flat mossy top, a pleasant place to rest, especially on a warm day. Unfortunately, this spot (and much of Sherwood Road) is strewn with cans, bottles, broken glass, toilet paper and other signs of uncaring humans. It seems that some people cannot tolerate being surrounded by nature without cluttering it with signs of their presence. This pathological compulsion to litter cuts across all segments of human culture (even some hikers, God forbid!). Please don't be one of the bad guys! Even better, do your part by picking up some of the litter to carry out with you. In this way you can thank Mother Nature for enriching your day.

As you drop to the most level portion of the route so far, look for 6873-foot Hull Mountain 40 miles away in Mendocino National Forest. Contour past M.7.07 (3 miles from trailhead) and drop gradually to a saddle around 3¼ miles. Then you descend slightly to a large clearcut with an expansive view. Cahto Peak is to the north, while Sherwood Peak (on your route) is northeast. From here you can also see two large logged areas, the left one a "selective cut," the one to the right a clearcut. The next ¼ mile is open and sunny, with spots near the road for picnics and sun bathing. Please do not trespass onto the adjacent timber lands. Along the road grow Douglas iris, Oregon grape, redwood sorrel, wild strawberries, sword ferns and an occasional calypso orchid.

At 4⅛ miles (near M.8.25), after a short climb, the road bends left around another clearcut. This stretch is mostly level with short drops and climbs to 5⅝ miles.

Then you begin another descent, dropping moderately around a clearcut to 5⅞ miles. In winter and spring, this section of road (and intermittently from here east) is often blocked with fallen trees from winter storms. One can generally find a way around these barricades, but bikers may have to walk or lift their bikes around or over the logs.

At 6⅛ miles your route climbs again gradually,

then moderately through a clearcut to 7⅜ miles. Past M.11.00, the road descends slightly around a large logging scar on the right. Just beyond a saddle near 7¾ miles is a corral on your right. Beside redwoods just beyond is Coon Camp, a tiny camp provided by Georgia-Pacific as an overnight stop or picnic spot. The rules are one night stay only, no fires, hikers and equestrians only. A covered spring box lies just east of camp; the water is brackish but potable. Please keep horses away from the spring.

After Coon Camp the trail climbs for the next 1¾ miles. A seasonal stream ¼ mile beyond the camp provides very cold and fresh water; it is better than the spring at camp, if it's still flowing. Two other seasonal streams also flow from the mountain on the left. At M.14.00, about 9⅞ miles from the trailhead, your route levels, then descends slightly. The peak to your left rises to 1550 feet above sea level. Most of the next stretch of Sherwood Road is level. Do not mistake the many side roads along this stretch for your trail. Most of them are blocked by a gate or a pile of dirt. The trail continues along the ridge.

At M.18.25, around 14⅛ miles, you pass the last county road marker for 12 miles. At 14½ miles Sherwood Road turns northwest at a junction, climbing past Marble Place. The county road continues, wandering back and forth from the north side of the ridge to the south side and back again. It's mostly well shaded by the forest on this stretch. Tanoak and ceanothus are prevalent.

Around 17 miles, you arrive at Wanhalla Camp on the south side of the road. The camp, provided courtesy of Mendocino Redwood Company, is in an open area overlooking the canyons of the Noyo River and the wooded ridges to the south. You are permitted to build a fire only in the fire box provided. Carry out your trash please. A 1250-gallon water tank provides drinking water (if it has been filled recently). Be sure to keep the tap turned off.

As you leave Wanhalla Camp, Sherwood Road climbs generally toward Sherwood Peak across timber lands designated as a tree farm. This continues for 4½ miles to a boundary about 28 miles from Fort Bragg. Just beyond the boundary are the remains of an old lumber mill, one of many in these hills abandoned in the 1950s with the centralization of lumber production.

114

Just over one mile from the mill, around 20¾ miles you come to a clear freshwater stream bubbling from the mountainside just above the road. You can fill your canteen year round with the sweet spring water. You have 4 miles to go.

Sherwood Road continues east, mostly ascending to the road's summit at 22⅜ miles. You're just below the 3209-foot summit of Sherwood Peak. The road offers spectacular views in this area, as Sherwood is the highest peak near the coast between Cahto Peak near Branscomb (4234 feet) and Cold Springs Peak near Philo (2736 feet). To the south many heavily timbered ridges line up to the horizon. On a clear day you can see more ridges extending to the glistening Pacific.

From the level area near the peak, the road drops gradually, then more steeply by sharp curves. Watch for motor traffic again as you are approaching the populated Sherwood Valley near Willits. Just over 2 miles from the summit the road levels, then comes to Octagon House, the official end of the trail at 24½ miles. If you watch carefully for traffic, you may continue the 8 miles into Willits, mostly downhill. It is even better if you have arranged to be picked up at the eastern trailhead.

23.

MENDOCINO HIKING & EQUESTRIAN TRAIL

PART TWO: HIGHWAY 20 TO SHERWOOD ROAD

While the Mendocino Hiking and Equestrian Trail was developed primarily for equestrians, it get very little use of any kind, so it offers a pleasant and uncrowded choice for a longer hike. I especially like this second part because, unlike the other two parts, it shares barely 2 miles of its route with motorized traffic. An especially pleasant hike follows the first 1¼ miles from Highway 20 down to Camp One on an old wagon road. Despite one giant old clearcut and several recent small ones, the wagon road offers an intimate downhill trek through the forest,

MENDOCINO HIKING & EQUESTRIAN TRAIL
Part Two:

DISTANCE: 7¾ miles one way, or 2⅝ miles round trip to Camp One.

TIME: Four hours one way, one hour round trip to Camp One.

TERRAIN: From ridge to river canyon to ridge to canyon, then climbing to a third ridge, traversing many habitats.

ELEVATION GAIN/LOSS: 1505 feet+/1825 feet-; 740 feet+/740 feet- round trip to Camp One.

BEST TIME: Late spring to late autumn.

WARNINGS: Trail is sometimes closed by logging operations; inquire at State Forest Office. North portions of trail cross private land by permissive use agreements. Stay on trail. Portions of trail are open to motorized traffic. Watch and listen for gunfire, especially deer season—August and September. Watch for poison oak.

HOW TO GET THERE, SOUTH END: Turn east off Highway 1 at M.59.8 (just south of Fort Bragg) onto Highway 20. Go east to M.8.02, where a logging road goes downhill on the left.

HOW TO GET THERE, NORTH END: Turn east off Highway 1 at Oak Street (M.61.3), near the center of Fort Bragg. Go 5.3 miles east to intersection where pavement ends; Sherwood Road continues ahead, Company Ranch Road (on the right) is the trail.

FURTHER INFO: Jackson State Forest (707) 964-5674.

but requires a steep climb on your return.

On the down side, be warned that the property owner at Company Ranch on the north end of part two of the Hiking and Equestrian Trail has not been honoring the agreement that created this as a public trail. He has chased some hikers and cyclists from his property. You certainly don't want to park on Company Ranch property and you might ignore the trail section's north end, north of the North Fork Noyo River bridge unless you need to pass through there on a longer hike.

After crossing Highway 20 at M.8.08, the trail turns west and parallels the highway briefly, then turns right to meet a logging road in 500 feet. Follow Road 90, marked on the yellow gate around the first corner, on a gentle descent for ¼ mile to a fork. Take the left fork and go 200 feet to where a tiny sign on a young redwood points right for the Hiking and Equestrian Trail. Your vague, hard-to-spot trail descends east, then north above a recently logged area, with Scotch broom growing in the bed of the old Camp One wagon road.

By ⅜ mile your trail meets a broad road and enters the giant clearcut. Go left on the road for 100 feet, then veer left on the old track, which starts north, then bends east descending along the edge of the clearcut. Before ⅝ mile you mercifully return to the forest. Contour along a ridgetop, then descend as the trail winds right and left through the forest, heading generally north.

Around one mile your trail promptly bends right and descends east with a clearcut below on your left. As you reach the bottom of the clearcut, a signed junction is on the left. The left fork offers an alternative descent on the narrow Camp One Loop Trail. The MHE Trail, signed SHERWOOD, continue down the old wagon road, descending southeast, then northeast, then north. Before 1¼ miles you come to a trail sign in a level campground. Continue north 350 feet to Road 360 opposite the Noyo Egg Collecting Station. This area, called Camp One because it was the first logging camp on the railroad line of the Caspar Lumber Company, has several free campsites—contact the state forest.

Turn right and follow Road 360 north alongside the North Fork of South Fork Noyo River. Watch for motorized traffic for the next ¾ mile as the trail shares the road with vehicles. You pass two pleasant campsites along this stretch: Wagon Camp and Tin Can Camp. Around 2 miles you come to a gate. If the gate is closed, you'll not encounter any motorized traffic for several miles.

Continue on Road 360 over a short steep hill and across the stream, which crosses to the right side of the road. Just beyond, you (and Road 360) take a sharp left and head up Brandon Gulch. (Road 361 is on the right, leading to the North Fork of South Fork Trail, #20.) After the turn, you should be heading northwest.

You come to another junction at 3 miles. Go left here on Road 362, climbing 800 feet in just over ¾ mile to Riley Ridge, where you meet Road 1000. Just across from the junction the Hiking and Equestrian Trail descends west by northwest, leading to the Noyo River in 2 more miles, a 1000-foot descent.

This section of trail crosses the property of Georgia-Pacific Company; stay on the trail and don't trespass. Descend a narrow path for ½ mile until it ends at a broad dirt road. Turn right and descend the road ¼ mile to cross a metal bridge and come to road's end at another road at 4⅝ miles. Turn left and ascend the road to an old homestead site with an apple orchard and daffodils at 5⅛ miles. This was the site of Sointula, a Finnish-American community that thrived in the 1930s.

Look for a narrow single track trail on your right at a big bend in the road. Turn right and descend the narrow trail along a winding creek. You ford a seasonal stream then pass through two dips. Descend the track northwest down a side canyon, contour past a marsh, then drop to ford a small creek around 5¾ miles. Your trail immediately climbs to meet a dirt road. Turn left and descend the road to its end at 6⅛ miles. Turn right and descend the broad road for 150 feet to the bridge over the North Fork Noyo River.

Company Ranch lies beyond the bridge. If you continue, you cross the Skunk Railroad tracks, then veer right briefly to Company Ranch Road. Turn left and ascend the county road 1⅜ miles to Sherwood Road at 7¾ miles, climbing 510 feet. Again you should watch for motorized traffic. Part One of the Mendocino Hiking & Equestrian Trail continues up Sherwood Road on the right. Fort Bragg is just 5½ miles west on Sherwood Road.

For Part 3 of the Hiking and Equestrian Trail, see Jackson State Forest South, near Mendocino (Trail #33).

24

JUGHANDLE NORTH HEADLANDS

GORGEOUS STRETCH OF COASTAL TRAIL

State Parks acquired the headlands north of Jughandle Creek just in time to keep the right-of-way for the California Coastal Trail (CCT). The surrounding subdivisions attest that the park acquisition was none too soon. You might see a few people on one of the pocket beaches along this hike, but most of the Jughandle North Headlands get very light use. You may wonder why if you visit on a sunny day when the beauty of this sparkling shoreline boggles the mind.

You can follow the entire described hike for a 4¾-mile round trip or take shorter hikes from any of the three highway access points. You can also walk north on Ocean Drive past the Pine Beach Inn to the road's end and visit tiny Pine Beach at the mouth of Mitchell Creek.

Follow the CCT, the obvious trail heading west from the dirt parking area. Head west through grasslands, passing shiny-leaved small trees, cascara sagrada. You soon enter a forest of shore pines where private property lies immediately to the north around ⅛ mile. Around ¼ mile, two trails fork right. Take the second one, leaving the CCT to cross a tiny creek and head north, then northwest through grasslands scattered with shore pines.

Come to the bluff's edge at ⅜ mile and follow it to Mitchell Point at ½ mile. From the point you overlook a rugged shoreline with deep water of many vibrant hues offshore. Cormorants perch on sea stacks offshore. You can see tiny Pine Beach to the east. Retrace your steps to the CCT where you left it.

Turn right and continue west on the Coastal Trail. The trees soon part to reveal a convoluted, rocky shore. Beyond ¾ mile you reach a narrow promontory with pocket beaches on both sides. You can take a side trail out to the narrow point if you'd like. Follow the CCT as it turns southeast along the bluff's edge, soon coming to a trail fork above tiny Bromley

JUGHANDLE NORTH HEADLANDS:

DISTANCE: 4¾ miles round trip, or one mile round trip to Mitchell Point or 2 miles round trip to Bromley Beach.

TIME: One to three hours.

TERRAIN: Level or gently rolling headlands near the shore, with one descent to the beach and a steep, rocky ascent back to blufftop.

ELEVATION GAIN/LOSS: 180 feet+/180 feet-.

BEST TIME: Spring and early summer for wildflowers.

WARNINGS: Never turn your back on the ocean. Use caution on short, steep rocky part of trail. Watch for the sharp spines of gorse in grasslands south of Bromley Beach. Don't trespass on adjacent private property.

HOW TO GET THERE: Turn west off Highway 1 at Milepost 57.49 south of Fort Bragg, north of Caspar onto Ocean Drive at Pine Beach Inn. Turn left into dirt trailhead parking just beyond Pine Beach Inn sign. (Other access from highway at M.57.15 north of Gibney Lane and M.56.75 north of Jughandle Creek bridge.)

FURTHER INFO: Mendocino State Parks (707) 937-5804.

Creek at ⅞ mile.

Turn right and descend beside the creek to secluded Bromley Beach, with a tall beached sea stack in its center. Cross the creek and walk southwest across the beach to its southern end at one mile. A steep, sometimes slippery footpath there requires scrambling up the bluff face. Once you reach the level headland on top, walk east briefly, then turn south and descend across another seasonal creek and climb up the other side. Veer right at a fork and follow the bluff's edge out to another point. This headland area offers some of the most natural, least disturbed coastal grasslands habitat you'll find on the north coast. Look for abundant brodiaea, coastal wild onion, Mendocino paintbrush and many more native flowers in spring. One of the densest concentrations of native plants grows on the rocky knoll around 1¼ miles.

Continue southeast along the bluff-edge path to another junction. Since private property lies to the south, you want the trail on the left that heads east, coming almost back to Highway 1 at 1¾ miles, directly opposite Gibney Lane and Annie's Jughandle Beach Inn. When you come to a gravel road, turn right and follow it south, paralleling the highway.

Shortly after the driveway turns right, you come to a private property sign. This is your cue to leave the road and head south, again paralleling Highway 1, this time through a grassy field which often has no obvious path. Watch for uneven footing and spiny gorse on this lightly traveled leg. Pick your way south until you find a broad track around 2⅛ miles, the Jughandle North Headlands Trail.

From here the CCT continues south briefly, then veers east under the highway bridge to meet the Jughandle Ecological Staircase Trail (Trail #25). Instead, you want to turn right and head west to the bluffs north of Jughandle Cove. As you pass several forks, always take the left path for the grandest views. (You'll return on the right.)

By 2¼ miles you gain vistas of the sea stacks off Jughandle Point to the south. Continue west on the narrowing double track, with Lost Coast views to

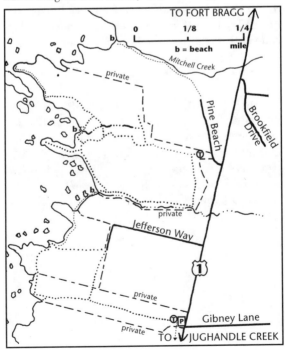

the northwest. In another 300 feet you reach the edge of the bluff. The surf-sculpted outer Jughandle Cove lies below you. The sandy beach of inner Jughandle Cove, however, isn't revealed until you reach the very tip of the southern point around 2⅜ miles.

From here you can continue circling the point counter-clockwise. You pass weather-shaped mounds of coast buckwheat and seaside daisy near the amazingly rocky bluff edge. By 2½ miles you come to the headland's western rim, but a point to the north extends further west. Continue north along the rim past a safe path down to the outer rocks— watch for waves if you go. At the westernmost point in 150 feet, native plants form a thick mat along the rim.

The trail continues north along the rim, coming to a final tidal access spur in 200 feet. From there the path turns east along the rim above a deep cove. After you reach the head of the cove, follow the trail as it veers southeast away from the shore. Climb gently past a pond and wetland on the left. Beyond the pond take the left fork before 2¾ miles. It heads due east, returning to the south parking area at 2⅞ miles. If you're returning to the northern trailhead at Pine Beach Inn, leave the path about 200 feet before the highway to head north-northeast cross country across the untracked field, heading for the east end of the tall stand of trees to the north. When you reach the gravel road in the trees around 3⅛ miles, retrace your steps to Bromley Beach, then follow the trail back to the trailhead.

OTHER SUGGESTIONS: CASPAR HEADLANDS STATE RESERVE lies just south of Caspar Creek. To visit this coastal access, you first must obtain a permit from state park headquarters. They'll give you a map indicating the precise location of access trails to the bluffs and adjacent tidepool areas surrounded by private property.

25

JUGHANDLE ECOLOGICAL STAIRCASE

SHOWPLACE OF COASTAL EVOLUTION

The unique area along Jughandle Creek became a state reserve in 1978. It had long been recognized as a prime example of the ecological history of the Mendocino coast, as well as one of the best preserved showplaces of coastal landscape evolution anywhere in the Northern Hemisphere. Its importance became recognized primarily through the pioneering work of botanist Hans Jenny, who identified the uplifted marine terraces occurring near the creek and the resulting varied botanical habitats.

The ecological staircase consists of five wave-cut terraces, each about 100 feet higher and 100,000 years older than the next. The youngest terrace, at the start of the hike, emerged from the sea about 100,000 years ago. The oldest terrace has been above sea level for more than 500,000 years. Each terrace was raised above the younger one as a result of the tremendous tectonic forces that have built the coast ranges as the Pacific (offshore) tectonic plate collides with the North American (onshore) continental plate.

Though you may find it difficult to imagine such dynamic change as you hike the coast's placid forests and grasslands, to the trained eye the evidence of this tectonic uplifting can be seen at many places up and down the Mendocino coast. This hike up Jughandle Creek explores the first, second and third terraces, passing through some of the clearest examples of the progressively uplifted marine terraces to end at the pygmy forest on the third terrace, helping us to understand and recognize the powerful forces which shaped, and continue to shape, the western edge of our continent.

The name Jughandle originated with the shape of the cove at the mouth of the creek. Today the Jughandle State Reserve covers 778 acres including the lightly traveled headlands north of Jughandle Creek (see previous trail) stretching a mile north to Mitchell Point. This hike's eastern end

JUGHANDLE ECOLOGICAL STAIRCASE:

DISTANCE: 5 miles round trip.

TIME: Three hours.

TERRAIN: Across wooded and open headlands, through creek canyon, then climbing gently over ancient marine terraces through tall forest on ancient dunes to pygmy forest.

ELEVATION GAIN/LOSS: 280 feet+/280 feet-.

BEST TIME: Spring to autumn.

WARNINGS: May be muddy after heavy rains. Wear waterproof boots in rainy season.

HOW TO GET THERE: Turn west off Highway 1 north of Caspar and just south of Jughandle Creek bridge at M.56.1 into Jughandle parking lot.

FURTHER INFO: Mendocino State Parks (707) 937-5804.

explores the adjacent lands of Jackson State Forest, protected in the Pygmy Forest Reserve.

The trail heads west from the parking lot and picnic area, passing through mixed forest dominated by introduced Monterey pines, but also with native Bishop and shore pines. You quickly come to the grassy coastal prairie, where more than a dozen species of wildflowers bloom in spring and summer. You may see the uncommon Mendocino paintbrush and coast wild onion as well as purple seaside daisy, poppy, angelica, goldfields, sea thrift and lupine. After passing a spur trail on the left before ⅛ mile that leads south to Caspar, follow the trail west to the point at ¼ mile. Where the trail turns north, you can follow a spur trail west about 200 feet to the tip of the point. From the point, you look west to offshore sea stacks and northeast into bowl-shaped Jughandle Cove with its broad sandy beach.

The grassy headlands form the first terrace, uplifted gradually over the last 100,000 years. The

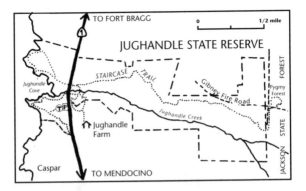

gradually sloping shoreline and tidal area below will eventually become the next terrace as it is uplifted above sea level by the collision of the two tectonic plates along the San Andreas fault about a mile offshore.

From the point, turn north and circle the headlands clockwise above the cove, passing gum plant and iris. Around ⅜ mile you pass two steep paths down to separate beaches. (No dogs on the beach please: prime wildlife habitat.) Beyond the second spur, continue east into forest where Sitka spruce, grand fir and wax myrtle mingle with the pines. Before the parking lot, veer left around ½ mile on the trail heading north past red flowering currant. You soon pass a spur on the left, the best trail to the sheltered beach of Jughandle Cove. The Staircase Trail angles northeast past coast silktassel, twinberry, ceanothus and abundant wildflowers including paintbrush, hedge nettle and false lily of the valley, then turns east to pass under the highway bridge. About 150 feet beyond the bridge, take the left fork, descending a stairway to Jughandle Creek around ⅝ mile. The creek is tidal to just above this point. You may see it flowing upstream if the tide is rising. (Before the trail crosses the creek, a wonderful little side trail leads upstream. Known as the Doree Diamond Trail, this spur leads through a beautiful swamp on a narrow boardwalk for 300 feet before continuing on drier ground into tall Sitka spruce forest.)

Cross the creek on the sturdy bridge, then continue along a raised boardwalk. Before climbing back up to the first terrace, you pass through a stand of red alder. Many Native American tribes used the blood red sap of this tree as a dye. Watch for stinging nettles growing in the shade of the alder. Notice

125

these plants and avoid them.

The trail climbs toward the highway, passing poison oak, sticky monkeyflower, canyon gooseberry, ceanothus and invasive Scotch broom. At the top of the hill, a vague spur forks left, leading under the highway bridge to the headlands north of Jughandle Creek (see Trail #24). The main trail turns east through mixed pine forest and grasslands, a good area for spotting deer.

Around ⅞ mile from the trailhead, you walk through a small tunnel of brush, climbing gradually. A big blackberry patch is on your left. The trail steepens as you ascend from the first to the second terrace around one mile. Here grand firs and Douglas firs begin to mix with the pines, with thimbleberry in the understory. Around one mile you pass through an old homestead site before entering a tall forest of Sitka spruce, grand fir, western hemlock and Bishop pine. Lichens, redwood sorrel and sword ferns cover the forest floor.

Around 1⅛ miles the forest floor becomes dominated by a carpet of false lily of the valley, lush green plants with heart-shaped leaves and tiny white flowers. As you climb gradually along the second terrace, other plants appear on the forest floor: first fairy bells and corn lily, then wax myrtle and salal mix with the false lily of the valley. Then red huckleberries grow on your right, quickly followed by red alders, evergreen huckleberries, rhododendrons and tanoak. Soon Labrador tea with pungent little white flowers and shiny leaves appears. Near 1¼ miles you begin to see Oregon grape (holly like leaves, yellow flowers in May, followed by blue "grapes").

You encounter an old fence line running north and south, perpendicular to the trail. You're leaving the old homestead and entering what was once timber company land. The area ahead was logged in 1961. As you walk on, notice how well a forest can recover from logging in less than 40 years.

Just 30 feet beyond the fence, the trail forks. Take the right fork, remembering this turn in the trail for your return trip (many hikers have mistakenly ended up on Gibney Lane not far to the north). Continue through the young-growth forest dominated by Bishop pines and young hemlocks with evergreen violet abundant on the forest floor. Before 1½ miles you come to a partial clearing, created when the logged area was burned to clear slash (logging debris). Notice how the hardwood species and grass intruded on the forest after the fire. Now, however, the conifers are growing to dominate the intruders.

Around 1⅝ miles notice the orange-brown soils along the trail. This hardpan soil is one of the first steps in the creation of the pygmy forest environment. Eventually the hardpan will become so thick that most plant roots will not penetrate it. As you enter a drier habitat, manzanita and wood rose occur.

Heading east, you soon cross under a power line. This was the right of way of the Caspar Railroad, which ran from the mill at the mouth of Caspar Creek and up Jughandle Creek in the early 1870s. The first "rails" were made of wood, because of a shortage of iron after the Civil War. The timber-laden cars were pulled by oxen until 1875, when the coast's first steam locomotive was brought in pieces by schooner from San Francisco, reassembled and put into service on the wooden rails. The engine, dubbed "Jumbo," raced along at a top speed of 10 miles per hour, a great improvement over the oxen. About 1880, after Caspar Lumber Company bought more timber land to the north, they built a huge wooden trestle spanning the deep chasm of Jughandle Creek.

The trestle, located where the power line crosses today, was 1000 feet long and 146 feet high. At that time it was the world's largest wooden railroad bridge. It carried many huge loads of timber before folding like an accordion in the 1906 earthquake.

Continuing east, you immediately encounter the first young redwoods along the trail. They form a pleasant grove on your left. The raised berm beside the grove was probably created in developing the rail line. Suddenly the clover-like leaves of redwood sorrel are abundant. Continue east past rattlesnake plantain, fat Solomon's seal and trillium. At 1¾ miles the first large redwood stump, a charred cylinder, stands on your left. The rise it grew on is an ancient sand dune, created 200,000 years ago by waves and wind at the base of what is now the third terrace. The sandy, well-drained soil of the dune creates an excellent growing environment where the redwoods and Douglas firs grow tall and healthy, especially in contrast to the hardpan of the pygmy. The trail soon turns left and climbs onto the dune.

A different group of shade-loving plants join redwood sorrel and trillium on the forest floor here: sword fern, the tiny pink starflower, clusters of red clintonia blossoms (replaced by dark blue inedible berries in summer) and an occasional calypso orchid. For the next ¼ mile you climb gradually onto the third terrace through the tall forest. Many more clintonia line the trail. Mature Bishop pines join the redwoods and firs.

The trail soon follows the ridge of the dune through beautiful forest on the rolling terrain around you. Dip through a gully at 2⅛ miles that feeds Jughandle Creek. Rhododendrons line the trail. Around 2¼ miles you come to a stand of big western hemlocks, which love moisture and thrive on less well-drained soils. Deer ferns grow on the forest floor here. They look somewhat like sword ferns, but their leaflet edges are smooth. Continue along the crest of the ancient dune, a steep drop into Jughandle Creek canyon on your right.

You're climbing into the transition zone between the well-drained dune soils at the front (west end) of the third terrace and the pygmy forest at the back of the third terrace. Notice that the conifers are neither as tall here nor as vigorously growing. Less demanding hardwood species like tanoak and wax myrtle are competing with the conifers for the available light, soil and moisture. The hardwoods do better in hardpan soil than do most conifers.

Your trail soon veers left, leaving the edge of the canyon, then the forest for transitional pygmy, a drastic change in the landscape at 2½ miles. The trail here may be a bit confusing: go north on a raised gravel path atop a broad fire break. You cross the Gibney fire road running east-west at a beach-sandy intersection.

Continue north 300 feet to where the trail leaves the fire break at 2⅝ miles, veering to the right onto a boardwalk into the heart of the pygmy forest. Typical of pygmy soils, this area does not drain well; there may be standing reddish brown water after rain, highly acidic—pygmy soils can be 1000 times more acidic than the soil of the redwood forest—and known as pygmy tea. Walk 50 feet to #33 where a Bolander pine grows on your left. The Bolander is a variation of the species *Pinus contorta*, which grows as lodgepole pine (straight and tall to 80 feet) up to 11,000 feet in the Sierra Nevada, and as shore pine (dense and scrubby) near the coast north to Alaska. The Bolander variation occurs only on pygmy soils and seldom grows much taller than this 16-foot-tall example.

Continue to a deck and raised viewing platform. Two other species limited primarily to pygmy soils also grow along the boardwalk. Mendocino cypress grows as the predominant tree in this pygmy forest. Low growing Fort Bragg manzanita with small shiny leaves, grows a bit farther along the boardwalk. It's not easily confused with its bigger cousin hairy manzanita, which also occurs sparsely in the pygmy forest. Other unusual plants that grow in or around the pygmy forest habitat include sphagnum moss, reindeer lichen, bunchberry and the insectivorous bog-loving tiny sundew. In May dwarf rhododendrons produce pink blooms of all sizes. Mushrooms may be abundant in the rainy season, but please no picking allowed in the delicate habitats of the Pygmy Forest Reserve. Looking southwest you can see the tall forest you walked through and to the east you may see more tall forest growing on the front of the fourth terrace ¼ mile away.

Most of the plants here grow to only about eight feet, with many cypresses under four feet tall show-

ing mature characteristics and bearing cones. A few
Bishop pines and Mendocino cypresses grow up to
30 feet tall here. The roots of these trees have broken through the pygmy hardpan to reach underlying pockets of nutrients.

At 2¾ miles you reach the end of the short pygmy
forest loop. You come to the last item in the interpretive brochure. The drainage ditch before you
shows the layers of soil underlying this pygmy bog:
thin humus, thick leached podsol, reddish brown
and iron-rich hardpan, then beach sand and gravel
underlaid with graywacke sandstone bedrock. Imagine trying to grow your vegetable or rose garden in
such soils. That is what many coastal residents have
to do.

Turn right and follow the ditch downhill for about
150 feet to the Gibney fire road. There you continue
west another 250 feet, then turn left on the north-
south fire road back to the big forest to rejoin the
main trail going west above the creek canyon. It's
about 2 miles to the trailhead.

OTHER SUGGESTION: The BEACH TRAIL
branches off main trail north of parking area, leading down to the beach of Jughandle Cove.

26.

POINT CABRILLO PRESERVE
GRASSY HEADLANDS ROLLING TO A RUGGED SHORE

*Point Cabrillo Preserve was snatched from the hun-
gry jaws of land speculators when the Coastal Conservancy completed its acquisition in 1992. The
preserve's 300 acres offer a prime example of the
abundance of the northern California coast's rich
biological diversity. You may see whales, seals and
sea lions offshore, and a rich selection of raptors
and other birds, deer, wildflowers and perhaps even
river otters within the preserve boundaries. Human
history is abundant too. The farming community of
Pine Grove sprang up here around 1860 and the
lighthouse service established the still operating light
in 1909.*

POINT CABRILLO PRESERVE:

DISTANCE: 3 miles round trip.
TIME: One to two hours.
TERRAIN: Wooded, then grassy headlands along spectacularly rugged shoreline.
ELEVATION GAIN/LOSS: 160 feet+/160 feet-.
BEST TIME: Spring, but anytime is good.
WARNINGS: Open sunrise to sundown. Some uneven footing requires caution beyond the lighthouse. Please observe marked closed areas.
HOW TO GET THERE: Turn west off Highway 1 south of Caspar and north of Mendocino at Milepost 54.66 onto Point Cabrillo Drive. Go 1.7 miles to Point Cabrillo Preserve. This section starts from the new paved parking lot just north of Lighthouse Road.
FURTHER INFORMATION: Point Cabrillo Preserve (707)937-0816.

This hike explores the California Coastal Trail's route across the gorgeous headlands around the lighthouse plus a loop north to the preserve's northern boundary where tiny Frolic Cove was the site of an important nineteenth-century shipwreck. The Baltimore sailing ship Frolic *wrecked on the offshore rocks here in July 1850 en route to gold-rush San Francisco from China with a load of oriental trade goods expected to bring top dollar in the booming City. After the shipwrecked officers reached San Francisco by lifeboat, entrepreneur Henry Meiggs sent a salvage crew to the wild Mendocino coast. They never found any salvage—the local Pomo people got there first—but the salvagers returned to the City to tell Meiggs of the vast redwood forests around Big River. Meiggs immediately shipped a sawmill and another crew to establish modern commerce on the Mendocino coast.*

Walk north from the parking lot and follow the narrow north road west out of the cypress grove and down the hill, enjoying expanding ocean vistas. From ⅛ to ¼ mile you pass bushy cypresses. Other com-

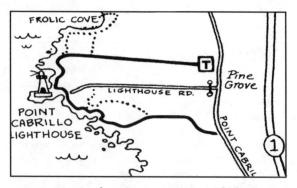

mon species in the upper preserve include poppy, huckleberry, iris, wax myrtle and coyote brush.

After passing a cotoneaster bush on the left beyond ⅜ mile, the path forks. Take the side trail on the right to head north past native strawberry and blackberry, cow parsnip and angelica. The path ends beyond ½ mile at a "T" intersection. Turn right to follow the side trail down to Frolic Cove. After it wraps left around a split rail fence, turn left to descend to Frolic Cove at ⅝ mile at the preserve's northwest corner.

Retrace your steps to the "T" intersection at ¾ mile. Then walk west paralleling the edge of the bluff. Around ⅞ mile you reach the point southwest of Frolic Cove. To the north you can see Caspar Point with the Lost Coast visible beyond on the clearest days.

Your trail angles southwest following the bluff edge above a rocky shelf at the high-tide zone. Look for abundant goldfields in spring, purple seaside daisy, lupine and sea thrift, with asters in late summer.

After entering the marine reserve boundary and crossing a wooden bridge across a tiny creek, the trail turns south toward the lighthouse. After you meet the western end of the north-road path, your trail dips across another old wooden bridge at 1⅛ miles. You soon pass through a fence line and come to the paved lighthouse road west of the lightkeeper's houses.

You can take a short detour west along the pavement for a closer look at the vintage lighthouse, to use the picnic tables, or to explore the eroded tip of Point Cabrillo northwest of the lighthouse. The side trip to the very point is only ¼ mile round trip.

Follow the Coastal Trail east along the pavement briefly. In about 300 feet, opposite the second house, follow the Coastal Trail as it turns right on a semi-paved track angling southwest over the grassy headlands. (An outhouse is 250 feet east along the paved road.) Where the semi-paved track ends at 1⅜ miles, veer west then south on a grassy track. It soon follows the bluff's edge where offshore rocks beyond a small cove often have harbor seals resting. Follow the grassy track south along the blufftop past gum plant, coast buckwheat and yarrow, then across a sturdy bridge over a small creek where mimulus grows at 1½ miles. Pass through a fence line and follow the track south toward a rocky point.

As you reach the point before 1⅝ miles, the trail dips, then veers left up a short hill into lush growth. A short spur on the right leads to the rocky shelf and views of a cove with surge tunnels and a small waterfall. To the south you can see the Mendocino headlands with the round swell of Stillwell Point rising beyond Little River.

Follow the CCT as it veers left to cross a bridge over a verdant creek just above where its waterfall plunges over a cliff into the sea with the surge tunnel invisible below. Follow the trail as it passes a razor-thin promontory on your right, then turns northeast past a healthy patch of kinnikinnick sheltered by ceanothus and coast silktassel. The trail continues northeast to circumvent a deep cove to the south. At the head of the cove, the trail turns east then south, becoming vague briefly. Before 1¾ miles, just north of another shimmering cove, you meet a track climbing northeast through the grasslands toward a broad pine up the hill. From here the CCT climbs northeast then east and southeast to leave the preserve and head for Russian Gulch State Park.

If you're day hiking you'll probably want to turn back at the last cove around 1¾ miles, retracing your steps back to the lighthouse, then taking the north road trail back to your starting point at 3 miles.

RUSSIAN GULCH STATE PARK

INCLUDES THE NEXT THREE TRAILS

Russian Gulch State Park was established in 1932. Just two miles north of the town of Mendocino, the 1305-acre park includes varied habitats: coastal headlands and pine forest, a verdant stream canyon and wooded ridges.

Local Indian tales told of seeing hunters with large ships landing at this cove in the late eighteenth century. They fit the description of the Russian fur hunters, thus the name Russian Gulch.

A fine network of trails winds through the park, three of which are described in the following pages. Other trails are mentioned in the text.

27.

WATERFALL LOOP

LUSH CANYON TO A WATERFALL

Here, unhindered by motorized traffic, you can bicycle, wheelchair or walk through a lush riparian canyon. The 2¼-mile-long (4½ miles round trip) paved bike path is one of the most beautiful in California, allowing an intimate visit with a small coastal stream and its verdant habitat. To go on to the waterfall, one must continue on foot. Nevertheless, the trail remains gentle, affording a non-strenuous 6½-mile outing. Add an extra mile to continue over the ridge beyond the waterfall for a somewhat more arduous but still pleasant hike.

The trail starts just east of the campground, where the main park road is blocked to motorized traffic. (From November to March when the campground is closed, you will need to start ½ mile further west) The paved trail winds alongside the stream in the bottom of this lush canyon. The canyon is heavily forested, though not with the big trees abundant before the early logging here. Now the conifers (redwood, grand fir, western hemlock and Douglas fir) dominate the sides of the canyon, while deciduous water-loving trees (alder, willow, big leaf maple,

WATERFALL LOOP:

DISTANCE: 4⅝ miles round trip or 6¼-mile semi-loop. Wheelchairs and bikes can only do the first 1⅝ miles, 3¼ miles round trip.

TIME: Two to four hours.

TERRAIN: Gentle creek canyon, heavily forested, leading to 36-foot waterfall.

ELEVATION GAIN/LOSS: To falls: 220 feet+/220 feet-. Full loop: 500 feet+/500 feet-. Bike path only: 90 feet+/90 feet-.

BEST TIME: Late winter or spring, but anytime nice.

WARNINGS: Watch for poison oak.

HOW TO GET THERE: Turn west off Highway 1 at M.52.95 north of Mendocino, then left to park entrance. After kiosk, descend under highway and into canyon. Distance from kiosk to parking: 0.4 mile to year-round parking by clubhouse or 0.9 mile when campground open.

FURTHER INFO: Mendocino State Parks (707) 937-5804 or at the kiosk.

FEES: Day use: $5/vehicle. Camping: $16/night.

tanoak) dominate the canyon bottom. Lichens and ferns abound here as do other water-loving plants like hazel, wild ginger, nettle, thimbleberry and various wildflowers.

The first mile offers a gentle climb. At ⅝ mile you pass a rock wall on your left that weeps from seeps. Round a second high mossy rock at ⅞ mile. Then you climb moderately as the creek picks up speed. The trees get larger as you proceed up the canyon. From 1¼ miles you ascend beneath a dense forest canopy. At 1⅝ miles the paved path ends at a picnic area beneath redwoods. Cyclists will want to lock their bikes at the bike rack here and continue up the canyon on foot. Wheelchairs might get a bit farther, but the terrain quickly gets rougher and steeper.

Just 100 feet beyond the picnic area, the North

Trail forks left to climb above the canyon heading west by northwest, a good but steeper alternate return route for hikers (2⅝ miles back to campground). Continue 75 feet to the start of the waterfall loop. Take the left fork, noticing that Russian Gulch Creek also forks here. Wild rose and trillium grow near the junction. In ⅛ mile the trail climbs by steps as the canyon becomes steeper. Near a wooden bridge just beyond grows a clump of columbine.

A little farther, as a second wooden footbridge crosses a tiny tributary, rhododendrons stretch for light beneath a dense forest canopy. Climb a series of stone steps.

Approximately ¾ mile from the trail fork, you come over a rise and the falls are before you. Dropping over a flat shelf of hard Franciscan sandstone, the falls tumble 36 feet, sending clouds of spray into the air. Notice the many plants growing in the mist at the base of the falls. The sun seldom penetrates the deep forest here to light the waterfall. Photographers do best with fast film, though early afternoon may bring a few patches of sunlight to the falls. If the day is hot, you might want to venture into the spray at the base of the falls.

You can return by the same trail for the shortest, easiest hike. Or you can continue the loop up over the ridge south of the falls. You might at least climb the trail switchbacking to the top of the falls for a look at the stream above the falls. Bear grass, huckleberry and rhododendron form a garden through which the placid stream wanders before plunging over the brink. At the top of the falls, the trail is

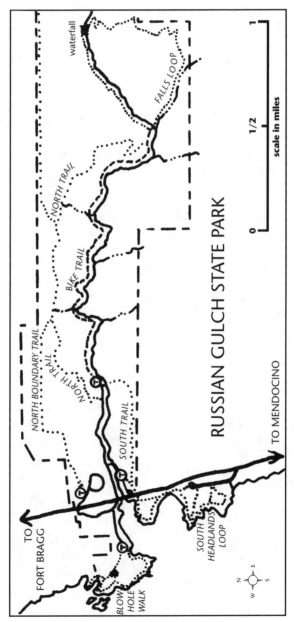

RUSSIAN GULCH STATE PARK

carved out of the bedrock in a series of stone steps.

If you continue, the trail parallels the placid stream briefly. The sound of the falls roars behind you. The loop trail switchbacks right, climbing away from the creek. At the switchback another path drops back to streamside amidst a gentle garden with nice blanket picnic spots. If you can ford the stream, it continues as a volunteer trail, eventually climbing to the North Boundary Trail about ¼ mile from the Horse Camp. Climbing onward up the loop, you don't see the falls again except for a glimpse at the westernmost switchback about ¼ mile after leaving the falls. Rhododendrons now begin to dominate the forest understory, mixed with Oregon grape and tanoak trees.

At ⅜ mile beyond the falls, you top the ridge. The trail stays atop this wooded ridge for another ⅝ mile. Your high ground trail traverses the headwaters of several feeder streams of Russian Gulch Creek. The moist habitat here brings more dense underbrush. About a mile beyond the falls, the trail drops abruptly through brushy forest into the deep canyon on the south. This is the fork of the creek you left at the start of the falls loop. The roar of the creek grows louder as you drop ¼ mile to streamside and the return trail.

Turn right and head downstream, returning to the loop junction in ⅜ mile. Total loop is about 2½ miles, although the sign claims 3 miles. That makes 7½ miles total from the trailhead. Return down the canyon to your car.

OTHER SUGGESTIONS: The NORTH TRAIL climbs the north side of the canyon from campsite #24, coming back to the main trail near the picnic area at the east end of the bicycle path (2⅝ miles each way).

The NORTH BOUNDARY TRAIL leaves from the park headquarters and climbs high above the canyon to follow the park boundary for 2¾ miles before coming out at a horse camp on Road 409 at M.3.35.

The SOUTH TRAIL heads south from the Group Camp, climbing to the south canyon rim, then descending to the east end of the park road near campsite #30, a distance of ¾ mile.

28.

BLOWHOLE WALK

TUNNEL-RIDDLED HEADLANDS

The ⅛-mile trail to the venerable old blowhole of Russian Gulch, also known as the Devil's Punchbowl, offers an easy and rewarding walk. Technically the blowhole is a decadent blowhole, meaning one where the action of the waves no longer spews above the lip of the pit. You can continue beyond to explore the entire promontory riddled with wave tunnels and natural bridges, with wildflowers and grand views thrown in as a bonus.

From your car, walk west to the fence around the blowhole. A blowhole forms when part of a wave tunnel collapses. Both are worn by strong tidal action over millennia. Eventually the tidal pressure causes the water to surge into, and sometimes to gush out of, the blowhole's abyss. Though this blowhole is too large to erupt like a geyser, watching the power of the wave action still impresses. This giant measures more than 100 feet in diameter, 400 feet in circumference and about 80 feet deep. The inlet is at the southwest corner. If the surf and tide are high, go to the sea cliff directly south of the blowhole and marvel at the raging waves which surge into the blowhole tunnel.

From the blowhole, walk farther west onto the narrow point. Looking back toward the punchbowl, you can see that the ocean has nearly worn another tunnel into the blowhole from the west. Across the small cove to the south is a sturdy natural bridge. Yet another wave tunnel undercuts the point beneath your feet. Land's end is a bit farther. You can see more wave tunnels and natural bridges to your north, northeast and east. On the grassy headlands around you, Douglas iris bloom starting in February, soon joined by sea thrift, beach strawberry, ice plant, yarrow, poppy and a profusion of other wildflowers.

Retrace your steps to the foot of the point, then turn south. You can walk out to the head of the southern point if you like. From here, return by walking

BLOWHOLE WALK:

DISTANCE: ¼ mile round trip to blowhole or ⅝-mile semi-loop.

TIME: Fifteen minutes to one hour.

TERRAIN: Gradually sloping grassy headlands with giant blowhole, wave tunnels and natural bridges.

BEST TIME: Spring for wildflowers. High tide for best blowhole action.

WARNINGS: Stay out of the blowhole—dangerous! Stay back from the very edge of the cliff. Watch for poison oak.

HOW TO GET THERE: Turn west off Highway 1 at M.52.95, 2 miles north of Mendocino. Turn left again to state park entrance kiosk, then go .1 mile. Turn right and go .25 mile to parking and trailhead.

FURTHER INFO: Mendocino State Parks (707) 937-5804.

FEES: Day use: $5/ vehicle. Car camping: $16/night.

along the south edge of this headland where you see great views of Russian Gulch to the east and Mendocino Headlands to the south. It's a short walk uphill to the parking lot. A pleasant picnic area with outstanding views is ⅛ mile east. You can follow a trail east from the parking area along the south rim of the headland to reach the picnic area if you prefer.

29.

SOUTH HEADLANDS LOOP

FOLLOWING THE CROOKED SHORE

The lush, wooded south headlands overlooking Russian Gulch offers great vistas of the sheltered cove's sparkling waters and one of the few heavily wooded headlands in the Mendocino area. You'll find abundant and diverse wildflowers on this walk. Amazingly you'll often have this lovely corner of the park to yourself. Once again this blufftop hike fol-

lows the California Coastal Trail.

Beginning across the park road from the Group
Camp, your trail climbs through lush vegetation—
skunk cabbage, elderberry, coffeeberry and ferns—
beneath grand firs and alders to get above the canyon, then follows the canyon rim heading west. Soon
you come to the junction with the South Trail on
your left, which goes east above the canyon for ¾
mile. Stay to the right past red flowering currant
and ascend west through a eucalyptus grove beside
the highway. Take the right fork at an unmarked
junction and follow the trail under the highway
bridge.

Soon the trail forks again next to an immense
forked grand fir. Your return trail is on the left. Take
the right fork through Bishop pine/grand fir forest
growing to the cliff's edge. Douglas iris, slim
Solomon's seal and fairy bells tangle with poison oak,
salal, thimbleberries and blackberries on the forest
floor. The deep waters of Russian Gulch cove appear on your right around ¼ mile. Two tiny wooded
peninsulas on the right offer grand views encompass-

141

SOUTH HEADLANDS LOOP:

DISTANCE: ¾-mile single loop or 2⅛-mile double loop.

TIME: One half to one hour.

TERRAIN: Lush wooded headlands with commanding views of Russian Gulch, then grassy headlands with views south.

ELEVATION GAIN/LOSS: 220 feet+/220 feet-.

BEST TIME: Anytime.

WARNINGS: Stay back from the cliff edge. Watch for poison oak.

HOW TO GET THERE: Follow directions in #28, but go straight at the junction after the kiosk for .3 mile. Turn right and park at the Group Camp. Trailhead is on south side of road.

NOTE: No fee parking is available along old Highway 1. Turn west off Highway 1 at M.52.00 onto Road 500D. Go .4 mile to end of road.

FURTHER INFO: Mendocino State Parks (707) 937-5804.

FEES: Day use: $5/vehicle.

ing a tiny wooded island or sea stack, one of the southernmost such islands on the Pacific coast to support tree growth. Continue west as angelica and paintbrush join the tangle of coastal scrub.

The trail winds south to a marvelous wooded point, then east following the bluff's edge overlooking another cove to your south. You climb past zygadene lily and vanilla grass to a junction before ½ mile. You can turn left here to return to the trailhead (¾ mile total). Our described trail turns right for a longer hike.

A right turn follows the cliff edge south, paralleling Highway 1 for ⅛ mile past a toyon bush on your left as aster and honeysuckle join the coastal scrub. You come to a paved cul-de-sac, an old section of Highway 1. Follow the paved road for 350 feet. Then turn right on a narrow trail that dips, then winds west through a headland pine forest. At ¾ mile you reach an open grassy headland, very different from the wooded headland to the north. Continue west to the tip of the point where you look north to the ocean entrance of Russian Gulch. The gulch itself hides behind the wooded point from which you just walked.

The loop turns south paralleling exposed tidal rocks for about 100 feet. At the south edge of the point before ⅞ mile, the Mendocino headlands stretch out before you. The north edge of the village of Mendocino is visible, but nearly all the "old" town lies hidden on the south (sunny) side of the point.

Follow the bluff trail east. When the trail forks near the trees, take the right fork and follow it along a spectacular rocky shoreline. It leads to the paved road before 1⅛ miles. Turn right and walk the pavement south 200 feet to overlook an ancient blowhole tucked in the trees immediately west of the road. In the afternoon the light plays on the waves in the blowhole's inlet tunnel. State park property continues south nearly ¼ mile. From the blowhole, it's just over one mile back to the trailhead.

OTHER SUGGESTION: If you continue on the road beyond the Group Camp, you'll come to lovely RUSSIAN GULCH BEACH, a great spot to launch a sea kayak or to stroll barefoot in the fine sand along the water's edge.

TOWN OF MENDOCINO

Mendocino was once known as "The Jewel of the North Coast." Though its sawmill has been gone for sixty years, the town survives today as a haven for artists and a popular tourist destination.

Mendocino was founded in 1852 when San Franciscans came north looking for salvage from the wreck of the sailing ship Frolic, *but instead found the immense redwood forests along the coast. They established the first successful sawmill on the Mendocino coast, shipping the redwood lumber south to supply California's gold rush boom. The first mill was located at the tip of the point, near the blowhole. (A tidal-powered mill had been started earlier that year at Albion, but was destroyed by killer waves in the winter of 1853.) In 1854 a larger mill was built for Mendocino, located ½ mile upriver from Big River Beach. It operated nearly continuously until it shut down in the 1930s.*

The town was originally known as Big River or Meiggsville, but the first post office opened in 1858 with the name Mendocino. Many woodsmen and other settlers came to Mendocino from New England, helping to establish the town's distinctive New England style. By 1877 the township of Mendocino had the highest population (3100) and property valuation in Mendocino County, $1.5 million, one-quarter of the county's total valuation.

After the sawmill closed, the town teetered on the brink of oblivion for a few years. Its biggest fame during that time came from being the location for the filming of two Oscar-winning movies, Johnny Belinda, *starring Jane Wyman (1948), and* East of Eden, *starring James Dean (1955). The mansion used in* East of Eden *burned in 1956. In 1959 the Mendocino Art Center was established on that site, giving new life to the town as an artists' community.*

Today Mendocino and its magnificent coast are renowned far and wide. Crowds of visitors strain the systems of the old town, especially during summer months and on weekends. When Mendocino is crowded, parking and traffic become a problem. Since it takes only about ten minutes to walk across town, it is best to plan on walking after you find a precious parking spot. (What the town really need is a giant underground parking garage and a ban on cars along Main Street.)

Water and public toilets are also scarce in Mendocino. The town has always had a water shortage (hence the many water towers). When the crowds descend in summer, the problem becomes acute. Notice the two public restrooms on the map; there are no other public restrooms. For its small size, Mendocino has an active cultural life. Many shops (including two bookshops) and art galleries provide shopping and browsing opportunities. Plays and musical events occur year round.

30

MENDOCINO HISTORY WALK
JEWEL OF THE NORTH COAST

*Today Mendocino thrives as a busy artistic and rec-
reational community. As you walk its streets, think
back to the booming lumber town that created most
of what you now see.*

*Reflecting the times in which it grew, the town of
Mendocino had a two-tiered social structure. The
elite owned the mill, banks and mercantile stores.
They were well aware of their superior wealth and
education and did not socialize with the working
men. The loggers and mill workers worked long
hours six days a week, then played hard when they
brought their pay to town. At the peak of the lumber boom, nineteen saloons served the town. The
east part of town was known as Fury Town because
of the mood on Saturday night.*

*By 1865 Mendocino's population had reached 700.
The 1880 census counted 3100 people in Big River
Township (which included the coast from Caspar
to Albion). Today the population is about the same
as in 1880.*

1. MENDOCINO PRESBYTERIAN CHURCH
(est. 1868) is the oldest continuously used Protes-
tant church in California. Built of locally milled redwood, the building faces south because the original
coast road passed between the church and Mendocino Bay. Also on the south side of the church is the
EIDSATH HOUSE (est. 1909).

Across Main Street, slightly to the east is:

2. THE McCORNACK HOUSE (est. 1882, now the
Mendocino Village Inn) Also known as the Doctor's
House, this two-story white house was built by Dr.
William McCornack and later served as a residence
for three other doctors. The original exterior orna-
mentation has been restored.

The next house to the west is:

3. LANSING HOUSE (est. 1854?, now private) was
built by Captain David Lansing, one of the town's
first settlers. A sea captain and superintendent of
shipping operations at the Mendocino Saw Mill,

DISTANCE: 1¼-mile loop.
TIME: One to two hours.
TERRAIN: Mostly level on paved streets.
BEST TIME: Anytime.
HOW TO GET THERE: Three streets enter the town
of Mendocino from Highway 1:
    Lansing Street at M.51.5
    Little Lake Street at M.50.8
    Main Street at M.50.55
Our History Tour starts at the Presbyterian Church
on the east end of Main Street, but you can start the
tour from most anywhere around the town center.
FURTHER INFO: Kelley House Museum, 45007
Albion Street, (707)937-5791.

Capt. Lansing imported redwood lumber from San
Francisco to build the house because early lumber
from the local mill was roughly milled. Lansing installed the state's first railroad line in 1853 to facili-
tate ship loading on the point. It was 180 feet long at
the start, soon expanded into a maze of tracks on
the point.

*Walk west on Main Street, passing Howard and
Lansing Streets and the old Ex-Lax Building on the
corner (now Mendocino Mercantile). The next building is:*

4. KELLEY HOUSE (est. 1861, now a museum,
open Friday through Monday, 1–4 p.m., daily in
summer) was built by William H. Kelley, who ran
the company store after arriving in 1852. The Kelley
family acquired much land over the years. They
preserved the original character of this two-block
area until the 1970s. Then R.O. Peterson bought
the Kelley House and donated it to Mendocino Historical Research, Inc. The large lot includes the
house, lawn and gardens, the water tower and the
duck pond.

*Walk west to the duck pond. Visible directly
behind it, one block north is:*

5. MacCALLUM HOUSE (est. 1882, now a hotel
and restaurant) was built as the residence for

Alexander MacCallum, a junior partner of William Kelley, when he married Kelley's daughter Daisy. An 1882 article in the Mendocino Beacon marveled at the house's modern amenities: "Hot and cold water can be had in three different places, and there is a bathroom with sprinklers overhead for family use."

On the other side of Main Street, 100 feet west, is:

6. FORD HOUSE (est. 1854, now the State Park interpretive center, public restrooms to the east) was always known as the Company House, because the mill superintendent lived there. The west section was built first. The original kitchen and dining room were underground (for reasons unknown). The first birth in Mendocino occurred in this house. The first grammar school classes were also held here. Stop in to see the wonderful scale model of Mendocino as it was in 1890, plus other exhibits.

Walk west on Main Street for 200 feet to:

7. MENDOCINO HOTEL (est. 1878) was one of eight hotels along Main. The back part of the building is even older, having been moved to the back of the lot when the new addition was built in 1878. The Bever brothers operated it as the Central House for 25 years. It later became the Mendocino Hotel. It had a pool table, tavern and cheap rooms until 1975.

Farther west along Main Street, at the end of the block, is:

8. JARVIS-NICHOLS BUILDING (est. 1874, now

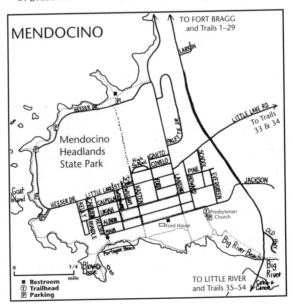

Gallery Bookshop) was built by (or for) Lauriston Morgan, whose father died trying to establish a shipping point at Bear Harbor (see Trail #5) in 1868. Morgan established a "new and elegantly fitted up store" at this location in 1874, according to a local newspaper report. In 1870 the fire that destroyed the older building on this site and 25 buildings west of here started at this location. After the fire, the center of town moved eastward. By 1879 this building became the Jarvis-Nichols store, which served the community for 39 years. As late as 1960 it was still a store, owned by Chet Bishop. It was seen in the movie *Johnny Belinda*. Gallery Bookshop started in the market's old store room in 1962.

Across Kasten Street is:

9. BANK OF AMERICA BUILDING (est. 1908, now Out of This World), originally the Bank of Commerce, was restored in 1985. Before the 1870 fire, this was the location of the Chung Kow Wash House. Clothes were hung out over Kasten Street to dry.

Walk north one short block to Albion Street. Turn left, then go 300 feet. On your right is:

10. TEMPLE OF KWAN TAI (est. 1857?). One of the few old Chinese temples left in California, this tiny Taoist shrine was a focal point for the coast's Chinese community. The first Chinese are said to have come to the area when their goldrush-bound junk, far off course, was shipwrecked near Caspar. By the 1880s, 250 Chinese lived in Mendocino, about 600 total on the coast.

Walk west to the next cross street (Woodward). After you turn right, on your left is:

11. CROWN HALL (est. 1901), built as a social hall for the Portuguese community, is now used for community events.

Walk east on Ukiah Street for 350 feet to:

12. LISBON HOUSE (a.k.a. PAOLI HOTEL, est. 1881, now various shops) served the community for years with lodging, a hard-liquor bar (for men only) and a ladies' parlor where soft drinks were served. It was refurbished in 1984.

Walk east to the corner of Kasten Street. On the right:

13. ODD FELLOWS HALL (est. 1878, now William Zimmer Gallery) was built for $2000. It has been beautifully restored.

In the next block on the right, next to the

windmill is:

14. KASTEN-HEESER HOUSE (est. 1852, now part of the Mendocino Hotel) was the first house built of sawn lumber in Mendocino. Modified from its original saltbox style, over its first century it was home to several prominent pioneers: William Kasten, William Kelley, William and August Heeser.

Across Ukiah Street and east slightly is:

15. THE BEACON BUILDING (est. 1872, still the Mendocino Beacon headquarters and various shops) was the site of the second bank north of San Francisco, established 1870. In 1877 William Heeser started the Mendocino Beacon here, a weekly paper covering the entire coast.

Continue east on Ukiah Street to:

16. BAPTIST CHURCH (est. 1894, now Corners of the Mouth Natural Foods). William Kelley built it for his wife Eliza who wanted a church of her own faith. It was used only until 1914, but has been lovingly maintained, like the other Kelley properties.

Continue east to the corner of Lansing Street. On the left is:

17. MASONIC TEMPLE (begun 1866, completed 1872) This is Mendocino's most famous building. It was built by Erik Albertson as fast as Lodge finances would permit. He carved the top statue of Father Time and the Virgin out of one chunk of redwood.

Walk north up Lansing Street (the former coast road and highway) to the second corner, Little Lake Street, and turn left. Walk one block to Ford Street, where kitty corner across the intersection is:

18. BLAIR HOUSE (1888, now an inn) built by J.D. Johnson for Elisha Blair who worked for the mill for 24 years, then opened an office in Packard's Drug Store to cash mill checks at regular bank rates. You might recognize this house as the television residence of Jessica Fletcher on *Murder, She Wrote*.

This and the three other houses on this block are among the most grand houses in town. The prominent citizens of Mendocino built their houses here because they expected the county courthouse to be built across the street, but when tiny Ukiah became the county seat in 1859, no courthouse was ever built in Mendocino. The lot, however, was kept open just in case. Now the Heider field has been preserved as open space by the Mendocino Land Trust.

This concludes the history tour of Mendocino. If you want to learn more about Mendocino's history and landmarks, go to the Kelley House Museum between Albion Street and Main Street. They conduct group history walking tours by appointment. Also available is a booklet with a more extensive walking tour, *A Tour of Mendocino*. It covers 32 buildings, including the grand old houses along Little Lake Street.

31.

MENDOCINO HEADLANDS WEST and NORTH

COVES, PROMONTORIES, WAVE TUNNELS AND WHALES

Like the town, the bluffs and bay are full of history. The Pomo Indians had a village upriver from Big River Beach called Booldam (big river). California's first railway was built on the point in 1853. Mendocino was one of the first doghole ports in California where longshoremen loaded ships with freshly cut redwood lumber. They used an apron chute located near the blowhole on the point, a dangerous task even without the often treacherous sea conditions. One story tells of a lumber schooner being sucked into a 700-foot wave tunnel in high seas, never to be seen again. The crew jumped to safety.

Another story claims that the blowhole on the point was connected by an underwater passageway to a deep pool about two miles up Big River. This submerged tunnel was said to be the source of mysterious moaning sounds heard for years by people crossing the prairie between Little River and Mendocino. After many seasons of floating timber down Big River to the mill, the deep hole upriver became filled with debris and the moaning stopped.

The first large and continuously producing sawmill on the California coast north of Bodega was at Mendocino. It operated for 82 years, making Mendocino the county's leading community and providing a large share of the redwood that built San Francisco, then rebuilt it after the 1906 earthquake.

After the Mendocino mill closed in the 1930s, the company's lands were purchased by Fort Bragg's

DISTANCE: 3½ miles round trip or 3-mile loop.

TIME: One or two hours.

TERRAIN: Mostly level, grassy headlands bordered by steep cliffs.

BEST TIME: Spring for flowers, but anytime is good.

WARNINGS: Stay back from the edge of dangerously steep cliffs; every year people are hurt and/or trapped because they venture too close to the edge or do not heed the tides. DON'T LET IT BE YOU! Don't let rising tides trap you at the base of impassable cliffs. Watch for poison oak in the tangle of vegetation on the bluffs.

HOW TO GET THERE: See directions for Trail #30, Mendocino History Walk. Go to the very west end of Main Street, where more parking is usually available. The trail description starts from there, where Main Street ends at Heeser Street. Other trails lead to the same headlands from Heeser Drive.

FURTHER INFO: Mendocino State Parks (707) 937-5804.

Union Lumber Company. In the 1960s, when Union Lumber was acquired by the Boise-Cascade Corporation, the new owner announced plans to develop the Mendocino headlands with condominiums and townhouses clustered around the bluffs surrounding town. Many residents were appalled by the plan, but one resident led the fight to save the town's headlands. Artist Emmy Lou Packard, who had studied with Diego Rivera and been friends with Frida Kahlo, led a movement for Mendocino's south headlands to be purchased as state park land. She helped get the town listed on the National Register of Historic Places and with the help of many, got the state to add Mendocino's south headlands to Mendocino Headlands State Park, which now consists of 376 acres.

From the Main and Heeser Streets trailhead, walk south to explore the headlands along the California Coastal Trail on the outer Mendocino Bay and ocean

sides of Mendocino. Go right at the first main trail junction in 100 feet. (A left turn leads to Trail #32.) The trail winds west, forming a broad promenade past benches along the bluff's edge as the waves below you splash on Portuguese Beach and surge through the blowhole. The trail narrows and swings left heading south toward the point. Beyond ⅛ mile you can look east to the mouth of Big River beneath the curve of the highway bridge.

You soon come upon the blowhole, surrounded by a low fence, on the point east of the trail. If the tide is right you might see a kayak glide through the tunnel. Two big iron chains anchored to the earth west of the blowhole were used from 1852 until the 1930s to tie down ships here to load lumber. You can walk out on the point just southeast of the blowhole to see the remains of the loading chute, but stay back from the edge. It's also a good place to spot ospreys, egrets and oystercatchers foraging in the bay.

The broad trail continues to the southern point past oddly carved virgin redwood beams which were also old ship tie-downs. Around ¼ mile the trail turns west, circling the point. You pass a final iron chain tie-down. A fork left drops to tidal rocks, but stay to the right and continue west.

At a second fork, you can take either path. The idea from here on becomes to follow your muse, taking your best path around the headlands, generally following the marvelous bluff's edge above its dramatic meeting with the Pacific. My favorite choice follows an obvious track along the top of the rock area exposed below the loamy bluffs. Or you can stay to the right and follow the California Coastal Trail generally along the edge of the blufftop. Either way beyond ⅜ mile you'll be on the blufftop path as the trail rounds a series of deep little spectacular coves. (For an early return to town, take either of the next two right forks.) As you reach the west end of the first cove around ½ mile, pause to peer down into the three-way wave tunnel and surge channel below.

Continue west past a spur on the left that leads south to the point west of the cove. Your blufftop track reaches the second cove in only 200 feet. This cove is more exposed to the force of the ocean. Come to its sheltered northwest corner by ⅝ mile. Follow the trail south along the rim of the cove, coming to a south-facing point before ¾ mile. The path rounds the point to turn north along the bluff's edge above the open ocean, with rocky shelves between you and the sea. You pass a plaque commemorating Mendocino's bond with its sister city, Miasa, Japan, then come to a large parking lot.

Circle the west end of the lot, then follow the bluff edge east until you can follow it north. As you turn north, look west to see a natural bridge near the point north of the lot. Further north across the inlet to the cove below you stands Goat Island, named for the animals that local farmers once grazed on the grassy top of the islet. As you follow the bluff north, the trail draws alongside Heeser Drive briefly, then meanders northwest with the bluff's edge. By 1⅛ miles you meet a side trail that leads west to the rocky tip of the Mendocino headlands' westernmost point. From the point you survey an aqueous world punctuated by rocky islets and sea stacks.

Return to the main trail and follow it east and north along the bluff edge. It soon draws back beside Heeser Drive briefly, then comes to a junction. The spur on the left leads out to a narrow promontory, while a spur on the right leads to a small parking lot. You continue north, returning to the bluff's edge above a cove studded with offshore rocks and popular with divers. The track leads to a side trail on your left out to a north facing promontory. From here you have a grand view of the several islets to the west and Point Cabrillo and its lighthouse further north.

Follow the trail east along the northern blufftop. It once again draws beside Heeser Drive briefly, then continues east along the rim of the bluff. Around 1⅝ miles it drops down a hill and meets a well beaten trail north to one last point (¼ mile round trip to point). A small path there leads down to a tiny beach. Turn right and climb into a wind-shaped cypress grove, then make your way south to the north rest rooms at 1¾ miles. A picnic area and drinking fountain lie between the comfort station and its parking lot. The park boundary lies not far to the east.

Return as you came. Or you may head east to Lansing Street where a right turn brings you back to town in ⅜ mile. Or you can take the shortcut path past Mendocino High School. Take the trail that's 50 feet west of the driveway across Heeser Drive from the north parking lot. Walk south up a hill and through the Mendocino High School grounds, then descend Kasten Street to Main Street and walk Main Street or the south headlands path back to your starting point.

32.

MENDOCINO SOUTH HEADLANDS to BIG RIVER BEACH

BLUFFS, BEACHES & HISTORY

This walk is a quick getaway from the crowds on busy days in the town of Mendocino. Or in the off-season, especially on weekdays, you may have the entire headlands to yourself. This easy hike follows the California Coastal Trail. The headlands are a wild garden of escaped domestic plants: hedge rose, calla lilies, holly, the lily called naked ladies, cabbage family plants, creeping myrtle, mint, coto-

SOUTH HEADLANDS TO BIG RIVER BEACH:

DISTANCE: 1¾ miles round trip.

TIME: One hour.

TERRAIN: Mostly level, grassy headlands bordered by steep cliffs with paths to two pleasant beaches.

BEST TIME: Spring for flowers, but anytime is good.

WARNINGS: Stay back from the edge of dangerously steep cliffs; every year people are hurt and/or trapped because they venture too close to the edge or do not heed the tides. DON'T LET IT BE YOU! Don't let rising tides trap you at the base of impassable cliffs. Watch for poison oak in the tangle of vegetation on the bluffs.

HOW TO GET THERE: See directions for Trail #30, Mendocino History Walk. Go to the very west end of Main Street, where more parking is usually available. The trail description starts from there, at the corner of Main and Heeser streets. Other trails lead to the same headlands from Main and Kasten and from Main and Lansing streets.

FURTHER INFO: Mendocino State Parks (707) 937-5804.

neaster, Scotch broom, tamarisk and nasturtiums.

On this hike you have the chance to visit two pleasant beaches. Tiny Portuguese Beach shelters at the base of the steep bluffs explored by this trail. Its sheltered southern exposure allows for sunbathing here even when the chilly north wind blows. Big River Beach at the end of this trail offers an expansive strand at the mouth of the river. This locale makes the configuration of the beach a constantly evolving wonder. It's popular with surfers, families and just about anyone who loves Mendocino.

From the corner of Main and Heeser Streets, a trail heads south through the fence. In just 100 feet, the broad path splits in two. This report takes the left fork. In another 25 feet, a short spur trail on the left leads to a plaque commemorating the efforts of artist Emmy Lou Packard to preserve these headlands for public use. The main trail immediately

forks again before the bluff's edge. The right fork
leads to a blowhole on the point and the Headlands
West and North trail (see Trail #31). The hike in
this report takes the left fork, quickly coming to
benches near the bluff's edge and a stairway to little
Portuguese Beach.

The trail turns left and heads east along the bluff,
passing an invasive tamarisk shrub on your right.
You follow the route of an old logging railway. What
may have been the first rail line in California was
built on this point in 1853. Teams of oxen pulled the
cut lumber to the point for loading onto ships. In
places you can see the old crossties in the path.

Continue east with views of Main Street, Mendocino Bay, the mouth of Big River and the river canyon to the east. Beyond ⅛ mile you cross a small
boardwalk and come to wooden steps dipping
through a small gully. You come to a fork on the far
side. Left leads north to Main and Kasten streets.
Continue east to another trail fork. You can choose
the scenic right fork, wandering close to the bluff's
edge or the more direct left path along the hedge
roses. Both head generally east toward Big River
Beach. Our description follows the right path, passing two small islands directly offshore at ¼ mile and
Douglas iris and checker lilies in spring. As you come
to a small point before ⅜ mile, several old Bishop
pines balance on the bluff's edge. On your right an
overlook surveys the popular surfing spot off Big
River Beach. Your trail takes a sharp left past coyote brush, wax myrtle, salal and angelica. Pass
through a small dip where mimulus and silverweed
grow, then come to another junction. The left path
leads uphill to the corner of Main and Lansing
streets.

Take the right fork to head for Big River Beach, winding south then east. Old Bishop pines thrive near another small point. Continue along the bluff-edge path as it winds toward the landmark Presbyterian Church to ½ mile. Then your trail turns east again, passing coffeeberry, iris and poison oak. The trail starts descending toward the beach. On your right grow paintbrush, sticky monkeyflower, beach morning glory and poison hemlock.

You come to a stairway. Descend the steps, coming to Big River Beach at ⅝ mile. The beach's fine light sand extends east for about ¼ mile. On the left grow sand verbena and bush lupine. A seasonally marshy area lies at the base of the cliff. Though state park property ends at the highway bridge, the beach continues east along the north side of the river.

Return to the headlands by the same path, then take whichever path you choose into town. The path on the right at the top of the stairway winds north to the Presbyterian Church on the east end of Main Street.

33.

MENDOCINO HIKING & EQUESTRIAN TRAIL

PART THREE: LITTLE LAKE ROAD TO HIGHWAY 20

The Mendocino Hiking and Equestrian Trail, also called the Little Lake-Sherwood Trail, was developed primarily for equestrians but is available for the use of hikers and cyclists as well. The lightly used route runs 44 miles through rugged terrain between Mendocino on the coast and Willits on Highway 101. Much of it, including this section, passes through Jackson State Forest, while the easternmost part, described in Trail #22, crosses private timberlands via the old Sherwood stage road, a county road. This section describes the trail's southern end, most of which follows another county road that was once a stagecoach route. The trail starts 3 miles east of Mendocino, following a mixture of back roads and trails.

MENDOCINO HIKING & EQUESTRIAN TRAIL
Part Three:

DISTANCE: 10 miles one way.

TIME: Five to six hours each way.

TERRAIN: Through tall forest, then pygmy, dropping to headwaters of Russian Gulch before climbing along ridges with fine views.

ELEVATION GAIN/LOSS: 1320 feet+/990 feet-.

BEST TIME: Spring to autumn (except deer hunting season August through September).

WARNINGS: Watch and listen for motorized traffic. Occasionally closed due to logging; inquire at Jackson State Forest before taking trail. Watch and listen for gunfire.

HOW TO GET THERE: South end: at Mendocino, turn east off Highway 1 at M.50.85 onto Little Lake Road. Go 2.75 miles to trailhead, where parking is limited. Trail starts at M.2.78, just west of the 3-mile "Y." North end: from Highway 1 at M.59.8 go east on Highway 20 to M.8.08. For the north portion of the Hiking and Equestrian Trail, see #23.

FURTHER INFO: Jackson State Forest (707) 964-5674. For map, get Jackson State Forest map.

ENVIRONMENTAL CAMP: Berry Camp is located 8.7 miles from the south end of the trail. This is an old camp where settlers from all over the county came to pick and can berries in the summer.

The unobtrusive trailhead, signed LITTLE LAKE-SHERWOOD HIKING & EQUESTRIAN TRAIL—MENDOCINO WOODLANDS 2 MILES, lies next to a redwood on the north side of the road. The well-beaten, mostly level path leads north through mixed forest of Bishop pines, redwoods, tanoaks and firs. You pass several side trails, but stay on the obvious main trail. Manzanita, rhododendron, Labrador tea, wax myrtle, evergreen huckleberry and young western hemlock line the trail. Bear right at a fork in 300 feet. Pass golden chinquapin trees growing on the right at ⅛ mile.

At ¼ mile you swing left (north) and meet a forest road. Your trail turns right and follows it for the next leg. Soon your track swings right to head northeast through tall mixed forest. Your trail soon swings right again, passing a log barrier and meeting a bigger road (Road 770) just short of ½ mile. Little Lake Road is about 250 feet south of this junction.

Turn left here and follow Road 770 (watch for motorized traffic) as it quickly drops into the canyon of South Fork Russian Gulch Creek, then climbs steeply up the other side. At ⅝ mile the road levels. You enter transitional pygmy forest (dwarf trees mixed with a few taller conifers), where you find Fort Bragg manzanita, Mendocino cypress and Bolander pine. In the next ½ mile, three spur roads branch left; stay on the main road (intersections marked with trail signs).

Just beyond 1⅛ miles, you come to a bigger intersection. Continue on Road 770, heading northeast through the pygmy forest.

At 1⅞ miles our route leaves the road it has been following and takes the left spur, plunging steeply into the canyon of Russian Gulch Creek. (Cyclists may have to walk this heavily rutted stretch of road.) The habitat becomes more moist as you approach the sound of running water; hemlocks, rhododendrons and thimbleberries line the road. You quickly come to a rough crossing of the headwaters of Russian Gulch Creek at 2⅛ miles. You might want to rest here and look down the gulch at tall, mixed redwood forest.

Beyond the creek the road climbs quickly to a "T" intersection with another unmarked road (Road 760). Turn left and climb northwest on Road 760. Around 2½ miles the road bends right and climbs.

Continue climbing eastward for the next ½ mile, up a steep hill to meet Road 409 on the ridge, just over 3 miles from the trailhead. (For a shorter loop of 5¾ miles, cyclists can turn right here, proceed to Little Lake Road and return 2½ more miles to the trailhead.)

The trail continues on the north side of Road 409, bending around a big log that keeps four-wheeled vehicles off the trail. You head generally northeast through tall mixed forest of redwood, fir and Bishop pine. Your route quickly turns east as you meet the old ridge road. Follow that to 3¼ miles, where a sign at the junction tells you to take the left fork. Between you and the sign grow deer ferns; note the smooth edge of the fern's leaflets, unlike the serrated

edges of the sword ferns nearby.

Continue northeast on the ridge, descending slightly. At 3½ miles, head-high bracken ferns grow along the trail. The trail forks just beyond. The trail marker indicates the left fork. Descend to a big landing where pampas grass and 20-foot-high ceanothus grow. Your trail continues east, then drops down to another landing. Not far up a short hill you come to Little Lake Road, the old stage route you follow north. The trail sign calls it Little Lake-Sherwood Trail, 4.7 miles to Berry Camp. The Mendocino Woodlands Road junction is just 50 feet northeast.

From the 4-mile point (watch for motor traffic from here on), climb moderately through tall forest. At 4¼ miles you can look west into the Caspar Creek watershed, the ocean beyond. Mile 4½ finds you climbing steeply, ascending the next ½ mile to near the top of 1057-foot-high Great Caspar. Also known as Observatory Hill, this high point was used as a lookout to coordinate logging operations in the gulches below, and also to watch for wildfires. You pass the Forest History Trail (Trail #34) on the right (M.6.95) just before the top.

Beyond 5 miles your road stays on the ridge, Big River's watershed on your right and Caspar Creek's on your left as you head generally north. The road climbs, then drops, then climbs again, repeating this pattern for the next 4 miles along the ridge. Side roads lead off to the left and right, but stay on Road 408.

At 8⅜ miles you come to a junction with Road 500. The trail continues east on 408, but go right for ¾ mile to Berry Camp if you plan to camp. Just beyond M.11.00, Road 408 veers right, but your trail takes the left fork, dropping down to the crossing with Highway 20, 10 miles from the trailhead. Use extreme caution crossing the busy highway. The trail continues with Part Two of the Mendocino Hiking and Equestrian Trail (Trail #23).

> OTHER SUGGESTION: OLD MILL FARM is an old homestead east of Mendocino surrounded by forest. You can sleep in their Hiker's Hut or Family Cabin for a reasonable fee (reservations and two-night minimum required). You can incorporate it with a hike along part three of the Mendocino Hiking and Equestrian Trail or ask owner Chuck Hinsch about other trails near the farm. (707) 937-0244.

34.

FOREST HISTORY TRAIL
RAILROAD GULCH & OBSERVATION POINT

This loop trail offers a variety of choices for the hiker. It provides a good aerobic workout through pretty forest highlighted by occasional views. It also has an informative interpretive brochure, though it's out of print as this edition goes to press. We'll discuss some of the highlights of the interpretive loop for those who are interested. You can hike the entire 5⅜-mile loop with its tangential leg on the bottom end for a considerable 980-foot elevation loss/ gain, you can hike the 3⅝-mile loop itself, or you can take an easy 1⅛-mile stroll just to enjoy the view of Big River from Observation Point.

If you're planning to hike the entire Forest History Loop, you might contact the Jackson State Forest office in Fort Bragg to see if they've reprinted the free interpretive brochure.

At M.6.95 on Road 408 (Little Lake Road), a sign marked F. HISTORY TRAIL points across the road. The trail descends southeast to follow a ridgetop through

DISTANCE: 5⅜-mile semi-loop with Cookhouse and Observation spurs, or 3⅜-mile loop with Cookhouse, or 1⅛ miles round trip to Observation Point.

TIME: Two to four hours for semi-loop, one half hour to Observation Point.

TERRAIN: Along a ridge, down through logged areas, then up a creek canyon to a peak.

ELEVATION GAIN/LOSS: 980 feet+/980 feet-. For Observation Point: 350 feet+/350 feet-.

BEST TIME: Spring for wildflowers, but anytime is good.

WARNINGS: Watch for poison oak along the trail. The trail, though well-graded, has steep climbs. Don't overdo it.

HOW TO GET THERE: Turn east off Highway 1 at M.50.85 onto Little Lake Road. Go 6.95 miles (last mile is dirt) to a level spot where a trail sign points across the road.

FURTHER INFO: Jackson State Forest (707) 964-5674.

mixed forest around ⅛ mile. Descend gradually along the ridge, passing the big, weathered stumps of virgin redwoods cut by hand long ago. The interpretive brochure discusses redwood forest ecology along the first part of the trail (one of the interpretive brochure's five sections).

At ¼ mile you meet a junction with the pleasant Manly Gulch Trail (unmarked) on the left, which descends north and east for 2¼ miles before coming to the Mendocino Woodlands Camp property. Continue along the ridge, climbing gradually to the junction with the Forest History Loop at ⅜ mile. (To go directly to Observation Point, turn left, go ⅛ mile, then turn right for the short climb to the top. See description near end of this report.)

Veer right at the junction to follow the Forest History Trail, heading southwest to the start of the Demonstration Forestry segment of the interpretive trail. Walk along a side slope, rocky in spots, that drops steeply on your right into Railroad Gulch.

Watch your step! After a rest bench, at ½ mile you contour past a rock outcrop with lichens and moss.

At ⅝ mile your trail swings to the east. Item #20 (of the interpretive brochure) describes propagation experiments with clones of redwoods. Clones are cuttings taken from the tops of healthy, fast-growing redwoods. A similar process is used with roses in the home garden. Tanoaks thrive on these cutover slopes. As you begin to descend, pass another rock outcrop, then a pocket of California nutmeg trees (no relation to the spice) with dark green pointed needles. As you pass a big redwood stump at ¾ mile, notice how well the second-growth redwoods are growing in this gully.

Your descent ends before 1¼ miles. You follow a ridgetop, contouring then descending gently south past abundant yerba de selva and Oregon grape beneath young fir trees.

As you resume your descent, a large clearcut area lies below you to the right of the trail. Consider how drastically the clearcut has changed (you might say demolished) the forest environment. Compare it with the healthy second-growth forest through which you are walking.

Continue on an easy descent past abundant ceanothus in regenerating forest. The trail descends southeast, then south. At 1½ miles you pass a spur on the right, the main trail signed FOOT TRAFFIC ONLY. Your trail descends northeast and east to a junction at 1⅝ miles. For the full Forest History Trail, turn right and descend southeast, then south into Cookhouse Gulch, one of the prettiest parts of the trail. In ⅞ mile from the junction, around 2½ miles from the trailhead, you come to the lower trailhead at the boundary with the Mendocino Woodlands.

Turn around and follow the trail back up the hill, ascending northwest up Cookhouse Gulch. You pass through forest near the stream, then come to an open meadow after 300 feet. In another 200 feet, you come to a stand of young Douglas fir. While the interpretive brochure points out that Douglas firs do not live as long as redwoods, some live 1000 years.

At 2⅝ miles you begin to climb above the redwood flood plain of the canyon floor. As you climb along a small side stream, notice how many young redwoods are growing on the flat below and the hillsides around you. This is a prime area for redwood regeneration.

At 2¾ miles you are alongside the eroded gully of the creek. You soon cross a wooden footbridge, then climb more steeply. Your trail switchbacks to the right and up onto a ridge. As you continue to climb by switchbacks to 3 miles, the ridge becomes more open. At 3⅛ miles you pass a rest bench. The trail descends slightly, then ascends through more open forest, returning to the junction with the loop at 3⅜ miles.

Climb north on the start of the Native American segment of the trail. After crossing a wooden bridge at 3½ miles, you climb by rough wooden steps. Item #30 of the brochure describes edible and medicinal plants of the Pomo. They ate fiddlenecks, the edible young shoots of bracken fern. Poison oak, the toxins of which the local Pomo were immune to, provided berries for eating and to remove warts. They used the sap as a black dye. Though they ate the berries, don't try it.

Just short of 3¾ miles, you switchback twice, climbing into deep forest. If you are on the trail in summer or autumn, you may be able to snack on huckleberries growing here.

After another rest bench at the start of the Early Logging History segment of the trail, you climb more steps, cross a small bridge and continue climbing to #34 at 3⅞ miles.

The brochure speaks of timber cruisers in the past tense, but they are still used today. Timber cruisers inventory and measure the trees of the forest. As a former timber cruiser, I would classify cruisers as an endangered species due to a surplus of foresters and modernization and improved sampling techniques in forestry.

The next section of trail climbs steeply to a rest bench. You gain a ridgetop briefly around 4 miles, then leave the ridgetop to ascend a steep east slope. Continue climbing, then drop briefly through another gulch, coming to another bench around 4⅛ miles.

Continue 200 feet to #39. Just below the trail here, a small flat area held a steam donkey engine. Invented about 1880 by a Humboldt County logger, this device replaced the teams of oxen used until then to move logs. Imagine the noise and activity here when the donkey was working. (You can see a steam donkey at the Depot in Fort Bragg.)

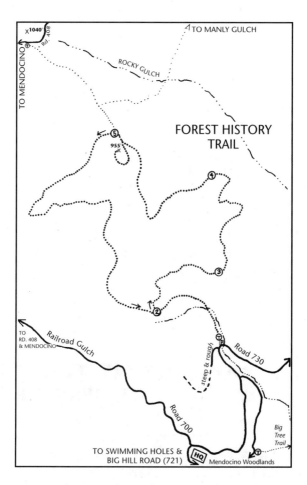

After dipping through a gulch which early loggers climbed to get to work, climb the steepest hill yet to a rest bench at 4¼ miles. Continue climbing to another rest bench at the start of the Forest Management section at 4⅜ miles.

Your trail ascends, soon gaining the ridgetop. Here you will learn the history of reforestation in this area. Though the interpretive brochure states that the Great Depression put an end to early reforestation efforts, fortunately tree planting is a common practice in modern forestry.

A short downhill stretch along the ridgetop is quickly followed by more uphill. Just before 4¾ miles, a short (900 feet) side trail on the left spirals to Observation Point, a 995-foot-high peak with a fine view south and west into the heavily wooded canyons of Big River. Near the bench at the top grows California torreya or nutmeg.

Returning to the main trail, descend west and northwest to the junction you passed early in your hike. Stay to the right here and follow the ridge north to return to the upper trailhead on Little Lake Road, your starting point. If you hiked the entire trail including the Cookhouse Gulch and Observation Point spurs, you covered 5⅜ miles of steep trail.

OTHER SUGGESTIONS: Take the trail down MANLY GULCH to the Woodlands boundary and return, 4½ miles round trip. Call Mendocino Woodlands Camp, (707)937-5755, to ask for permission to hike the Forest History Trail from its lower trailhead. You may also ask them about their own fine network of hiking trails. Access is usually granted when camp is not in session.

35.

MONTGOMERY WOODS STATE RESERVE

HIGHLAND VIRGIN REDWOOD FOREST

This narrow creek canyon at the headwaters of Big River has the most impressive stand of virgin redwoods remaining in Mendocino County and some of the tallest trees in the world. The reserve, established in 1945 from a seminal donation of nine acres, now comprises 1484 acres, though both trail and virgin redwoods cover only a small center portion. The trail follows Montgomery Creek beneath coastal sempervirens up to 14 feet in diameter, many over 300 feet tall. I suggest you stop and hug one. Trees give out good grounded energy.

An interpretive brochure, describing the "climax forest" environment and flora, may be available at the trailhead (April through October).

The main hiking trail starts west of the parking area, heading south up Montgomery Creek through young redwood forest. You quickly come to a sturdy bridge across the creek. Cross the bridge and turn left, ascending the old wagon road toward Montgomery

DISTANCE: 1¾-mile loop.

TIME: One or two hours to hike, plus one hour driving time from Mendocino or Ukiah.

TERRAIN: Up a hill into steep-walled canyon with redwood flood plain containing immense virgin forest.

ELEVATION GAIN/LOSS: 220 feet+/220 feet-.

BEST TIME: Spring for wildflowers, summer good too.

WARNINGS: May be impassable during rainy season. Watch for poison oak. Winding, often narrow road to get there. Drive slowly and carefully.

HOW TO GET THERE: Turn east off Highway 1 at M.50.00 onto the Comptche (Comp-chee)-Ukiah Road. Go 30 beautiful paved but winding miles. Park in lot just east of bridge at M.29.6. OR from Highway 101, exit at M.25.9 just north of Ukiah, taking paved Orr Springs Road 14 miles west to Montgomery Woods State Reserve.

FURTHER INFO: Mendocino State Parks (707) 937-5804.

Grove. You immediately enter a small stand of large redwoods, Orr Memorial Grove. Beyond the outhouse, a side trail on the left leads south through the grove, coming to picnic tables.

The main trail continues up the broad track, climbing a steep hill. Take your time ascending this steep incline, as it's the only difficult part of the trail. In a few hundred feet, look down to your left at a small waterfall on the creek. The redwoods here are about five feet in diameter. At ⅛ mile you're still climbing steeply, angling away from the creek. The trail continues the steady ascent, passing abundant California hazel and tanoak in the understory. At ¼ mile the path levels and forks. The main trail goes downhill on the left. An old trail in the center continues south. The fire road swings to the right and climbs steeply. You can take the latter for an overview of this virgin canyon.

Take the gentle descent on the left dropping to a broad redwood flat in the creek canyon. Trilliums, redwood sorrel and sword ferns abound. Where the trail flattens out, you come to redwoods to 11 feet in diameter. These old giants of the Grubb Memorial Grove stand about 320 feet tall. If you leave the trail here, step very carefully; tiny calypso orchids bloom from late March to May.

The loop trail begins here. Stay on the right. You soon come to #1 of the guided nature trail, about ⅜ mile from the trailhead. Continue across the broadest part of the canyon to a moss-draped rock ridge on your right, defining the boundary of the redwood flat. Five-finger ferns grow nearby. Poison oak is profuse in this area, both as a bush and as a vine; in the fall, it adorns many of the trees with its yellow and scarlet leaves. A California hazel 20 feet tall grows on the left.

Continue along the edge of the flood plain. Three-leaved vanilla leaf thrives on the steep rise on your right. A bit farther, at marker #3, woodwardia ferns grow in a dense thicket to the left of the trail. They grow six or seven feet tall in this protected canyon. Other ferns growing nearby include licorice, wood, bracken and gold back. A redwood growing directly on the left side of the trail has a burl the size of a

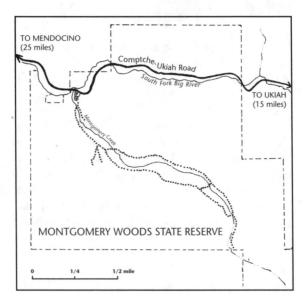

portable television. When the author walked this trail on Easter 1986, the quiet canyon reverberated with a sound like a wooden machine gun; a woodpecker, hidden high above, drilled for bugs in the redwood bark.

You come to marker #4 on your left around ½ mile. A large redwood with a massive goose-pen fire scar grows by the trail. Early settlers actually used hollows like this to house their poultry. In their 1000- to 3000-year lives, these giants have withstood many major lightning-caused fires and many fierce storms and floods. In another 300 feet, you pass the MacCallum Grove. Then your trail leads you under a giant fallen redwood, splintered from its jarring fall. The trail briefly follows a small side stream.

The forest is more wild and undisturbed on this upper end, away from the heavier foot traffic. Large clumps of ferns and huckleberries thrive here. In between grow redwood sorrel, calypso orchids, false Solomon's seal and other shade-loving wildflowers.

At ⅝ mile, standing directly in the trail, a ten-inch-diameter, seven-foot-long redwood branch (or top) has fallen in a storm, wedging itself immovably into the forest floor. When I first saw it, it was sprouting, even though it landed top first. Redwoods' ability to sprout from almost any cell is a characteristic unique among trees.

The next section of trail follows an old logging "skid" or corduroy road. Until recently there were boards in the trail bed, put down so that teams of oxen could drag huge cut logs down the canyon, clear of the often muddy ground. They washed away in the winter of 1998. Another 100 feet brings you to the Kellieowen Grove on the right. Named to memorialize early Mendocino pioneers (as in the Kelley House in Mendocino village), this grove has smaller trees but is beautifully situated in a small, flat side canyon. Redwood benches provide a resting spot.

Just 100 feet beyond Kellieowen Grove, the trail once again follows the verdant and rocky edge of the canyon, then climbs along the steep slope. In 300 feet, look to your left at one of tallest trees in the world. This tree measures 13½ feet in diameter, 42½ feet in circumference and easily 350 feet tall, perhaps more. At ¾ mile your trail descends back to the flood plain, ducks under a fallen giant and passes below a huge rock outcrop on the right that sprouts leather ferns.

Your trail continues past more ferns, then climbs steps carved into a fallen redwood. You can walk on top of this log for about 150 feet. Notice how the redwood flat has built a new level up canyon from this log, burying another three feet of the butts of the redwood giants just ahead. Over centuries this process of fallen redwoods forming natural dams has helped create this redwood flat. Now the trail continues east briefly beyond the stepped fallen log.

At ⅞ mile you come to Kistiakowsky Grove. The main trail turns left, crossing the stream bed and the canyon. Those more adventuresome can go right, following a volunteer trail that becomes vague in ⅛ mile, leaving the virgin forest for selectively logged, but still large, forest. This small trail leads toward the headwaters of Montgomery Creek. At ⅛ mile the spur comes to an immense mossy rock outcrop where poison oak and canyon live oak thrive. Beyond the outcrop the trail becomes a bushwhacker's delight.

The trail toward the car: after crossing to the north side of the canyon, the trail turns southeast following the north canyon wall. You'll soon see the first Douglas fir intrusion (marker #10) on this virgin redwood forest. Duck under another fallen giant. At one mile the trail passes through three fallen, now cut giants. Soon the track rises above the redwood flood plain, dropping back to the flat at 1⅛ miles. Your trail climbs gently back up the slope, looking out over the flood plain filled with giants. Continue along the slope or its base until a fork. Either fork quickly leads to another large moss-covered rock outcrop (#12) at 1¼ miles. Follow a boardwalk for 150 feet then continue along the canyon's edge. At the far end of this is a bench where you can rest.

Your trail soon leaves the canyon wall and crosses two small footbridges, then veers to the right past glassy, blue-green pools along the creek which reflect the ferns and redwoods. Come to marker #13, a fine display of upended redwood roots. Your trail bends to the left to cross the canyon and rejoin the start of the loop at Grubb Grove. You've come just over 1⅜ miles. Climb the hill out of the grove and drop down the hill, cross the bridge and return to the trailhead at 1¾ miles.

Before you leave, take a few minutes to wander up the paved road along the headwaters of South Fork

Big River. Alders, big leaf maples, and beautiful
Pacific dogwoods (bloom in spring) mix with Douglas firs and redwoods along the stream. Bright red
Indian warriors, pink farewell-to-spring and orange
California poppies grow in sunny clearings. Think
about the time when the north coast was dominated
by immense virgin redwood groves similar to the one
you have just explored.

36.

CHAPMAN POINT &
SPRING RANCH HEADLANDS

SOUTH OF MENDOCINO BAY

This trail traverses sloping, grassy headlands scattered with pines and wildflowers, then descends to the rugged, eroded ocean bluffs of a marvelous shoreline. This land was part of the original Beall ranch, settled in the 1850s by one of the earliest pioneer families. The Bealls sold to the Kents in 1857. The Kents sold to the Spring family in 1969, who recently sold the 162 acres of their ranch west of the highway to state parks. With the two adjacent parcels acquired in 1975, you now have 315 acres of gorgeous public land, including a mile of shoreline, to enjoy here. Old maps refer to this area as Chaparral or Mason. The walk is notable for its rugged rocky shoreline with uplifted sand deposits, its postcard views of Mendocino and abundant wildflowers. Once again you follow the California Coastal Trail along the shore.

These headlands offer a fine vantage point to watch for whales, seals, pelicans, cormorants and other sea life. Hawks, kites and many smaller birds live onshore. Wedged into the sea stacks offshore are the remains of a wrecked fishing boat. Only the mast is visible at high tide.

The trail heads due west from the parking area,

CHAPMAN POINT & SPRING RANCH HEADLANDS:

DISTANCE: 3 miles round trip.

TIME: One or two hours.

TERRAIN: Gently sloping grassy headlands leading to eroded coastal bluffs.

ELEVATION GAIN/LOSS: 130 feet+/130 feet-.

BEST TIME: Spring, but anytime is good.

WARNINGS: Watch for killer waves near the bluffs. Stay off adjacent private property. Littering on this pristine land is considered a capital crime.

HOW TO GET THERE: Go 1.6 miles south from Little Lake Road in Mendocino. There, on the west side of Highway 1 at M.48.94 cautiously drive onto the rough dirt parking area opposite Gordon Lane.

FURTHER INFO: Mendocino State Parks (707) 937-5804.

between a cypress pole fence on the left and a row of planted Monterey pines on the right. Before ⅛ mile you descend gradually toward the shore as postcard views of Mendocino play peek-a-boo on your right. On a clear day, on the horizon beyond the village loom Point Cabrillo and the rugged mountains of the King Range Lost Coast.

The trail wanders through clumps of Douglas iris (bloom February to May), then tops a small rise where California rose grows overlooking a twisting grassy shoreline. Hidden to the right of the trail, a grassy hilltop offers a fine blanket picnic spot with superb views. Beyond the rise, follow the trail west as it drops steeply from the second to the first marine terrace.

Beyond ¼ mile your descent eases. When the trail forks, take the right fork heading northwest. Before ⅜ mile you pass short-needled shore pines on your right and come to level, open headlands. Stay right at the next fork and continue until the trail reaches the edge of the bluff above a small keyhole cove. Tidal action has worn away the softer rock, creating the keyhole shape. This cove may be the remains of an ancient blowhole.

USE CAUTION HERE: North Coast surf can be dangerous. Watch out for large waves breaking over these low headlands. Furthermore, these eroded cliffs are crumbly and unstable. They consist largely of sand, geologically uplifted from ancient beaches.

Continue north along the bluffs on the trail clinging to the edge. From the point beyond the cove you can see the Mendocino headlands. You may see harbor seals swimming below the point, bobbing in the rough surf. They may view you with as much curiosity as you view them.

Walk north past poppy, coast buckwheat, purple seaside daisy and sea thrift, following the bluff edge to the small point just before the fence marking the northern park boundary. Main Street of Mendocino village appears beyond the fence. Beyond the fence at bluff's edge, a small natural bridge is visible. Mendocino Bay and the mouth of Big River hide just beyond the arch. Native Pomo shell middens lay at your feet.

Return south along the bluff edge, circling the keyhole cove and continuing along bluff's edge. Between you and the sea a steep sandy incline marks the lip of the wave cut terrace. At ⅞ mile you come to a point with a broad sandy "beach" sloping toward another small cove.

Turn east and walk through a new break in the

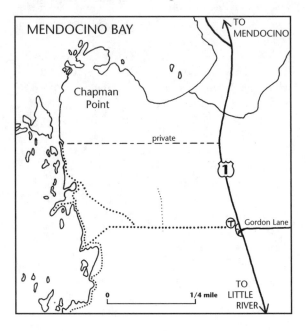

fence to explore the recently acquired Spring Ranch headlands. Walk south along the bluff's edge of the old Spring Ranch. As the trail becomes vague, you simply want to follow the bluff's edge winding east and south.

At 1⅛ miles the trail and the bluff turns west, passing above a pretty little pocket beach. Your path turns south through a fence, then veers west again across a tiny stream where watercress grows. When you reach the very western edge of the headlands, follow them south above rocky tidal shelves both on and offshore. After a jog east before 1½ miles, your bluff-edge path again turns south.

You quickly pass through a fence line, leaving the Spring Ranch portion of Van Damme State Park for land acquired in 1975. Your trail fords a tiny stream with seep-spring monkeyflower and more watercress, then meanders generally south near the bluff's edge, passing clusters of cypresses. You might notice two side trails on your left that explore the pine-spattered grasslands to the east.

Around 1¾ miles the Coastal Trail turns east, passing a short side trail that heads south to the tip of a wooded promontory. You might explore the spur trail to take a look at the deep rocky cove on its left. While the Coastal Trail winds east to return to Highway 1, this promontory offers an ideal turnaround point for this hike. Retrace you steps north along the blufftop until you pass through the last broken fence line, then turn east to ascend the trail back to your starting point.

OTHER SUGGESTION: Not far to the north, MENDOCINO BAY VIEWPOINT TRAIL offers a short stroll from Brewery Gulch Road to a sweeping vista of the bay, thanks to the hard work of the Mendocino Land Trust. Another nearby walk offers a very different outing; the CHARLOTTE HOAK PYGMY FOREST TRAIL can be found 2.6 miles up Comptche-Ukiah Road. On the right the trail provides a ¼-mile walk with a ⅛-mile loop through dwarf forest at the headwaters of Little River.

37.

LITTLE RIVER POINT

PRIME WHALE WATCHING & HIDDEN COVES

Like Chapman Point, one mile to the north, Little River Point was part of the original Beall Ranch. This was ranch land, while most of Little River was devoted to logging. In 1975 the state acquired these 80 acres, now administered as part of Van Damme State Park.

This easy walk follows a lightly traveled path to a stunning hidden shoreline. This seems to be one of the trails that always changes between editions, adding some adventure to exploring these glorious headlands. First in 1987, the original access at the end of Peterson Lane was blocked by an electronic gate. Then when I wrote it up for the second edition, State Parks hadn't mowed the trail here, making it sound like a tiny wilderness. As of this writing, it's a bit more manicured. Don't hold your breath, however, but do visit.

Park on the southwest corner of Highway One and unmarked Peterson Lane and cautiously walk north along the highway for 250 feet, then head west through a break in the fence. On this hike, bring your own litter bag. There are no garbage cans, and no one will follow along to pick up your mess. PLEASE PACK IT OUT!

The break in the fence is north of Rachel's Inn, beside a yellow caution sign. The trail now parallels the highway north across grasslands for 300 feet, then swings west across land that provides wet

DISTANCE: 1 to 1⅝ miles round trip or loop, plus optional ¼-mile side trip.

TIME: One half hour to one hour.

TERRAIN: Gently sloping headlands spotted with cypress and Monterey pines leading to convoluted, rocky shore.

BEST TIME: Any sunny day that is not too windy. High overcast also good.

WARNINGS: Stay off private property. On bluffs or tidal rocks, watch for killer waves. Trail can be very wet after heavy rains.

HOW TO GET THERE: At M.48.35 on Highway 1 at the north end of Little River, turn west onto unmarked Peterson Lane (south of Rachel's Inn). Park in the dirt lot on the left just west of highway. The trailhead is 250 feet north along the west shoulder of Highway One.

FURTHER INFO: Mendocino State Parks (707) 937-5804.

walking after rains.

By ⅛ mile you reach higher and drier ground at a large, grassy clearing dotted with pines. Continue west past a junction in 200 feet. (All trails here reach the headlands eventually; this description takes the shortest route.) The path west contours, then descends to a second junction beyond ¼ mile. Continue west, descending gradually through more open prairie with blue-eyed grass, Douglas iris, a lovely orange-flowered holly bush, and scattered pines, coming to the rim of the headlands at ½ mile. There the Kissel family memorial bench offers a comfy spot with a grand view of the rocky shore.

Behind the bench you meet the California Coastal Trail. From the bench you can follow it north or south along the shore. If you go north, you cross a creek and pass a small point, then reach the fence line of the old Spring Ranch boundary in ⅛ mile. You can follow the convoluted bluffs north for up to a mile to the end of state park property. That route is described in Trail #36.

Following the shoreline south from the bench, your trail winds among cypresses that punctuate the grand view. You soon come to a point with a view south, when clear, all the way to Navarro Head six miles away. Even when the fog is in, flat rocky shelves directly offshore are a favorite haul out for harbor seals. Beyond the rocks the ocean rapidly drops off to a deep channel where migrating whales come very close to shore, giving the whale watcher a great vantage point.

Continue south above the shoreline. Beyond ⅝ mile a deep cove blocks your route south, though you cannot see it for the dense trees. Follow the trail east for 250 feet to a fork, then turn right and follow a dead-end path south. It leads 375 feet along a promontory lined with cypresses, passing a junction at ¾ mile and ducking through a cypress thicket, to end on a grassy point where brilliant blue iris grow overlooking the mouth of a deep and narrow blue lagoon. An ultramodern home stands on private property beyond the azure inlet.

Retrace your steps 150 feet to the junction and turn right. This path follows the wooded edge of the lagoon. Three spurs on your right survey the awesome cove—it's worth a look! When this path ends, a left turn returns the way you came (via the bench), 1⅝ miles round trip.

Our described hike turns right to explore the rest of these convoluted headlands. As you head east on the narrow path through grasslands, one last short spur on the right explores the finger cove. Continue up a slight hill 100 feet to an unmarked junction.

You can turn right on this dead-end spur for a ¼-mile side trip to explore yet another finger cove hiding beyond the first one. That path heads south, then swings west to avoid a house on private property. Just ⅛ mile from the junction you come to the lip of the bluff. From there you can see the second finger cove paralleling the first and bisecting the headlands before you. Return to the junction.

From the junction the main trail heads east and northeast, then turns north. Beyond one mile you veer right to head northeast, climbing gently and passing to the right of the orange-flowered holly bush. At another junction, you turn right to climb gradually east. In 165 feet, as the mowed path veers to the right toward houses, you veer left on a faint

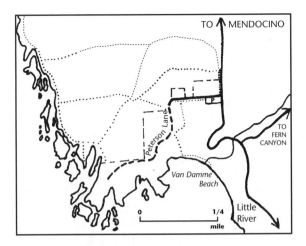

but well beaten path that heads east toward a shiny leaved cascara sagrada shrub, then turns north to climb past a bog where tiger lilies bloom in spring and early summer.

Beyond the bog, you quickly reach a junction at 1⅛ miles with the north path you came out on. Turn right and retrace your steps east then south to the trailhead at 1⅜ miles.

OTHER SUGGESTION: A short, pretty trail leads to the beach north of the mouth of Little River. Walk west on Peterson Lane for .1 mile from parking area, then follow the trail south to the beach (⅝ mile round trip).

38.

VAN DAMME STATE PARK
FERN CANYON TRAIL

This very popular trail follows a mostly paved old road built by the Civilian Conservation Corps in 1936. It's often crowded with nature lovers during the summer months. My favorite time of year to visit this deep verdant canyon is in winter or early spring. On a weekday in March, I saw only four other people in the entire canyon. If the water is high, you may have to ford Little River in a spot or two, but the old wet fords that this hike once featured

179

VAN DAMME STATE PARK:

DISTANCE: 5 miles round trip.

TIME: Two to three hours.

TERRAIN: Gently sloping bottom of deep lush canyon. May require fording stream in winter.

ELEVATION GAIN/LOSS: Round trip from summer trailhead: 180 feet+/180 feet-. From beach lot: 230 feet+/230 feet-.

BEST TIME: Spring to autumn.

WARNINGS: Watch for poison oak and stinging nettles along trail. You may have to ford Little River at 1½ miles in rainy season when water runs high.

HOW TO GET THERE: Turn off Highway 1 at M.48.05 into Van Damme State Park. Go .5 mile east on the road to the Lower Campground. Off season the trail leaves from campsite #26. In summer the road is open .2 mile farther to signed Fern Canyon Trailhead.

FEES: Day use: $5/vehicle. Car camping: $16/night. Environmental Camps: $10/night. No fee parking available on west side of Highway 1.

FURTHER INFO: Mendocino State Parks (707) 937-5804.

have now been replaced by bridges, improving the chances for steelhead and salmon to make it upstream. An interpretive brochure available at the trailhead discusses the lives of salmon and steelhead and recent efforts to preserve their run in Little River.

The CCC road mostly follows an old skid trail used to haul cut redwoods down the canyon by oxen teams from 1864 through 1893. In summer, and whenever the upper end of the lower campground is open, you can start this hike at the Fern Canyon Trailhead and the end of the park road. In winter you may have to park at the restroom just before campsite #26 and start from there, adding ¼ mile to the total

distance. Or you can park free in the beach lot, adding about ⅝ mile in each direction.

The following types of ferns occur in Fern Canyon: western sword, bracken, deer, five-finger, lady, licorice, horsetail, wood, bird's foot, and occasional gold back (or stamp) ferns.

Starting at the summer trailhead, head east on the narrowing paved road. By ⅛ mile you're surrounded by steep canyon walls draped with ferns and other moisture tolerant plants. The change to a natural environment is sudden and complete. Ferns grow nearly everywhere in the canyon: both north- and south-facing slopes, on trees and stumps, and out of rocks. Other common species in the understory below second-growth redwoods, firs and hemlocks include California hazel, redwood sorrel, salal, fairy bells, coastal manroot, stinging nettle, columbine, elderberries, thimbleberries, red and evergreen huckleberries, salmonberries and raspberries.

Before ½ mile you pass a short spur trail to streamside and the first of many rest benches. The lower canyon features moss-draped rocky cliffs. A low sign marks the trail's ½-mile-point beside a rocky

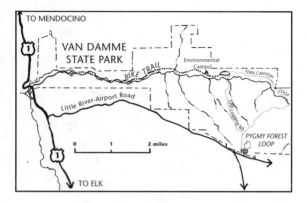

cascading side stream on your left.

You cross a small wooden bridge across the river beyond ¾ mile. The second crossing is just beyond. After the third bridge, five-finger, sword and lady ferns grow next to the trail. Uphill by a tiny waterfall on the right grows wild ginger. You soon pass pig-a-back plant growing in shade on the right.

Continue up the canyon, crossing Little River at the fourth, fifth and sixth bridges up to the 1⅜-mile point. Beyond the sixth bridge, the canyon broadens.

After crossing the stream for the seventh and eighth times around 1½ miles, the latter one of the original concrete CCC-built fords, you climb to the first of ten pleasant environmental (walk or bicycle-in) camps at 1¾ miles. This quiet, pristine spot offers a real treat for anyone who wants to escape the crowds elsewhere in the park. The upper canyon is more gradual and open but still has the dense carpet of lush vegetation in the understory. Other plants in the understory here include trail plant, wood rose, Solomon's seal, inside out flower, Oregon grape and the poisonous baneberry.

At 2¼ miles the road forks into a small loop. It runs ¼ mile before the paved road ends. At the end of the loop, two dirt trails lead off in different directions. They form a more arduous 3½-mile loop (see Trail #39). The fork on the right which fords the river is open to mountain bikes while the rougher trail up the canyon is not.

Return down the canyon to your starting point.

OTHER SUGGESTIONS: The 3½-mile UPPER FERN CANYON LOOP starts where the paved trail ends. Or reach the loop at its top end from the

39.

PYGMY FOREST/UPPER FERN CANYON LOOP

TREES FROM PYGMIES TO GIANTS

*You have two excellent choices here, an easy short
walk along the ¼-mile fourth-terrace Pygmy Forest boardwalk or an invigorating 3⅝-mile loop into
upper Fern Canyon and back. Because the Pygmy
Forest Loop is obvious from the no-fee parking lot
on Little River-Airport Road, we'll leave you to explore it on your own and we'll describe the loop hike
here. For more information about the pygmy forest
and the uplifted marine terraces, see Trail #25.
Please note that not only is the raised boardwalk
fully wheelchair accessible, but also that wheelchair
riders can explore for up to one mile round trip on
the level left fork of the main trail or up to ⅞ mile
round trip on the right fork (¼ mile beyond the junction).*

*The upper Fern Canyon Loop explores the tran-
sition from pygmy forest to redwood forest and
riparian stream canyon and back, offering an intimate visit with the upper reaches of the lovely small
stream called Little River. For a longer hike you
can combine this loop with the trail down Fern Canyon (see Trail #38).*

From the parking area, take the broad path behind
the silver gate (west of the boardwalk) It contours
northeast, in 450 feet passing through a corner of
the pygmy forest. Your path is primarily surrounded
by tall pine forest. Where the trail forks beyond ⅛

DISTANCE: 3⅝-mile loop, plus ¼-mile boardwalk
  loop.
TIME: Two or three hours.
TERRAIN: Level pygmy forest contrasts with steep
  trail in and out of the canyon and gradual trail along
  upper river.
ELEVATION GAIN/LOSS: 470 feet+/470 feet- (none
  for Pygmy Forest).
BEST TIME: Spring.
WARNINGS: Bikes allowed on 1¼ miles of left fork.
  Bikes not allowed on rest of loop. Watch for poison
  oak, especially in the upper canyon. Upper canyon may be muddy or impassable in wettest months.
HOW TO GET THERE: Turn east off Highway 1
  south of Little River at M.47.5 onto Little-River-
  Airport Road. Go 2.85 miles to the signed parking
  lot and trailhead on the left.
FURTHER INFO: Mendocino State Parks (707)
  937-5804.

mile, take the left fork. The described hike returns
by the right fork.

Beyond the fork your broad path contours northwest. By ¼ mile the vegetation becomes more dense
as you near the edge of the canyon to the north.
Redwood, Douglas fir and chinquapin join the pygmy
forest plants. By ⅜ mile abundant evergreen violet
and salal cover the forest floor.

Begin a gradual descent by ½ mile. By ¾ mile the
descent turns moderate as your path narrows. Look
for trillium, fairy bells, clintonia and redwood sorrel which flower in spring. Your trail switchbacks to
the right before one mile and descends toward Fern
Canyon.

By 1⅛ miles you'll hear the Little River burbling
below as you pass deer fern, trail plant and thimbleberry. Drop into a side canyon where wild ginger
grows around 1¼ miles, then descend gently to the
ford of Little River. Climb briefly to reach the end
of the paved Fern Canyon Trail (Trail #38) and the
junction with the upper Fern Canyon Trail at 1⅜

miles.

Turn right and follow the narrow footpath up the canyon, following the north bank of Little River through its canyon lush with ferns beneath young redwood forest punctuated by giant charred old redwood stumps. You soon cross a bridge over a side canyon and climb above the river. Watch for abundant poison oak and the shiny leaves of redwood ivy, also called inside-out flower.

By 1⅝ miles you've climbed high above the Little River. Descend back to streamside and follow it east. Dip across a small bridge over a moss-lined tributary at 1⅞ miles. At 2 miles you overlook the confluence of a rocky tributary where it cascades into the river. Red huckleberries and sword and lady ferns overhang the spot. Cross a long, sturdy bridge over Little River, then promptly cross another span over the meandering stream. Watch for Oregon grape, wood rose, cascara sagrada and yerba de selva as you continue up the bottom of the canyon. Climb above the stream again, then return to its side.

Around 2¼ miles you cross a bridge over a side stream where Fern Canyon fans out over a broad, flat flood plain. Giant stumps indicate that it once grew immense redwoods, but now ferns blanket the flat. Cross a tributary on a long bridge at 2⅜ miles. Abundant raspberries and thimbleberries line its banks with coltsfoot and ginger beside the stream. Continue on very sandy, then very slippery tread right beside the very Little River. Two fords here should be dry-foot crossings in all but the wettest

months, when it might be impassable.

Suddenly the bottom of the canyon becomes very narrow at 2½ miles. You cross a short bridge over Little River and leave streamside by climbing a fancy switchback. Suddenly you find yourself going down canyon on a gradual ascent along the dark slope, overlooking the stream and the streamside trail. Veer away from Fern Canyon and cross a trickling side stream. You turn east by 2¾ miles, ascending moderately up a side canyon. Climb steeply by rough steps briefly to get beyond a fallen fir.

As you make your way up the canyon's steep slopes, notice how many big stumps still speak for the awesome forest that once graced this land. Around 3 miles your steady ascent eases as fir forest replaces redwoods here. Pass through a small clearing beyond 3⅛ miles, then mixed forest of Bishop pines and hardwoods takes over.

Around 3¼ miles you pass a big mound of bear grass on your right. Relax. You're back home on the fourth terrace. Your trail's nearly level from here back to the trailhead. Contour to the junction at 3½ miles, turn left and follow the broad path to the parking lot just beyond 3⅝ miles.

40.

NAVARRO-BY-THE-SEA
SWEEPING VIEWS FROM THE OLD HIGHWAY

This short hike along the California Coastal Trail climbs to and follows the old coast highway to spectacular views of the Navarro River mouth, its sandy beach and the surrounding rocky coast.

As you drive the access road to the beach and trail, you pass the few buildings that remain from a nineteenth century logging town called Navarro that thrived here from the 1860s until the early 1900s. Navarro Ridge immediately to the north was the northern limits of the territory of the Central Pomo people, although the only known villages were south along the coast near the Garcia River.

The unmarked, sometimes overgrown trail heads into dense vegetation opposite the campground

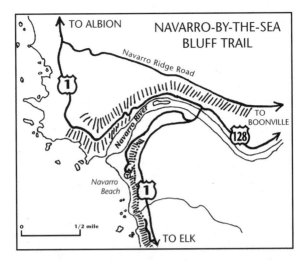

information sign near the end of the paved road. Unless it has been cleared recently, the path often gets overgrown with coastal scrub for the first 200 feet. The trail heads east, then northeast. You rapidly climb the steep hill as the trail gets very rough from 100 to 150 feet, where it ascends by two steep switchbacks through the dense undercover. The path winds beneath a lone cypress. Climb the rough track for another 200 feet to reach the pavement of the old highway.

Here you have a grand view of the Navarro River mouth and beach. Offshore are several sea stacks including the Arch of the Navarro. Harbor seals can often be seen in the river near the mouth. They gorge themselves on the salmon and steelhead that have come to spawn upriver. The seals feast playfully as seagulls chase after them for fish scraps.

Turn right on the pavement and climb gradually along the bluff. The coastal scrub surrounding the asphalt is rapidly overcoming the pavement. Dominant species include ceanothus, coyote brush, lupine, Douglas iris, blackberry and sticky monkey-flower. Other plants include coast buckwheat, Indian pink, mugwort, angelica, fiddleneck phacelia, sedum, redwood penstemon, poppy, purple seaside daisy, blue-eyed grass, yarrow, wood rose and beach morning glory.

Soon you come to a fallen rusted old guardrail. Where the road surface has been eroded, you can see the old redwood supports of the road. Just beyond, a mudslide, now overgrown with vegetation,

187

DISTANCE: 1 to 1¼ miles round trip.
TIME: One half hour.
TERRAIN: Old road across steep, brushy headlands with commanding views of ocean and river mouth.
ELEVATION GAIN/LOSS: 200 feet+/200 feet-.
BEST TIME: Anytime.
WARNINGS: Watch for poison oak as you climb the trail. First part of trail is steep and rough, may be overgrown, especially in winter and spring.
HOW TO GET THERE: On Highway 1 just south of the Highway 128 junction and the Navarro River bridge, turn west at M.40.15. Go .75 mile to unmarked Navarro Bluff trailhead.
FURTHER INFO: Mendocino State Parks (707) 937-5804.

covers the pavement. Uphill a stunted grand fir grows. At ¼ mile an old turnout provides views south to Point Arena on a clear day.

In 300 feet you come to another large mudslide. In another 200 feet, rocks cover the pavement. Watch for falling rocks here, especially in wet weather. Above you a house sits precariously at the top of the rock slide.

You soon pass a windblown cypress on the steep slope below you. On the uphill side, wild red columbine and sticky monkeyflower bloom in spring. At a major sinking of the old roadbed, the trail veers left and hugs the cliff. Though the sunken road looks unstable, it is not likely to slide away under your feet.

A bit farther you come to a recent slip out nearly at the top of the bluff. While you may be able to get around it, it may not be worth your while. Just beyond, ½ mile from your starting point, the road reaches still-maintained pavement and a sign, the back of which warns ROAD CLOSED BECAUSE OF STORM DAMAGE AND SLIDES. A small cluster of houses lies just beyond.

You have climbed to an elevation of 160 feet. Looking west from here, you can see where the water changes from milky blue-green to a deep blue, indicating deep water. Looking back from where you have come, you see a bird's-eye view of the beach, river mouth and the 600-foot rise of the steep headlands beyond the Navarro River. When you have had your fill of the view, return by the same path.

If you are not ready to return to your car, you can walk north from where the trail drops to the beach. The trail goes almost ⅛ mile before coming to a fence marking private property. Please do not go beyond this point. Notice how the environment changes to an entirely different shady riparian habitat. Here stinging nettles, red alders, sword ferns and thimbleberries thrive in the cool shade of the north-facing hillside. Moss and lichen even grow directly on the old road surface, helping to return it to a more natural state.

OTHER SUGGESTIONS: A walk along the broad NAVARRO BEACH is an easy alternative to climbing the bluffs, though in summer it is often packed with campers. If you go in winter, be sure to watch for killer waves.

The many swimming holes among the redwoods along the NAVARRO RIVER southeast of here can be reached from Highway 128.

Especially for mountain bikers and equestrians, NAVARRO RIDGE ROAD is a county road running along the ridge north of the river. The 13.35-mile road has very light traffic on its easternmost 8 miles. It is unpaved for the eastern 10 miles. Access is at M.11.60 on Highway 128 on the east end and at M.42.35 on Highway 1 on the west end. Watch and listen for gunfire; avoid in hunting season.

If you're heading north on Highway 1, the HERITAGE HOUSE COASTAL ACCESS PATH lies west of the road at M.45.25, about .25 mile south of the Heritage House main driveway. There a dirt path descends between a wooden fence and a driveway to a stairway which drops by 77 steps to a marvelous beach below steep cliffs at the mouth of Dark Gulch. At low tide the beach extends up to ⅛ mile from cliff to cliff. (½ mile round trip)

HENDY WOODS STATE PARK

Hendy Woods represents the only link to what Anderson Valley was like before logging began around 1860. About 100 acres of the park's 845 acres are virgin forest. The climate of the valley is warmer and drier than it was when the first settlers arrived because so much of the forest has been removed. Anderson Valley was the territory of the Northern Pomo people.

All the trail descriptions for Hendy Woods begin at the picnic area beside the river at the end of the road.

41.

GENTLE GIANTS LOOP
ALL ACCESS TRAIL

The pleasant picnic grounds sit on the bank of the Navarro River in a partial clearing sprinkled with native riparian hardwood species like California buckeye, Oregon ash, valley oak and big leaf maple.

Go south from the parking area toward the tall redwoods, quickly entering the relatively cool shade of the forest. In about 300 feet you enter the even cooler virgin redwood forest of Big Hendy Grove. The redwoods here have diameters to eight or nine feet and range to 270 feet tall. Little grows beneath the giants except clover-like redwood sorrel, ferns and scattered bay laurels. Your level trail winds left and right. Soon a huge, fire-scarred redwood with an oblong base stands on your right. The narrow side is "only" 12 feet, the longer side nearly 17 feet!

Cross a bridge beyond ⅛ mile and come to a signed junction opposite a scarred giant. The Discovery Trail (Trail #42) forks left. Gentle Giants Trail continues on the right, heading through deep forest where little sunlight penetrates and crossing another bridge. Beyond the span, the Hermit Hut Trail forks left. Gentle Giants All Access Loop continues west through the grove. More abundant vegetation in the understory here includes tanoak, evergreen violet and hedge nettle.

DISTANCE: ⅜-mile loop or ½-mile round trip.

TIME: One half hour.

TERRAIN: Level path in virgin redwood forest.

BEST TIME: April through October.

WARNINGS: Watch for traffic on paved road.

HOW TO GET THERE: Leave Highway 1 at M.40.28. Go south on Highway 128 to M.20.15 where you turn right. Go .5 mile to state park entrance on the left. Follow this road to the picnic area at its end, 1.8 miles. (Note: Highway 128 runs from Highway 101 at Cloverdale northwest to Highway 1 at the Navarro River mouth—about 10 miles south of Mendocino.)

FURTHER INFO: Mendocino State Parks District Office (707)937-5804, Park Office (707)895-3141.

FEES: Day use: $5/vehicle. Car Camping: $16/night.

At ¼ mile the trail crosses one more very small bridge and promptly comes to the road. You can return the way you came or, with caution, turn right and go downhill on the road shoulder ⅛ mile to your car. Another choice is to cross the road and continue on the Campground Trail, then go right on the Eagle Trail to explore the Little Hendy Trail through Little Hendy Grove.

OTHER SUGGESTIONS: The HERMIT HUT TRAIL, 1¼ miles round trip, climbs to a park squatter's former residence. If you'd like to make this into a longer loop hike, continue west on the lower portion of the Water Tank Loop, then on the winding AZALEA CREEK TRAIL. It ends at the dump station, but you can head north across the main park road to follow the LITTLE HENDY TRAIL through Little Hendy Grove. Then continue east on the EAGLE and CAMPGROUND TRAILS to meet the southwest end of the All Access Trail near the parking area.

42

DISCOVERY LOOP

THROUGH GIANT REDWOOD FOREST

Follow the Gentle Giants Trail from the parking area for about ⅛ mile. Beyond a wooden bridge, fork left on the Discovery Trail. In about 200 feet you come to the root end of a huge fallen redwood tree. You stand on a flat river flood plain, a prime habitat for redwoods.

At ¼ mile from the parking lot you reach a forest clearing at the edge of the flood plain. The rise in front of you is the ancient riverbank. In 30 feet you come to a loveseat cut from a chunk of redwood on the right side of the trail. The next section of trail may be slippery after rains, watch your step. On this part of the flood plain, a small creek fans out to deposit silt and keep the forest floor moist. Notice that the redwood giants love it here.

You soon reach a memorial bench and grove, a fine place to sit and listen to the quiet of this place.

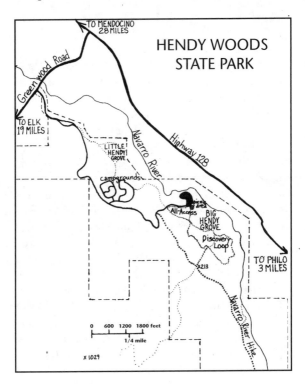

DISCOVERY LOOP:

DISTANCE: ¾-mile loop. (You can add the ⅝-mile outer loop or the Navarro River hike [Trail #43] for a longer trek.)

TIME: One half hour to one hour.

TERRAIN: Level flood plain through virgin redwood forest.

BEST TIME: April through October. Though trail may be wet in winter, it's still a fine walk with proper footwear.

WARNINGS: Watch for poison oak.

HOW TO GET THERE: Same as #41.

FURTHER INFO: Mendocino State Parks District Office (707)937-5804, Hendy Park office (707) 895-3141.

FEES: Day use: $5/vehicle. Car Camping: $16/night.

The uncommon woodwardia fern joins sword, lady and bracken ferns along the next section of trail. Near ⅜ mile your trail curves around a fallen giant. This tree left a 75-foot-high splinter when it fell.

In 100 feet your trail meets a main signed junction. The Discovery Trail turns left here. The Outer Loop trail straight ahead takes you on a ⅝-mile longer tour of the grove. You may take the Outer Loop without missing any of the Discovery Loop. On the right, the trail marked HENDY FIRE ROAD leads to the Navarro River hike (Trail #43).

The Discovery Trail continues northeast. Many green leafy plants grow on the forest floor: redwood sorrel, Pacific vanilla leaf (3 lobe-shaped leaves), salal, trail plant, evergreen violet, wood rose, huckleberry and sword and bracken ferns. Just 250 feet from the junction, the Outer Loop rejoins the Discovery Loop. Your trail continues straight briefly with a glimpse of the Anderson Valley hills through the foliage, then turns left. (A side trail leads out of the grove and down to a corral near the river.) You pass an old stump, evidence of the logging that occurred on the fringes of Big Hendy Grove before it became a state park in 1958. Around ½ mile from your starting point, the trail dips past a fallen redwood log. Just beyond, you can examine a redwood burl. Your trail winds among immense fallen logs, accentuating the marvel of the still standing, breathing giants.

You soon come to a rest bench. Here a redwood giant hangs over your head, leaning at a seemingly precarious angle. Redwoods have the ability to buttress themselves, however. When a redwood starts to lean, it puts on extra growth beneath the lean, counteracting the tendency to fall.

In 200 feet, your trail returns to the early part of the loop. Turn right and return to the parking area where you started.

43.

NAVARRO RIVER HIKE

THROUGH THE HENDY BACKWOODS

The Navarro River is the largest coastal river between Humboldt County's Eel and Sonoma County's Russian (all three pass through Mendocino County). While the Navarro here shrinks to hardly more than a trickle in late summer, in winter it can be a raging torrent. If you prefer to mountain bike this trail, you must start at the fire road that leaves the paved park road west of the Gentle Giants Loop.

At the junction on the Discovery Trail, take the right fork. From the redwood flat, you start climbing alongside a small mossy drainage where inside out flower grows. Beyond ⅛ mile the trail levels and comes to a gravel fire road. The gravel road immediately forks into two roads (trails for the purpose of this report). The main trail is on the left.

(You can take the right fork to extend the hike or as an alternate. Go uphill ⅛ mile to a fork in the road. Take the left fork. In another 200 feet, go left again, quickly crossing a small creek and continu-

ing uphill. You soon must climb over a large fallen log. About 900 feet beyond you come to the state park boundary. The trail, actually an old logging road, continues uphill onto private property.)

You're ½ mile from the picnic area. Taking the left fork of the fire road, your mostly level trail heads southeast. At ⅝ mile the trail bends to the right and heads up a slight hill. A little farther you cross a small creek; redwoods to seven feet in diameter and spice bush grow alongside. At ⅞ mile you pass a sign indicating a horse trail on the left, but your route continues on the gravel road. (The horse trail leads to the river where chatterbox orchids and azaleas grow on the far bank, then follows the riverbed back to the picnic area.) At one mile from the trailhead, the road has climbed above the forest floor on your left.

Around 1¼ miles the terrain to the left of your path steepens. You may be able to hear the Navarro River below you. In 300 feet another horse trail leads toward the river. Stay on the road, crossing another small creek. Soon the river is directly below you, about 60 feet down the hill. Just beyond, at 1½ miles, you come to the state park boundary and your turn-around point. From here the town of Philo is just about one mile southeast, but it's all private property in between.

Return along the same route by which you came.

44.

GREENWOOD STATE BEACH

CLIFFS, COVES AND SEA STACKS

The present town of Elk was first settled in the 1850s as Greenwood. Among the first settlers were four sons of mountain man Caleb Greenwood. Caleb was an organizer of the ill-fated Donner party. In fact, Caleb organized one of the expeditions that went to Donner Lake to rescue the survivors from their winter of horror. Two of his sons apparently went along to help. One of the many doghole ports along the Mendocino coast, Greenwood outlasted other nearby boom towns like Cuffeys Cove to the north and Elk River, Bridgeport and Alder Creek to the south.

Until recently, the sleepy town of Elk was one of the Mendocino coast's best kept secrets. Now sev-

197

eral fine inns and restaurants have brought Elk acclaim. But please try not to tell the whole world about it.

The trail leaves from the graveled parking lot opposite the Elk Store. (Several picnic tables and a toilet lie just west of the parking lot for those not willing or able to make the hike down to the beach.) In about 150 feet, the main trail to the beach goes left, while the right fork leads 250 feet to a fine picnic area with an expansive view of the beach below.

The main trail continues downhill below several private residences, then follows an old drainage ditch to the bottom of the hill, about ¼ mile. Here another picnic area is located on a flat, the site of one of Greenwood's lumber mills. Another restroom is nearby. A trail from the east meets the main trail near the picnic area. This leads upstream along Greenwood Creek briefly. Nasturtiums grow near the junction.

Walk west from the picnic area, coming to a large pile of driftwood marking the extreme high tideline. To the south across the creek, you can make out the remains of the spillway of an old dam, the lake of which was used to hold the logs before cutting at the

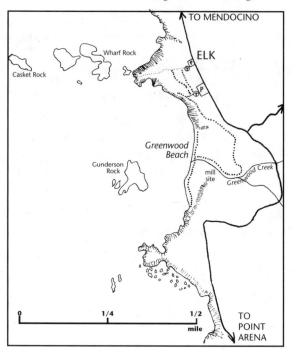

GREENWOOD STATE BEACH:

DISTANCE: ¾ to 1½ miles round trip.

TIME: One half hour to one hour.

TERRAIN: From coastal bluff down to beach in a protected cove at the mouth of Greenwood Creek.

ELEVATION GAIN/LOSS: 150 feet+/150 feet-.

BEST TIME: Anytime.

WARNINGS: Trail to beach is an easement across private property; please do not disturb occupants of adjacent houses. Never turn your back on the ocean. Always watch for rogue waves, especially in winter.

HOW TO GET THERE: In the town of Elk, 15.5 miles south of Mendocino, parking is on west side of Highway 1 at M.34.05, opposite Elk Market.

FURTHER INFO: Mendocino State Parks (707) 937-5804.

mill. Continue another 300 feet to the midpoint of the beach, from where you can follow the shore north or south.

Just offshore are several large sea stacks with wave tunnels. The one to the left is Gunderson Rock. To the right are Wharf Rock, with the flat top where a loading wharf was once anchored, and Casket Rock. Looking farther to sea between the latter two rocks, you can see Cove Rock, just south of jutting Cuffeys Point. Cove Rock was used by early navigators to locate Greenwood and Cuffeys Coves and safely steer their ships into anchor.

From the center point of the beach, you can walk about ⅛ mile south to the mouth of the creek. The beach continues for a few hundred feet beyond the mouth before coming to a cliff. To the north you may walk nearly ¼ mile before you come to an impassable cliff.

Return up the hill by the trail that you descended.

45.

MANCHESTER STATE PARK

GENTLE BUT WILD COAST

The hike is described from the north end, starting at Alder Creek, where the San Andreas fault leaves the land and heads north into the ocean. If you follow the trail as described, you'll be hiking the California Coastal Trail for most of the walk. Keep in mind that usually strong northerly winds may hamper your return progress. However, you may start at any one of the three access points. The long beach curves across prevailing ocean currents, forming a catch basin for sea debris, a beachcomber's paradise. At 5272 acres, Manchester State Park is the second largest state park on the Mendocino coast after Sinkyone Wilderness in the north.

A triangular lagoon sits at the mouth of Alder Creek. (The beach continues north of the lagoon for 1¾ miles to Irish Gulch, ending at impassable cliffs ½ mile beyond the gulch.) Walk west at the base of cliffs covered with wildflowers. In 300 feet a succulent garden grows on a cliff of fractured, jumbled rock; you are standing on the San Andreas fault. Short of ⅛ mile you come out on the broad, driftwood strewn beach. Head south toward the Point Arena lighthouse.

At ¼ mile the cliffs behind the beach are covered with sea grass, which has escaped from the dunes just south of here. At ½ mile the cliffs have ended; grass covered dunes lie behind the beach. In 300 feet a small gully runs through the dunes. If you walk up

MANCHESTER STATE PARK:

DISTANCE: 3¾ miles one way, Alder Creek to Garcia River mouth; 5 miles one way, Irish Beach to Garcia River, or any portion as a shorter round trip.

TIME: Two to three hours each way.

TERRAIN: Long beach backed by dunes and cliffs with lagoons, creeks and a river mouth.

BEST TIME: Spring and autumn. In summer, area is sometimes subject to high winds.

WARNINGS: Watch for rogue waves. Do not trespass on adjacent private property. Off-road vehicles are not allowed on the dunes. Fires permitted only in fire rings.

HOW TO GET THERE: From Highway 1 near Manchester, three access roads lead west to the park:

Alder Creek Road at M.22.48, go .7 mile to start of described trail.

Kinney Road at M.21.40, go .7 mile, where you go right for car and walk-in camping, or continue .3 mile to main parking at end of road.

Stoneboro Road at M.19.65, go 1.6 miles to end of road. Trail leads west.

FEES: Car camping & Environmental Camps: $12/night.

FURTHER INFO: Mendocino State Parks (707) 937-5804.

ENVIRONMENTAL CAMPS: Located near Davis Lake, ten pleasant Environmental Camps are reached by a trail (no dogs allowed) that leaves from the parking area at .7 mile on Kinney Road. It is approximately one mile from the trailhead to the camps. The pleasant trail leads north, then west past a pond, then turns north along the west shore of Davis Lake. The campsites are just north of the lake, in dunes and along a cypress windbreak. Register with the state park before you set up at the E Camps.

201

the gully, you'll reach the walk-in Environmental
Camps in about ¼ mile.

Continuing south along the beach, at ⅝ mile you
come to the broad outflow of Davis Lake. The narrow lagoon is 200 feet east of the beach. (You can
also get to the Environmental Camps by turning east
here.) Walking south, the driftwood strewn beach is
backed by more dunes. The dunes become quite high
at one mile.

At 1⅛ miles you come to a path leading out of the
dunes from the main parking area at the end of
Kinney Road. The beach becomes even broader here
as you continue south. The dunes are soon replaced
by wildflower-covered bluffs. A bright yellow sign
proclaims CABLE LANDING, this is where the trans-
Pacific cable heads west to Hawaii.

At 1⅝ miles from the Alder Creek trailhead, you
come to the mouth of Brush Creek. At 1¾ miles, to

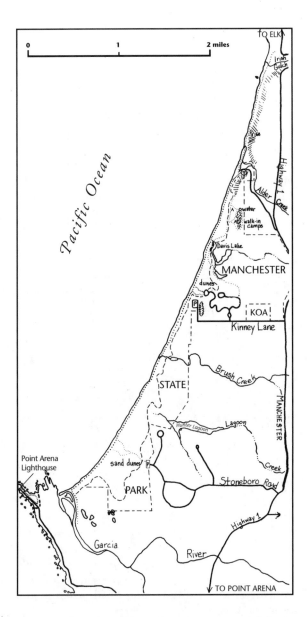

the east of the beach lies a lagoon strewn with large redwood driftwood. Though the lagoon is small, it marks the start of a broad wild area that is home to birds and other wildlife. In earlier days, Brush Creek was infamous for its large population of bears.

The beach continues southwest, the Point Arena lighthouse looming ever larger. At 2 miles large Hunter's Lagoon hides in the dunes ¼ mile east. Though only the west end of the lagoon lies within park boundaries, the mile-long, landlocked lake offers fine bird habitat. Climb the sand hills if you'd like a better look.

The long beach continues south, now backed by dunes up to 80 feet tall. Around 2¾ miles you meet two trails from the east. These lead through the dunes to the parking area at the end of Stoneboro Road. By 3¼ miles the dunes become narrower and lower.

At 3¾ miles you arrive at the narrow sand spit at the mouth of the Garcia River. Oddly eroded rocks grace the far shore. The river's estuary provides habitat for many birds. (In winter hundreds of tundra swans live two miles upstream.) The lighthouse stands less than ¼ mile to the west, with only the river and pastures between.

Unless you have arranged a shuttle at Stoneboro Road (1½ miles from here), you have no choice but to return the way you came.

46.

POINT ARENA LIGHTHOUSE & HEADLANDS

CLIMB TO VIEWS AND HISTORY

This is not a trail per se, but rather a climb to the top of a 115-foot lighthouse with fine views and fascinating history. Though the climb is short compared with other trails in this book, it will certainly get your blood pumping and relieve the road blues if you're traveling far that day. In spring, a short walk around the lighthouse grounds presents a wonderful variety of wildflowers and great views up and down the coast.

The Point Arena lighthouse was established in 1870 at one of the most treacherous sections of the Mendocino coast for ship traffic. Operated by the U.S. Lighthouse Service, the original oil lamp was visible for 18 miles or more.

The original tower stood slightly shorter than the one in place today. The earthquake that devastated San Francisco in 1906 shook, swayed, and finally cracked the original brick tower. Though it was the only brick building in Point Arena standing after the quake, it was severely damaged.

The Lighthouse Service razed the old structure and built the current tower, the first earthquake-resistant, steel-reinforced concrete lighthouse in the United States. It was later turned over to the Coast Guard.

After more than 100 years of human operation, the lighthouse was automated in 1977, putting an end to public access with the elimination of the Coast Guard staff. Local citizens formed a nonprofit organization to reopen the historic lighthouse to the public. In 1984 they received a 25-year renewable lease allowing them to open the tower to public tours. The group has established a small museum in the pre-earthquake Fog Signal Building. The fine little museum includes old foghorns, uniforms, flags and historic photographs of the lighthouse, earthquake damage, nearby shipwrecks and other local history. They also have a great map collection and an exhibit of native flowers.

Pay your admission at the museum before entering the lighthouse.

As you enter the tower, notice a brass plaque set in the first step. The cast iron steps were made in San Francisco in 1869. A sign warns that the 145 steps to the top are equivalent to a six-story building. Take your time as you climb the spiral staircase. Glass brick windows allow an occasional glimpse of the headlands and sea cliffs below you.

At step #145 you come to a landing where you will meet your tour guide. The center of the room is filled by cylindrical machinery, the center shaft of which held the original lamp. Looking up, you will see the amazing Fresnel (pron. franel) lens. This two-ton glass and brass lens was made in Paris (by the original Fresnel factory) in 1870, shipped around Cape Horn in pieces and assembled here, probably by a company representative sent with it. The apparatus was precisely engineered to magnify the intensity of the original oil lamp into a beam that carried 18 miles out to sea. (The current high-tech light is rated to carry only 25 miles!) The lamp rests on a mercury bath, strong enough to hold the weight yet fluid enough that the massive lens could be turned by a ⅛-horsepower motor.

At this level of the light tower, you can look out a

POINT ARENA LIGHTHOUSE & HEADLANDS:

DISTANCE: 145 steps to top of lighthouse (equivalent to 6 or 8 story building; it is 115 feet high). Also an optional headlands loop of ½ mile.

TIME: One half hour to one hour.

TERRAIN: Flat coastal headlands at end of long point. Steep stairs to top of lighthouse.

BEST TIME: A clear day. The headlands are best in spring when the wildflowers are at their peak— April, May best. March, June and July next best.

WARNINGS: Lighthouse is open 362 days a year, from 11 a.m. to 3:30 p.m. (from 10-3:30 on summer weekends and holidays). Closed Thanksgiving, Christmas and New Year's Day. Lighthouse is also closed during extreme winds or ferocious storms.

HOW TO GET THERE: Turn west off Highway 1 just north of Point Arena at M.17.05. Go 2.7 miles on bumpy but paved and scenic Lighthouse Road.

FEES: $3 for adults, $1 for children under 12.

FURTHER INFO: Point Arena Lighthouse Keepers (707)882-2777.

small door to the point and the rocky shoals beyond, site of many shipwrecks over the years. You can then go up eight steep steps to the top of the tower where the lens is located. A canvas curtain over the windows keeps direct sunlight off the lens; even a few seconds of direct sun on the powerful lens could start a fire. You may look behind the curtain at the wonderful view, but be sure to keep the curtain between you and the lens. Do not touch the lens, please, because the lighthouse keepers must keep it clean.

Descend the tower, perhaps reflecting on the marvels of engineering in the nineteenth century.

If you would like to walk more before leaving, a short loop leads east behind the vacation rental homes on an old road. It is about ½ mile around the flower studded headlands behind the homes, returning along the main road.

47

MOAT CREEK to
BOWLING BALL BEACH
GORGEOUS SECTION OF CALIFORNIA COASTAL TRAIL

Moat Creek Access, one of the hundreds of "Offer to Dedicate" (OTD) coastal access ways preserved by the 1972 California Coastal Protection Initiative, was the first OTD sponsored by a private group. Whiskey Shoals was a pre-Coastal Initiative subdivision north and south of Moat Creek. When California voters passed the initiative, the unfinished subdivision was shut down for not complying with the new laws, then acquired by the state when the developer defaulted on commitments to upgrade it. The Coastal Conservancy held the land for several years, then sold most of it to individuals, retaining a blufftop trail right of way from Moat Creek to Ross Creek.

The Whiskey Shoals Blufftop Trail is another link in the California Coastal Trail. Here I describe the rough, unimproved volunteer trail that exists as we go to press. In October 1998 the Coastal Conservancy announced that a $15,000 grant had been awarded to the Moat Creek Managing Agency to design, construct and manage an improved trail along the blufftop between Moat Creek and Ross Creek. Perhaps by the time you visit, this trail will be improved, especially the steep ascent from Moat Creek to the blufftop.

The name Whiskey Shoals harks back to the days of Prohibition when rum runners used these fog-shrouded cliffs to land their illegal cargoes.

From the Moat Creek parking lot, follow the path downstream to the cove at the mouth of the creek. When the tide is low, especially at minus tides, you can take a side trip north along the shore, perhaps getting as far as the point around ¼ mile from the creek.

Continue along the Coastal Trail as it turns left just before the cove to climb steeply southeast by a rough, sometimes overgrown path to the blufftop. From there the trail follows the bluff edge down the

MOAT CREEK TO BOWLING BALL BEACH:

DISTANCE: 3¾ miles round trip to Schooner Gulch
Beach, or 3 miles round trip to Galloway Creek or
½ mile round trip to Moat Creek Beach.
TIME: One or two hours.
TERRAIN: Along a creek to its mouth, steep ascent
to blufftop, then contour along blufftop until descent to Bowling Ball Beach.
ELEVATION GAIN/LOSS: Moat Creek to Schooner
Gulch trailhead: 230 feet+/190 feet-.
BEST TIME: Low tide for best beach access. Spring
and early summer for wildflowers.
WARNINGS: Use caution on undeveloped trail along
blufftop. Stay back from bluff's edge. Watch for
rogue waves on beach.
HOW TO GET THERE: Turn west off Highway 1
south of Point Arena at Milepost 12.9 into dirt
parking lot.
FURTHER INFO: Mendocino State Parks (707)
937-5804.

coast. Take your time and enjoy the views overlooking the blond striated cliffs, a striking feature of the
shoreline south of Point Arena. Around ⅜ mile your
bluff-edge trail veers left and circles around a horseshoe cove.

By ⅝ mile you reach the south end of the Whiskey
Shoals bluff. Descend due south toward the shore,
avoiding private property to the east. As you
approach the shore, veer left along the base of the
grassy bluff to the mouth of Ross Creek and meet
the Ross Creek access trail which heads east to Highway 1. Descend to the beach at ¾ mile. A small sea
stack stands in the tidal zone beside the creek.

If you hike through here at a tide higher than +2.0
feet, especially in winter, you may not be able to get
around the point ¼ mile south. If you can round the
point, you can continue southeast along the beach
from Ross Creek. The beach narrows and turns
rocky around ⅞ mile, then broadens and becomes
sandy as you approach the point at one mile. Around
the point you can see the strata of the cliff face as
they cross the tidal zone and run out to sea. These

are the bowling lanes of Bowling Ball Beach, which runs southeast from the point.

Walk down Bowling Ball Beach, passing fissures in the striated cliffs beyond 1⅛ miles. You soon pass large circular disks of yellow sandstone protruding from the cliffs of gray sandstone. These weathered concretions, which look like giant chariot wheels, formed deep below the ocean and were deposited under great pressure in concentric layers.

Continue along the beach past another narrow point around 1¼ miles, then past spherical concretions lying loose in the tidal zone. These "bowling balls," which gave the beach its name, are best viewed at low tide.

CCT continues along the beach to the mouth of Galloway Creek at 1½ miles. The beach angles south to an impassable rocky point. You might want to return from here for a 3 mile round trip. If not, just beyond the creek the Coastal Trail veers left to climb a narrow path to the blufftop and a junction at 1⅝ miles. The left fork contours east to Highway 1. CCT takes the right fork along the bluff edge. Near the southern tip of the bluffs around 1¾ miles, your trail turns east to drop past an outhouse to a junction overlooking the sheltered sandy cove of Schooner Gulch Beach.

At the junction turn right and descend for 175 feet to the logjam at the mouth of the creek, then continue to the beach at 1⅞ miles. When you're ready

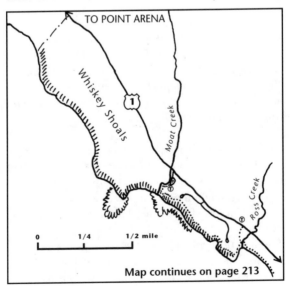

Map continues on page 213

to return, retrace your route to the Moat Creek Trailhead, 3¾ miles round trip.

48

SCHOONER GULCH NORTH to WHISKEY SHOALS

ISOLATED LOW-TIDE BOWLING BALL BEACH

The names of these places ring with history. Schooner Gulch was once the site of a ship-building operation to provide more doghole schooners for the Mendocino coast's booming lumber trade. Whiskey Shoals acquired its name during prohibition, when these isolated shores, hidden by their steep cliffs, were a popular spot for rum runners to land their illegal cargo. Today, however, the windswept bluffs produce only wildflowers, and the sea provides a few abalone and sea vegetables. The name Bowling Ball Beach stems from the fascinating geological formations found here.

State legislation and the Mendocino County Local Coastal Plan both promote the development of a five-mile coastal blufftop trail, a link in the California Coastal Trail, running from Point Arena to Schooner Gulch. The trail is currently a work-in-progress.

In the meantime, when the tide is +2.0 feet or lower, you can walk north from Schooner Gulch along a narrow, secluded strip of blond beach at the base of steep cliffs to Ross Creek at the southern end of the Whiskey Shoals property, a distance of 1⅛ miles each way. Be sure that your hike coincides with an appropriately low tide.

From the Schooner Gulch parking area, follow the beach trail for 500 feet to where it forks. Go right and climb southwest onto the headlands. Your trail soon bends right and heads north across headlands with beach strawberry, bush lupine, buttercup, blue-eyed grass and rattlesnake grass.

Where the trail forks in 300 feet, take the left fork, heading northwest. At ¼ mile from the trailhead, your trail merges with another path and descends

DISTANCE: 2¼ miles round trip.

TIME: One to two hours.

TERRAIN: Along verdant creek, up over headlands, then down to and along a sandy beach with intriguing rock formations.

BEST TIME: Tide of +2.0 feet or lower. Spring for wildflowers.

WARNINGS: Do not get trapped by rising tide. Watch for killer waves. Poison oak near Galloway Creek.

HOW TO GET THERE: Parking is on west side of Highway 1 at M.11.4, opposite Schooner Gulch Road. Take the lower trail beside redwoods.

FURTHER INFO: Mendocino State Parks (707) 937-5804.

to the mouth of Galloway Creek at ⅜ mile. Look for poison oak and checker lilies as you descend and sea rocket when you get to the beach.

If you are certain that the tide is low enough, head northwest along the beach toward cliffs with diagonal strata. Around ½ mile rocky shallows lie in the low-tide zone, a good place to explore at a minus tide.

Continuing along the beach, you soon find rock formations to the left of the beach that look like giant bowling lanes. Not far beyond lie many large spherical boulders, the bowling balls in the beach's popular name. Geologists call these concretions, because they are formed in concentric layers around a nucleus. Since they are harder than the surrounding sandstone, they have fallen to the beach as the Miocene-age strata in the cliffs above have eroded.

Just beyond ⅝ mile, you come to the narrowest point along the beach, marked by a cypress growing above a seep on the cliff face. This is where you should watch the tides to make sure you can return. Continue along the beach at the base of gray sandstone cliffs with pronounced diagonal strata. Circular discs of yellow sandstone protrude from the face of the cliff, concretions split in half that show the concentric layers in which they were formed. They

211

look like giant chariot wheels imbedded in the cliff. The most round one is nearly detached from the cliff, apparently ready to fall to the beach in the next few years.

Continuing to ¾ mile, you pass several deep fissures in alternating layers of stone, forming gullies with the help of runoff from the bluffs above. You then pass more concretions imbedded in the cliff.

At ⅞ mile you round a point where beach and cliff turn north. The bowling lanes off the point are loaded with seaweed. Before one mile you pass a private stairway leading to a house on the bluff. In another 300 feet, the sandy beach gives way to rock shelves and a narrow, rocky beach at the base of the cliff. At 1⅛ miles you come to the mouth of Ross Creek, where a sea stack sits in the tidal zone. A few feet beyond, the Ross Creek Trail heads northeast onto the bluff. It provides a convenient escape route if one were to be trapped by the rising tide. (It also provides easy access to this popular surfing and diving spot.) The trail leads to Highway One in ⅛ mile, at M.12.44.

If you have planned your tides correctly, however,

the easiest return to your starting point is back along the beach. After you climb onto the bluff south of Galloway Creek, you can take the left fork to cut ⅛ mile from the return distance.

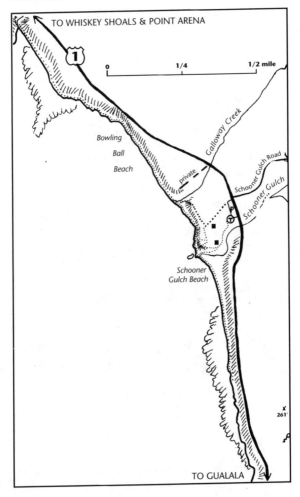

TO WHISKEY SHOALS & POINT ARENA

1

0   1/4   1/2 mile

Galloway Creek

Bowling
Ball
Beach

private

Schooner Gulch Road

Schooner Gulch

P

Schooner
Gulch Beach

261'

TO GUALALA

49.

SCHOONER GULCH

LOVELY WIND-SHELTERED BEACH

The state acquired this 53-acre jewel of a beach as a state park in 1985. It's the southernmost holding of the Mendocino State Parks. The protected beach provides sheltered sunning on windy days and access to tidepooling at low tide. This place prob-

213

SCHOONER GULCH:

DISTANCE: ¼ to 2 miles round trip, depending on tide.

TIME: Fifteen minutes to two hours.

TERRAIN: Along verdant creek to its mouth at protected pocket cove. At low tide, beach extends south along cliffs and north through a wave tunnel to a separate beach.

BEST TIME: Low tide, but main beach accessible even at high tide. Spring best for wildflowers, summer for berries.

WARNINGS: Parking area is on a dangerously blind stretch of Highway One; park facing south only and please don't turn around in this blind spot. Do not get trapped by rising tide if you go north or south from the main beach. Always watch the ocean for killer waves.

HOW TO GET THERE: Parking (facing south only) is on west side of Highway 1 south of Point Arena at M.11.4, opposite Schooner Gulch Road. Take the lower trail beside redwoods.

FURTHER INFO: Mendocino State Parks (707) 937-5804.

ably got its name from early day ship building that occurred here, though no written records exist. We do know there was a shingle mill here around the 1870s and 1880s.

The trail heads west into a tiny stand of redwoods, then turns south and drops towards the creek. You pass gnarled, burned-out redwood stumps with healthy young sprouts. After 200 feet the habitat changes to lush riparian. Thimbleberries and salmonberries grow in a dense thicket along the creek, intertwined with beach pea and other moisture-loving plants.

About 500 feet from your starting point, you come to a fork in the trail. The right fork leads up onto the headlands for wildflowers and fine views (see Trail #48 for a longer hike heading north). Take the left fork, which leads to the blond beach in about 200 feet. As you ford the creek over driftwood logs, you come to the beach of fine sand scattered with rocks, many of them rounded concretions like the bowling balls of the popular beach immediately to the north. If the tide is too high, you will not be able to get far to the south, while the north will be impassable.

The trail description continues as if you are there at a minus tide. Do not attempt the rest of the trail if the tide is higher, or if it has turned and is rising.

GOING SOUTH: The wide part of the beach extends about 300 feet. From there the sand strip quickly narrows, then ends, with cliffs on your left and algae covered, eroded rocks on your right. You must use caution on the slippery rocks. It is an easy scramble over the rocks to a flat, eroded shelf of sandstone, just like the "bowling lanes" of nearby Bowling Ball Beach. You have come ⅛ mile from the creek. Walk the smooth, slippery shelf for another 250 feet to its end. A jumble of tidal rocks extends about ¼ mile south to a sandy point. Extensive tidepools lie on your right, home to many varieties of seaweed, a few crabs, snails and anemones. If the tide is low enough, you may be able to continue around the sandy point.

GOING NORTH FROM THE CREEK: The beach extends about 300 feet, though you must again ford the creek. Here you encounter a wave tunnel, eroded from large, stratified, diagonal blocks of sandstone. You can peer through the tunnel to the cliffs and beach of Whiskey Shoals beyond. If you are sure the tide is not rising, you may continue.

Entering the tunnel, you come to a window after 50 feet. This looks out toward Point Arena to the northwest. Beyond the window the tunnel becomes more narrow, wet and slippery. Be careful. Gooseneck barnacles grow on the walls. In another 100 feet, you emerge onto tidal rocks at the far end of the tunnel. In 200 feet the tidal zone broadens to a rocky beach. In another 200 feet, you climb over a rocky ledge to a long, narrow beach with extensive tidal rocks offshore. Lovely Bowling Ball Beach, at the base of spectacular cliffs, extends more than a mile at low tide (see Trail #48).

You can return through the wave tunnel. Or you may take the easy trail just south of Galloway Creek that climbs to the grassy headlands, then heads east to the parking area.

GUALALA POINT REGIONAL PARK

The park sits in a spectacular setting on the south shore of the normally placid Gualala River, extending upstream from its mouth for about 1½ miles. The land was the northernmost portion of the Rancho German land grant, donated to Sonoma County when Oceanic Properties created the extensive subdivision called Sea Ranch. The park covers the diverse habitats of beach, rugged sea cliffs, grassy headlands, tidal river and redwood and bay laurel forest. It lies just across the Mendocino County line, at the extreme northwest corner of Sonoma County.

50.

HEADLANDS to BEACH LOOP
WINDBREAKS, WHALES AND WILDFLOWERS

The western portion of the park is covered by a fine network of trails offering several choices. Though the following trail report details the unpaved headlands-to-beach loop, a paved bicycle and wheelchair path can easily be followed out to the same beach and headlands area.

The modern visitor center fits nicely into the beautiful headlands landscape. The center has informative displays and provides a welcome refuge from the strong winds often blowing here.

From the visitor center, follow the paved path northwest for 200 feet. There you meet a grassy trail that continues northwest where the paved path swings west. Take the grassy path leading gently downhill through lush headlands. In 300 feet a trail on your right heads downhill to a nice picnic area near the river.

Continuing northwest, in 100 feet you meet another trail, on your left this time, which leads southwest on the leeward side of an old cypress windbreak to another picnic area. The main trail continues west by northwest around the windbreak, passing over

HEADLANDS to BEACH LOOP:

DISTANCE: 1¼-mile loop.

TIME: One half hour to one hour.

TERRAIN: Grassy headlands between river and sea cliffs leading to broad beach at river mouth, then to rocky point.

BEST TIME: Spring for wildflowers. Whale watching is best December through March. Anytime is nice.

WARNINGS: Watch for killer waves on beach: six people were swept into the sea here in February 1986; one of them drowned. Watch for poison oak tangled with other plants.

HOW TO GET THERE: Turn west off Highway 1 at M.58.2 (Sonoma County), about .25 mile south of the town of Gualala. Drive .5 mile to the visitor center. The trail starts there.

FEES: Day Use: $3/vehicle. Car camping: $14/night. Hike/bike camping: $3/person/night.

FURTHER INFO: Gualala Point Regional Park (707)785-2377.

headlands filled with wildflowers.

On your right the Gualala River offers prime habitat for aquatic birds. Many species of grasslands birds live near the trail.

Around ¼ mile, the footpath joins the paved trail, continuing to the beach near the river mouth. In late summer or early fall, you can ford the river near its mouth, continuing north to the end of the beach. At medium to high water, however, the river is not safe to ford.

Our trail description turns southwest on a fork of the paved path, quickly coming to a restroom and to the end of the paved path in about 300 feet. The grassy path continues south from here, following the edge of the bluff overlooking the beach.

The trail forks again in another 200 feet. Here you

can choose either the left path, protected behind a
row of cypress, or the right fork, continuing along
the spectacularly eroded sandstone bluffs above the
beach.

Before ½ mile, bear right into a "tunnel" through
the cypress trees. Here your trail heads west onto a
narrow rocky promontory known as Whale Watch
Point. It soon comes to sandy bluffs on the leeward
side of a cypress windbreak, overlooking ocean cliffs
on the south. You may continue 250 feet farther west
to the windswept point beyond the windbreak. From
here you look north for a fine view of the beach and
the town of Gualala. The wooded ridge beyond
extends west to the point of Haven's Neck and the
big sea stack called Fish Rock.

Returning to the sandy bluff east of the cypress
trees, take the right fork southwest along the bluff's
edge. You quickly come to a stairway on your right
leading to a flat, rocky tidal shelf (fishing access).
Continuing along the bluff, you soon plunge into a
broad cypress windbreak, a home for many small
birds. As you clear the cypress thicket, you meet
the windbreak trail forking to the left. (You may
return by that trail if your prefer.)

The trail continues southeast near the edge of the
bluff. Two benches along this stretch provide rest-

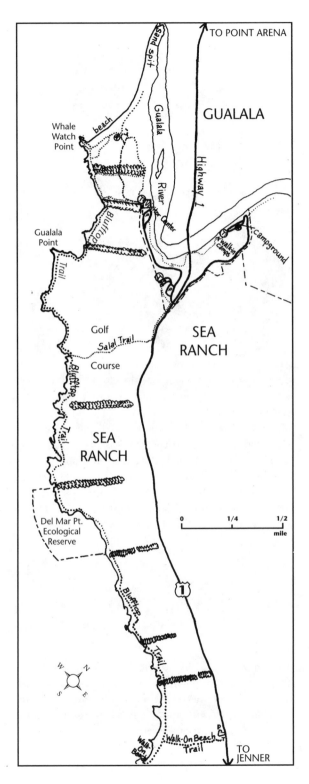

TO POINT ARENA

Sand Spit

GUALALA

beach

Whale
Watch
Point

Gualala River

Highway 1

Gualala
Point

Bluff Top

Trail

Walk-in
Camps

Campground

Golf

Salal Trail

SEA
RANCH

Course

Bluff Top

Trail

SEA
RANCH

0   1/4   1/2
                   mile

Del Mar Pt.
Ecological
Reserve

Bluff Top

1

N
W   E
S

Trail

Walk-On Beach
Trail

Walk-
On Beach

TO
JENNER

219

ing places with fine views of the coast. Just 300 feet after the second bench, you come to a fence and a sign indicating the park boundary. The northern end of the Blufftop Trail leads through the fence here (see Trail #52). You turn northeast here, following the fence and windbreak along the Sea Ranch boundary. In another 300 feet you enter a "tunnel" through pines. Leaving the tunnel, you meet the paved path in 20 feet. Follow the bike path for the 500 feet back to the visitor center and your car.

51.

RIVER TRAIL SOUTH

ALONG A QUIET STEELHEAD STREAM

The campground along the Gualala River lies at the western edge of a dense redwood forest on a quiet tidal stretch of the river. You can often hear the surf crashing just a mile to the west. The roar intrudes upon, but does not overcome, the quiet of the campground.

Though there are many large redwoods here, the

RIVER TRAIL SOUTH:

DISTANCE: One mile round trip (connects with 1¼-mile headlands/beach trail).

TIME: One half hour.

TERRAIN: Down the river canyon, under the highway bridge, then climbing the bluff to headlands.

BEST TIME: Spring for wildflowers, but anytime is good.

WARNINGS: Watch for poison oak and stinging nettles.

HOW TO GET THERE: Turn east off Highway 1 at M.58.2 (Sonoma County), about .25 mile south of the town of Gualala. Go .7 mile to the campground, then .1 mile farther to its south end.

FEES: Day use: $3/vehicle. Car camping: $14/night. Hike/bike camping: $3/person/night.

FURTHER INFO: Gualala Point Regional Park (707)785-2377.

ENVIRONMENTAL CAMPS: 7 walk- or bike-in camps are located from 75 feet to 400 feet along the trail in a dense bay laurel forest by the river.

many old stumps show evidence of pioneer logging. Most of these have springboard cuts still showing on their eroded surfaces, indicating that the trees were cut before the introduction of chainsaws. (The sawyers would stand on these springboards, five or ten feet above the ground to avoid cutting through the thicker, often scarred wood at the tree's base.) Many of these old stumps have new plants growing healthily from their tops. If you walk through the campground you will see the following plants atop stumps: elderberry, huckleberry, sword fern and bay laurel.

Where the redwood trees stop near the southwest end of the campground, bay laurels grow very large, with gnarled trunks to four feet in diameter.

The river trail leads south through this dense bay laurel forest from the south end of the campground. Seven walk- or bike-in campsites are located in this forest along the first 400 feet of trail. (They may be a bargain at $3 per person per night.) Just beyond the last campsite, the trail comes to a grassy clearing; a dense tangle of brush grows on your right between you and the river.

At ⅛ mile the trail swings right and follows the river bank. It continues through tall brush for the next 300 feet, crossing a sturdy bridge across a side stream.

Around ¼ mile you pass under the highway bridge. Many cliff swallows nest under the bridge, especially on its west side. From March through September, the swallows will be chattering and feeding over the river. Your trail then leads uphill away from the river, following a fence. Then, passing an old snag, you leave the grassy river flat and climb the face of the bluff. The tangle of brush along the trail includes many species: willows, bay laurel, ceanothus, blackberries, wild rose, paintbrush and poison oak. The trail switchbacks twice, coming to a bench where you may rest and enjoy the view.

As you come to the top of the bluff, the flora changes to bluff grassland, scattered with low cypress. Another ⅛ mile along the bluff's edge brings you to a pleasant picnic area. A few hundred feet beyond, you come to the visitor center. At this point you may return to the campground or continue to the network of headlands and beach trails (see Trails #50 and 52).

52.

BLUFFTOP TRAIL
ALONG THE SEA RANCH COAST

State law mandated this trail in 1980, after years of litigation that went all the way to the state appeals court. The entire trail was finally completed and opened in 1987. Today it serves as part of the California Coastal Trail. Though the trail passes many houses in the Sea Ranch subdivision, it provides the only public access to a marvelously convo-

luted coast with headlands rich in wildflowers. On one spring visit, the author counted more than two dozen varieties of wildflowers in bloom.

This description starts at the north end of the trail, where it meets the trails of Gualala Point Regional Park. You can also reach the Blufftop Trail via the Salal Trail (see Trail #53) and the Walk-On Beach Trail (see Trail #54).

From the visitor center at Gualala Point Regional Park, follow the paved path northwest for 200 feet. Then walk the pavement southwest for another 250 feet. Where the pavement turns right, take the dirt path that continues southwest through the trees and along the fence that marks the Sea Ranch boundary.

At ¼ mile a break in the fence marks the start of the Blufftop Trail. Turn left, heading through the fence and the cypress windbreak. Then the Blufftop Trail turns south, following the edge of the bluff. For the next ¼ mile, the nearby shore is mostly hidden behind dense cypress. At ½ mile you come to a small point with unobstructed views south to Gualala Point and northwest to Whale Watch Point.

Then your trail plunges through another windbreak. At ⅝ mile your trail jogs right, passing above a small, inaccessible pocket beach. You head southwest to Gualala Point, shrouded in bushy cypress. Gualala Point Island, just offshore, provides a nesting ground for Brandt's cormorants and other

BLUFFTOP TRAIL:

DISTANCE: 6½ miles round trip, 7 miles to Walk-On Beach round trip.

TIME: Three to four hours.

TERRAIN: Along headlands near the bluff's edge, crossing several creeks and passing through numerous cypress windbreaks.

BEST TIME: Spring and early summer for wildflowers.

WARNINGS: Do not trespass on adjacent private property. Watch for poison oak. Be careful along the bluff's crumbly edge. Stay on the trail and away from the edge.

HOW TO GET THERE: Turn west from Highway 1 at M.58.2 (Sonoma County) into the day-use area for Gualala Point Regional Park. Go to parking area at end of road (.5 mile).

FEES: $3/vehicle, day use.

FURTHER INFO: Gualala Point Regional Park (707)785-2377.

seabirds.

At ¾ mile you leave the cypress trees for open headlands. Your trail continues southeast, hugging the edge of the bluff. Near one mile you cross two small gullies and follow the rugged shore. Large yellow bush lupine lie scattered along the grassy headlands. You soon descend into a canyon where forest and soft chaparral plants mix. After crossing a creek at 1¼ miles, you meet the Salal Trail (Trail #53).

Climb the steps heading southeast up onto a headland with tall grasses, bush lupine, berry vines and Douglas iris. You wind along the lupine-covered bluff near the shore. Beyond 1½ miles your trail winds onto a point, passing the wind-sculpted end of a cypress windrow.

At 1⅝ miles you come to a creek with still pools overlooking the shore. Cross a bridge over the creek and come to a view of the waterfall where the creek drops to the ocean. Then continue generally southeast along the bluff.

At 1⅞ miles you cut in around a tiny cove and wind through more bush lupine, then head south. At 2 miles you approach another windbreak, this one marking the boundary of the Del Mar Landing Ecological Reserve. The Reserve was created to protect the rocky intertidal zone, habitat to an abundance of marine invertebrates. No fishing or collecting is allowed here.

The trail soon forks. Follow the right fork along the edge of the bluff. At 2⅛ miles a wooden beam and an old rusty stake mark Del Mar Landing, where lumber schooners were loaded around the turn of the century. Some unusual rock formations lie along the shore.

You soon come to the end of Del Mar Point. Your trail turns north briefly, then east. At 2¼ miles you pass a rock outcrop nearly buried in lush vegetation. Delicate hairy star tulips, or cat's ears, grow among the grasses nearby. Parallel paths lead across the bluffs. You may take either one, because they rejoin not far ahead. You pass through an old redwood split-rail fence at 2⅜ miles. Near 2½ miles you head into a broad windrow, then wind to cross a bridge over another small creek.

Continue southeast through the wildflower-dappled headlands. You soon find that you are alongside a rocky cliff with fantastically eroded rocks. The tafoni rocks here are similar to the more extensive rock formations at Salt Point, visible along the coast to the south. At 2¾ miles your path bends to the right and heads out to a small point, then heads east to cross a bridge. The small creek below is hidden in a dense tangle of vegetation. Beyond the creek grows a thicket of salal and cow parsnip.

Soon your trail splits in two. The right fork is the most scenic, heading out to a small point, then quickly rejoining the other fork. At 3 miles you approach another old windrow, which you promptly pass through.

In ¼ mile you come to the junction with the Walk-On Beach Trail, 3¼ miles from your starting point. You can go another ¼ mile southeast and descend the stairway to the beach. Or you can head northeast to the Walk-On Beach Trailhead, which would be perfect if you arranged a shuttle vehicle ahead of time. Otherwise, return along the Blufftop Trail to Gualala Point Regional Park. (You may also turn right when you reach the Salal Trail, follow that back to the park, then walk another ½ mile along the road to the visitor center.)

53.

SALAL TRAIL

COASTAL CREEK HABITAT

This short trail is one of my favorites because it offers such variety in a short invigorating hike, not to mention some very unusual habitats. The hike is even better if you loop back on the Blufftop Trail instead of the way you came.

The Salal Trail heads southeast from the restroom and parking area, then follows the south shoulder of the road to the park entrance on Highway 1. Your trail then parallels Highway 1 south for ⅛ mile.

A wooden post with the coastal access symbol marks where the trail heads away from Highway 1. Go through a dense berry patch, then down a stairway into the creek canyon at ¼ mile. This little creek canyon forms a habitat distinct from the coastal

SALAL TRAIL:

DISTANCE: 1½ miles round trip. (Or 2½-mile loop with the north portion of Blufftop Trail.)

TIME: One hour.

TERRAIN: Grassy headlands spotted with cypress, then dropping into narrow, wooded coastal creek canyon leading to rocky beach.

BEST TIME: Spring for azaleas and other wildflowers, but anytime is nice.

WARNINGS: Do not trespass on adjacent private property. Watch for poison oak and nettles along the trail.

HOW TO GET THERE: Turn west from Highway 1 at M.58.2 (Sonoma County) into the day use area for Gualala Point Regional Park. Take the first left inside the park, parking near the restrooms.

FEES: $3/vehicle, day use.

FURTHER INFO: Gualala Point Regional Park (707)785-2377.

grasslands adjacent to it. Many species thrive in the cool, damp, wind-protected environment, including fragrant wild azalea, madrone, salal, silktassel, alder, berries and oaks.

Your trail heads down the canyon, coming quickly to stands of redwoods, Bishop pines and droopy Douglas firs. You next come to a small wooden bridge, then to a paved road beyond ⅜ mile.

Cross the road and continue southwest, passing a pumphouse before the trail comes back alongside the creek in an area lush with willows, alders, sword ferns, skunk cabbage and salmonberries. These are soon joined by Bishop pines and cypress.

At ½ mile you cross a small bridge beside wild azaleas, then plunge into a dense tunnel of growth dominated by silktassel, alders and thimbleberries. In 300 feet you come to a more open portion of the trail where paintbrush thrives in a rocky spot. Then you

227

drop into another tunnel of brush, mostly bay laurel.

Near ⅝ mile you come to a dense stand of redwoods on the creek. The trees are snapped off just above the level of the surrounding grasslands, attesting to the protection this little canyon provides from prevailing strong winds. This pretty spot has a small waterfall. Continue along the left side of the creek. In another 300 feet, you find a dense salmonberry thicket beside the trail. Salmonberries ripen in May and June. Then you come to another paved path with miners lettuce growing beside it. The trail bends left and passes through a brushy area where you should watch for nettles.

Not quite ¾ mile from the trailhead, a small rocky beach comes into view at the mouth of the creek. The wooded habitat gives way to soft chaparral plants: skunk cabbage, cow parsnip, horsetail ferns, grasses and assorted wildflowers.

You come to a junction with the Blufftop Trail (Trail #52), which goes north for one mile to meet the trails of Gualala Point Regional Park, and south for 2 miles to meet the Walk-On Beach Trail. You can prolong your hike by going either left or right. Or you can simply descend the stairway to the tiny beach, enjoy the shore, and return the way you came.

54.

OTHER SEA RANCH TRAILS

SHORT AND SCENIC

THE WALK-ON BEACH TRAIL (¾ mile round trip) descends from the parking lot into a coastal scrub forest of madrone, willow, grand fir, cypress and Bishop pine. As you head south, watch for poison oak in the understory. Cross a paved road after 500 feet, then head southwest through grasslands west of a large cypress windbreak. Beyond ¼ mile you come to a junction with the Blufftop Trail (Trail #52). Go left here for almost another ¼ mile to reach the stairway and ramp at the far end of Walk-On Beach.

THE SHELL BEACH TRAIL (1¼ miles round trip) heads southeast through pines to a wooden bridge.

OTHER SEA RANCH TRAILS:

DISTANCE: ½ mile to 1¼ miles round trip.
TIME: One half hour to one hour (each trail).
TERRAIN: Coastal grasslands leading to small pocket beaches.
BEST TIME: Spring for wildflowers, low tide for best enjoyment of beaches and tidepools. These trails are nice anytime.
WARNINGS: Respect adjacent private property—do not trespass. Watch for rogue waves when on the beach. Trails are open 6 a.m. to sunset.
HOW TO GET THERE: All on west side of Highway 1 at the following Sonoma County mileposts (just south of Gualala):

    Walk-On Beach Trail: M.56.50
    Shell Beach Trail: M.55.20
    Stengel Beach Trail: M.53.96
    Pebble Beach Trail: M.52.30
    Black Point Beach Trail: M.50.83

FEES: Day use: $3/vehicle.
FURTHER INFO: Gualala Point Regional Park (707)785-2377.

Just short of ⅛ mile, you cross a paved road, then continue over grasslands scattered with trees. At ¼ mile you walk between houses, then cross a second paved road. In 300 feet you reach a stairway to the pleasant beach, protected somewhat by the point to the north.

THE STENGEL BEACH TRAIL (⅜ mile round trip) descends from the parking lot and heads southwest along a beautiful old cypress windbreak and a fence. In 500 feet you meet a private trail and a break in the fence. Your trail bends right and heads through the break to meet the stairway to broad, sandy Stengel Beach.

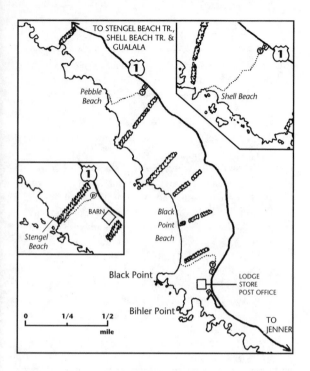

THE PEBBLE BEACH TRAIL (⅝ mile round trip) heads south between shore pines. At 250 feet you cross a private path at a right angle. The trail then leads west through Bishop pine forest. On your right runs a lush creek, home to skunk cabbage, ferns and other water-loving plants. At ⅛ mile you leave the creek for grassy headlands. Before ¼ mile the trail follows a cypress windbreak. You soon meet another private path on the left. Go right, crossing a small wooden bridge. In 150 feet you meet the stairway to Pebble Beach. The beach is gray, pebbly sand with good tidepools at low tide. Return by the same trail.

THE BLACK POINT BEACH TRAIL (⅝ mile round trip) goes north across lush, grassy headlands. After 300 feet you cross a private road. The trail turns west in 150 feet, heading directly toward the sea cliff. You cross a private Sea Ranch trail, then come to a sturdy stairway descending 86 steps to the south end of the beach. To the south is Black Point, a rock outcrop with windblown cypress, long a landmark to navigators on both land and sea. To the north the black sand and pebble beach extends about ½ mile. Return by the same trail.

OTHER SUGGESTION: If you rent a house in the Sea Ranch subdivision, you will have access to all the private trails there as well as trails described in this book.

COMMON & SCIENTIFIC NAMES
OF PLANTS ALONG THE TRAILS

* alyssum, *Lobularia maritima*

angelica, *Angelica tomentosa*

azalea, *Rhododendron occidentale*

baby blue eyes, *Nemophila menziesii*

baneberry, *Actaea rubra*

bay laurel (Calif. bay, pepperwood), *Umbellularia californica*

beach knotweed, *Polygonum paronychia*

beach morning glory, *Calystegia soldanella*

beach pea, *Lathyrus japonicus var. glaber*

beach primrose, *Camissonia cheiranthifolia*

beach sagewort, *Artemesia pycnocephala*

beach strawberry, *Fragaria chiloensis*

bear grass, *Xerophyllum tenax*

bedstraw, *Galium sp.*

bee balm (figwort), *Scrophularia californica*

big leaf maple, *Acer macrophyllum*

bird's foot fern (bird's foot cliff brake, poison fern), *Pellaea mucronata*

Bishop pine, *Pinus muricata*

black oak (Calif.), *Quercus kelloggi*

black twinberry, *Lonicera involucrata*

bleeding heart (western), *Dicentra formosa*

blueblossom (Calif. lilac), *Ceanothus thyrsiflorus*

blue dick, *Dichelostemma pulchellum*

blue elderberry, *Sambucus mexicana*

blue-eyed grass, *Sisyrinchium sp.*

* blue gum eucalyptus, *Eucalyptus globulus*

blue larkspur, *Delphinium decorum*

Bolander pine, *Pinus contorta ssp. bolanderi*

bracken fern, *Pteridium aquilinum var. pubescens*

brodiaea (tall brodiaea), *Brodiaea laxa*

buck brush, *Ceanothus cuneatus var. dubius*

bunchberry, *Cornus canadensis*

buttercup, *Ranunculus californicus*

California aster, *Aster chilensis*

California blackberry, *Rubus vitifolius*

California buckeye, *Aesculus californica*

California fuchsia, *Zauschneria californica*

California harebell, *Campanula prenanthoides*

California live oak, *Quercus agrifolia*

California nutmeg, *Torreya californica*

California poppy (golden poppy), *Eschscholtzia californica*

California rose, *Rosa californica*

* calla lily, *Zantedeschia aethiopica*

calypso orchid (redwood orchid), *Calypso bulbosa*

camas lily, *Camassia quamash*

canyon gooseberry, *Ribes menziesii*

canyon live oak, *Quercus chrysolepis*

cascara sagrada, *Rhamnus purshiana*

cattail, *Typha sp.*

chamise, *Adenostoma fasciculatum*

chatterbox (stream) orchid, *Epipactis gigantea*

checker bloom, *Sidalcea malvaeflora*

checker lily (mission bells), *Fritillaria lanceolata*

chicory, *Cichorium intybus*

chinese firecrackers, *Brodiaea ida-maia*

chinquapin, *Castanopsis chrysophylla*

cinquefoil (silverweed), *Potentilla egedei var. grandis*

clintonia, *Clintonia andrewsiana*

coast buckwheat, *Eriogonum latifolium*

coast eryngo (butter snakeroot), *Eryngium armatum*

coast lily, *Lilium maritimum*

coast silktassel, *Garrya elliptica*

coastal alum-root, *Heuchera pilosissima*

coastal manroot (wild cucumber), *Marah oreganus*

coastal onion, *Allium dichlamydeum*

coffeeberry, *Rhamnus californica*

columbine, *Aquilegia formosa*

common linanthus, *Linanthus androsacea*

* common tansy (tansy ragwort), *Tanacetum vulgare*

coral root orchid, *Corallorhiza sp.*

corn lily, *Veratrum fimbriatum, V. californicum*

*cotoneaster, *Cotoneaster sp.*

cow parsnip, *Heracleum lanatum*

coyote brush, *Baccharis pilularis*

coyote mint, *Monardella villosa*

cream bush (ocean spray), *Holodiscus discolor*

cream cups, *Platystemon californicus*

cream fawn lily, *Erythronium californicum*

* creeping myrtle, *Vinca minor*

cypress, *Cupressus sp.*

dandelion, *Taraxicum officinale*

deer fern, *Blechnum spicant*

dogwood (Pacific), *Cornus nuttali*

Douglas fir, *Pseudotsuga menziesii*

Douglas iris, *Iris douglasiana*

dune collinsia, *Collinsia corymbosa*

dwarf brodiaea, *Brodiaea terrestris*

elderberry, *Sambucus callicarpa*

elk clover, *Aralia californica*

* European beach grass, *Ammophilia arenaria*

evergreen huckleberry (Calif. huckleberry), *Vaccinium ovatum*

evergreen violet (redwood violet), *Viola sempervirens*

fairy bells, *Disporum smithii*

false lily of the valley, *Maianthemum dilatum*

false (fat) Solomon's seal, *Smilacina racemosa*

* fennel, *Foeniculum vulgare*

Fernald's iris, *Iris fernaldii*

fiddleneck, *Amsinckia intermedia*

* filaree (scissors grass, redstem storksbill), *Erodium cicutarium*

five-finger fern (maidenhair fern), *Adiantum pedatum var. aleuticum*

footsteps-of-spring (yellow mat), *Sanicula arctopoides*

Fort Bragg manzanita (dwarf manzanita), *Arctostaphylos nummularia*

* foxglove, *Digitalis purpurea*

fringe cups, *Tellima grandiflora*

giant chain fern, *Woodwardia fimbriata*

giant horsetail, *Equisetum telmateia*

godetia (farewell to spring), *Clarkia sp.*

gold back fern (stamp fern), *Pityrogramma triangularis*

golden aster, *Chrysopsis villosa var. bolanderi*

goldenrod, *Solidago sp.*

goldfields, *Lasthenia californica*

* gorse, *Ulex europaeus*

grand fir, *Abies grandis*

grass nut, *Triteleia laxa*

ground cone, *Boschniakia strobilacea, B. hookeri*

* groundsel, *Senecio vulgaris*

gum plant, *Grindelia stricta*

hairy honeysuckle, *Lonicera hispidula*

hairy manzanita, *Arctostaphylos columbiana*

hairy star tulip (cat's ear), *Hypochoeris radicata*

hazel (California), *Corylus cornuta californica*

hedge nettle, *Stachys rigida*

hen and chicks, *Dudleya farinosa*

* Himalayan blackberry, *Rubus procerus*

horsetail, *Equisetum sp.*

hound's tongue, *Cynoglossum grande*

Howell's spineflower, *Chorizanthe howellii*

huckleberry, *Vaccinium sp.*

* ice plant, *Mesembryanthemum sp.*

Indian paintbrush, *Castilleja sp.*

Indian pink, *Silene californica*

Indian warrior, *Pedicularis densiflora*

inside-out flower, *Vancouveria planipetala*

interior live oak, *Quercus wislizenii*

Kellogg's monkeyflower, *Mimulus kelloggii*

kinnikinnick (bearberry), *Arctostaphylos uva-ursi*

knobcone pine, *Pinus attenuata*

Labrador tea, *Ledum glandulosum var. columbianum*

ladies' tresses, *Spiranthus romanzoffiana*

lady fern, *Athyrium filix-femina var. sitchenense*

large godetia, *Clarkia purpurea*

laurel, *Umbellularia californica*

leather fern (leather-leaf fern), *Polypodium scouleri*

licorice fern, *Polypodium glycyrrhiza*

live-forever, *Dudleya sp.*

lovage, *Ligusticum apiifolium*

lupine, *Lupinus latifolius, L. littoralis, L. nanus, L. polyphyllus, L. variicolor, L. rivularis*

madrone, *Arbutus menziesii*

manzanita, *Arctostaphylos sp.*

Mendocino cypress, *Cupressus govenia ssp. pygmaea*

Mendocino paintbrush, *Castelleja mendosensis*

Menzie's wallflower, *Erysimum menziesii*

milkmaids, *Dentaria californica*

milkwort, *Polygala californica*

miners lettuce, *Montia perfoliata*

monkeyflower, *Mimulus guttatus ssp. litoralis*

* Monterey cypress, *Cupressus macrocarpa*

mugwort, *Artemisia spp.*

* naked ladies, *Amaryllis belladonna*

* narcissus, *Amaryllidaceae sp.*

Narrow-leaved mule ears, *Wyethia angustifolia*

* nasturtium (Indian cress), *Tropaeolum majus*

nettle, *Urtica sp.*

northern dune tansy, *Tanacetum douglasii*

one-leaved wild onion, *Allium unifolium*

Oregon ash, *Fraxinus latifolia*

Oregon grape, *Mahonia nervosa*

Oregon white oak, *Quercus garryana*

Pacific stonecrop, *Sedum spathulifolium*

Pacific waterleaf, *Hydrophyllum tenuipes*

Pacific willow, *Salix lasiandra*

paintbrush, *Castilleja latifolia, C. affinis, C. foliosa, C. hololeuca, C. wightii, C. mendosensis*

paintbrush orthocarpus, *Orthocarpus castillejoides*

* pampas grass, *Cortaderia selloana*

pearly everlasting, *Anaphalis margaritacia*

pennyroyal (western), *Monardella lanceolata*

phacelia, *Phacelia spp.*

pig-a-back plant (piggyback), *Tolmiea menziesii*

pink star tulip, *Calochortus uniflorus*

plantain, *Plantago sp.*

* poison hemlock, *Conium maculatum*

poison oak, *Toxicodendron diversiloba*

popcorn flower, *Plagiobothrys nothofulvus*

poppy, *Eschscholtzia californica*

* Port Orford cedar, *Chamaecyparis lawsoniana*

raspberry, *Rubus leucodermis*

* rattlesnake grass, *Briza maxima*

rattlesnake plantain, *Goodyera oblongiflora*

red alder, *Alnus rubra*

red clover, *Trifolium pratense*

red elderberry, *Sambucus racemosa*

red flowering currant, *Ribes sanguineum*

* red hot poker, *Kniphofia uvaria*

red huckleberry, *Vaccinium parvifolium*

red larkspur, *Delphinium nudicaule*

redwood, *Sequoia sempervirens*

redwood lily, *Lilium rubescens*

redwood sorrel, *Oxalis oregana*

rein orchid, *Habenaria elegans var. maritima*

reindeer lichen, *Cladina portentosa ssp. pacifica*

rhododendron (Calif. rose bay), *Rhododendron macrophyllum*

rosy johnny tuck, *Orthocarpus erianthus*

rush, *Juncus sphaerocarpus*

* St. John's wort (tinker's penny), *Hypericum anagalloides*

salal, *Gaultheria shallon*

salmonberry, *Rubus spectabilis*

sand verbena, pink, *Abronia umbellata*

sand verbena, yellow, *Abronia latifolia*

scarlet monkeyflower, *Mimulus cardinalis*

* scarlet pimpernel, *Anagallis arvensis*

* Scotch broom, *Cytisus scoparius*

scouring rush, *Equisetum hyemale*

scrub oak, *Quercus dumosa var. bullata engelmann*

sea blush, *Plectritis congesta*

* sea rocket, *Cakile maritima*

seaside daisy, *Erigeron glaucus*

sea thrift, *Armeria maritima var. californica*

sedge, *Carex sp.*

sedum, *Sedum spp.*

* self-heal, *Prunella vulgaris*

serviceberry, *Amelanchier alnifolia*

shining willow, *Salix lucida ssp. lasiandra*

shooting star, *Dodecatheon spp.*

shore pine, *Pinus contorta ssp. contorta*

Siberian miners lettuce (candyflower), *Montia siberica*

silky beach pea, *Lathyrus littoralis*

Sitka spruce, *Picea sitchensis*

skunk cabbage, *Lysichitum americanum*

slim Solomon's seal, *Smilacina stellata*

slink pod (fetid adders tongue), *Scoliopus bigelovii*

sneezeweed, *Helenium bolanderi*

snowberry, *Symphoricarpos albus*

soap plant (soaproot), *Chlorogalum pomeridianum*

* spearmint, *Mentha spicata*

sphagnum moss, *Sphagnum sp.*

spice bush, *Calycanthus occidentalis*

starflower, *Trientalis latifolia*

sticky monkeyflower (bush monkeyflower), *Diplacus aurantiacus*

stinging nettle, *Urtica lyalli*

stream violet, *Viola glabella*

sugarstick, *Allotropa virgata*

sundew, *Drosera rotundifolia*

swamp harebell, *Campanula californica*

sword fern, *Polystichum munitum*

tanoak, *Lithocarpus densiflorus*

tarweed, *Hemizonia corymbosa*

thimbleberry, *Rubus parviflorus*

thistle, *Cirsium brevistylum*

tidy-tips, *Layia platyglossa*

tiger lily, *Lilium pardalinum*

* tinker's penny, *Hypericum anagalloides*

toyon, *Heteromeles arbutifolia*

trail plant, *Adenocaulon bicolor*

* tree mallow, *Lavatera arborea*

trillium (wake robin), *Trillium chloropetalum, T. ovatum*

tule, *Scirpus acutus*

twinberry, *Lonicera involucrata*

two-eyed violet, *Viola ocellata*

umbrella plant, *Peltiphyllum peltatum*

valerian, *Valeriana scouleri*

vanilla grass, *Hierochloe occidentalis*

vanilla leaf (deer foot), *Achlys triphylla*

* vetch, *Vicia sp.*

vine maple, *Acer circinatum*

wallflower, *Erysimum cocinnum*

water hemlock, *Cicuta douglasii*

water parsley, *Oenanthe sarmentosa*

* watercress, *Nasturtium officinale*

wax myrtle (bayberry), *Myrica californica*

western coltsfoot, *Petasites palmatus*

western dog violet, *Viola adunca*

western hemlock, *Tsuga heterophylla*

western windflower, *Anemone deltoidea*

western yew, *Taxus brevifolia*

white alder, *Alnus rhombifolia*

white brodiaea, *Brodiaea hyacinthina*

whitethorn, *Ceanothus incanus*

wild ginger, *Asarum caudatum*

* wild mustard, *Brassica campestris*

wild rose, *Rosa sp.*

willow, *Salix sp.*

wintergreen, *Pyrola sp.*

wood anemone, *Anemone oregana*

wood fern, *Dryopteris arguta*

wood rose, *Rosa gymnocarpa*

woodland star, *Lithphragma affine*

woodwardia fern (giant chain fern), *Woodwardia fimbriata*

wooly sunflower, *Eriophyllum lanatum var. arachnoideum*

yarrow, *Achillea millefolium*

yellow mat (footsteps of spring), *Sanicula arctopoides*

yerba buena, *Satureja douglasii*

yerba de selva (modesty), *Whipplea modesta*

zygadene (star lily), *Zigadenus fremontii*

* Introduced (feral) species

FURTHER READING

Adams, Rick and Loiuse McCorkle, *The California Highway 1 Book*, Ballantine Books, New York, 1985. (o.p.)

Alt, David D and Donald W. Hyndman, *Roadside Geology of Northern California*, Mountain Press Publishing Co., Missoula, MT, 1975.

Bear, Dorothy and Beth Stebbins, *Mendocino Book One*, Mendocino Historical Research, Inc., Mendocino, CA, 1973.

Bear, Dorothy and Beth Stebbins, *A Tour of Mendocino*, Bored Feet Press, Mendocino, CA, 1996.

Becking, Rudolph, *Pocket Flora of the Redwood Forest*, Island Press, Covelo, CA, 1982.

Borden, Stanley, *California Western Railroad, Western Railroader, Volume 20, #8*, San Mateo, CA, 1965.

Borden, Stanley, *Caspar Lumber Company, Western Railroader, Issues 315–316*, San Mateo, CA.

Brown, Vinson and Douglas Andrews, *The Pomo Indians of California and Their Neighbors*, Naturegraph Publishers, Happy Camp, CA, 1969.

California Coastal Commission, *California Coastal Access Guide*, Fifth edition, University of California Press, Berkeley, 1997.

California Coastal Commission, *California Coastal Resource Guide*, University of California Press, Berkeley, 1987.

Carpenter, Aurelius, *History of Mendocino County*, Pacific Rim Press, Mendocino, CA, reprint of 1914 edition. (o.p.)

DeWitt, John B., *California Redwood Parks and Preserves*, Save-the-Redwoods League, San Francisco, 1982.

Hayden, Mike, *Exploring the North Coast*, Chronicle Books, San Francisco, 1982. (o.p.)

Hyman, Frank J., *Historic Writings*, self-published, Fort Bragg, CA, 1966. (o.p.)

Jackson, Walter A., *The Doghole Schooners*, Bear & Stebbins, Mendocino, CA, 1977. (o.p.)

Jenny, Hans, *The Pygmy Forest Ecological Staircase*, Nature Conservancy, 1973. (o.p.)

Keator, Glenn and Ruth Heady, *Pacific Coast Berry Finder*, Nature Study Guild, Berkeley, 1978.

Keator, Glenn and Ruth Heady, *Pacific Coast Fern Finder*, Nature Study Guild, Berkeley, 1978.

Konigsmark, Ted, *Geologic Trips: Sea Ranch*, GeoPress, Gualala, CA, 1994.

Kroeber, A. L., *Handbook of the Indians of California*, Dover Publications, NY, 1976.

Layton, Thomas N., *The Voyage of the 'Frolic:' New England Merchants and the Opium Trade*, Stanford University Press, Stanford, CA, 1997.

Levene, Bruce et al., *Mendocino County Remembered: An Oral History, Volumes I and II*, Mendocino County Historical Society, 1980. (o.p.)

Lyons, Kathleen and Mary Beth Cuneo-Lazaneo, *Plants of the Coast Redwood Region*, Looking Press, Los Altos, CA, 1988.

Mendocino Historical Review, Volume IV, Number 4, Summer 1978, Mendocino Historical Research, Inc., Mendocino, CA.

Mendocino Historical Review, Volume IX, Number 1, Spring 1986, Mendocino Historical Research, Inc., Mendocino, CA.

Munz, Philip A., *California Spring Wildflowers*, University of California Press, Berkeley, 1961.

Munz, Philip A., *Shore Wildflowers of California, Oregon and Washington*, University of California Press, Berkeley, 1973.

Niehaus, Theodore F. And Charles L. Ripper, *Field Guide to Pacific States Wildflowers*, (Peterson Field Guide Series) Houghton Mifflin, Boston, 1973.

Randall, Warren R., Robert F. Keniston and Dale N. Bever, *Manual of Oregon Trees and Shrubs*, Oregon State University Bookstores, Corvallis, OR, 1978.

Russo, Ron and Pam Olhausen, *Pacific Intertidal Life*, Nature Study Guild, Berkeley, 1981.

Ryder, David W., *Memories of the Mendocino Coast*, Taylor and Taylor, 1948. (o.p.)

Sholars, Robert, *The Pygmy Forest and Associated Plant Communities of Coastal Mendocino County*, California, self-published, Mendocino, CA 1973. (o.p.)

Watts, Phoebe, *Redwood Region Flower Finder*, Nature Study Guild, Berkeley, 1979.

Watts, Ted, *Pacific Coast Tree Finder*, Nature Study Guild, Berkeley, 1973.

Wurm, Ted, *Mallets on the Mendocino Coast*, Trans-Anglo Books, Glendale, CA, 1986. (o.p.)

Young, Dorothy King, *Redwood Empire Wildflowers*, Third edition, Naturegraph Publishers, Happy Camp, CA, 1976.

INDEX

ABOUT BORED FEET

We began Bored Feet Press in 1986 to publish The Hiker's hip pocket Guide to the Mendocino Coast. We've grown our company by presenting the most accurate guidebooks for California, including our series on California's Coastal Trail.

Updates on our publications are now available on our website, **boredfeet.com**, where you can also easily provide your feedback on any of our books, or order any of our products. If you'd rather have a catalog, please send or call in your name and address. The list below represents only 20% of our books, with many of our bestsellers. We also have hiking and recreation maps to many areas of the west.

Hiker's hip pocket Guide to Sonoma County, 2nd ed.	$15.00
Hiker's hip pocket Guide to Humboldt Coast, 2nd ed.	14.00
Hiker's hip pocket Guide to Mendocino Coast, 3rd ed.	15.00
Hiker's hip pocket Guide to Mendocino Highlands	16.00
Day Trips with a Splash: The Swimming Holes of CA	18.95
Day Trips with a Splash: The Swimming Holes of the SW	18.50
Hiking the California Coastal Trail, Vol.1: Oregon-Monterey, 2nd ed.	19.50
Hiking the California Coastal Trail, Vol. 2: Monterey-Mexico	19.00
Hiking the California Coastal Trail, Complete Set	37.00
Trails & Tales of Yosemite & the Central Sierra/ Giacomazzi	16.00
Mendocino Coast Bike Rides/ Lorentzen	16.00
Napa Valley Picnic/ Burton & Stanton	15.00
Sonoma Picnic/ Burton	13.00
Great Day Hikes . . . Napa Valley, 2nd ed./ Stanton	15.00
Geologic Trips: San Francisco & Bay Area/ Konigsmark	13.95
Geologic Trips: Sierra Nevada/ Konigsmark	17.50
A Tour of Mendocino: 32 Historic Buildings / Bear	7.00
Wood, Water, Air & Fire: Anthology of Mendocino Women Poets	19.00

Please add $3 shipping for orders under $30, $6 over $30 ($5 / 8 for rush)
For shipping to a California address, please add 7.25% tax.
PRICES SUBJECT TO CHANGE WITHOUT NOTICE.

BORED FEET PRESS
P.O.Box 1832
Mendocino, CA 95460
888-336-6199
707-964-6629
FAX 707-964-5953
www.boredfeet.com

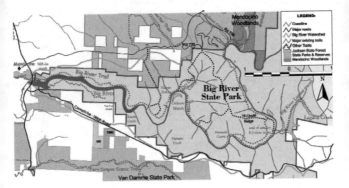